Resisting James Bond

Resisting James Bond

Power and Privilege in the Daniel Craig Era

Edited by
Lisa Funnell and Christoph Lindner

BLOOMSBURY ACADEMIC
NEW YORK · LONDON · OXFORD · NEW DELHI · SYDNEY

BLOOMSBURY ACADEMIC
Bloomsbury Publishing Inc
1385 Broadway, New York, NY 10018, USA
50 Bedford Square, London, WC1B 3DP, UK
29 Earlsfort Terrace, Dublin 2, Ireland

BLOOMSBURY, BLOOMSBURY ACADEMIC and the Diana logo
are trademarks of Bloomsbury Publishing Plc

First published in the United States of America 2023

Volume Editors' Part of the Work © Lisa Funnell and Christoph Lindner
Each chapter © of Contributors

For legal purposes the Acknowledgements on p. x constitute
an extension of this copyright page.

Cover design by Eleanor Rose
Cover image: Daniel Craig as James Bond © Collection
Christophel / Eon Productions / ArenaPAL

All rights reserved. No part of this publication may be reproduced or transmitted
in any form or by any means, electronic or mechanical, including photocopying,
recording, or any information storage or retrieval system, without prior
permission in writing from the publishers.

Bloomsbury Publishing Inc does not have any control over, or responsibility for,
any third-party websites referred to or in this book. All internet addresses given in this
book were correct at the time of going to press. The author and publisher regret any
inconvenience caused if addresses have changed or sites have ceased to exist,
but can accept no responsibility for any such changes.

A catalog record for this book is available from the Library of Congress.

ISBN:	HB:	978-1-5013-8826-2
	PB:	978-1-5013-8830-9
	ePDF:	978-1-5013-8828-6
	eBook:	978-1-5013-8827-9

Typeset by Integra Software Services Pvt. Ltd.

To find out more about our authors and books visit www.bloomsbury.com
and sign up for our newsletters.

Contents

List of Figures	vi
Foreword: Bond is Dead. Long Live 007 *Marwan M. Kraidy*	vii
Acknowledgements	x

Introduction: Resisting James Bond in the Daniel Craig Era
Lisa Funnell and Christoph Lindner 1

Part One   Embodiment

1 James Bond, Environmental Injustice and 'Slow Violence' in
the Craig Era *Tatiana Konrad* 11

2 'Do You Expect Me to Talk?': Bond the Torture Critic
Ron E. Hassner 29

3 The Thrusting Tip of the Spy Business: Discovering Resistance in
the Modern Moneypennys *Colin Burnett* 45

4 Highland Rape: Scotland's Traumatic Past in *Skyfall* *Mary M. Burke* 63

5 'Do You Consider Your Employment to Be Psychologically Stressful?':
Gender, Trauma and Resilience in Daniel Craig's James Bond
Bridget E. Keown 79

Part Two   Disembodiment

6 For Your Servers Only: Surveillance and Infonationalism in
Craig-era Bond *Kathryn Hendrickson and John Brick* 99

7 Spectres of Capitalism: Globalization in the Craig-era Bond Films
Milo Sweedler 115

8 Bond, Race and Coloniality: No Time to Die(versify) …
Harshad Keval 131

9 Licence to Urbicide: Defusing Bond's Acts of Terrorism for a
New Era *Fernando Gabriel Pagnoni Berns* 157

Afterword: 007 and Ableism *Lisa Funnell*	172
Contributors	180
Index	183

Figures

1.1 *Casino Royale* (Eon Productions et al. 2006) 17
1.2 *Spectre* (Eon Productions et al. 2016) 18
1.3 *Skyfall* (Eon Productions et al. 2012) 20
2.1 *Goldfinger* (Eon Productions et al. 1964) 31
2.2 *The World Is Not Enough* (Eon Productions et al. 1999) 33
2.3 *Casino Royale* (Eon Productions et al. 2006) 40
3.1 *Skyfall* (Eon Productions et al. 2012) 52
3.2 *Vargr* (Dynamite Entertainment 2015) 56
3.3 *Dr. No* (Eon Productions et al. 1962) 57
3.4 *Moneypenny* (Dynamite Entertainment 2017) 59
4.1 *Skyfall* (Eon Productions et al. 2012) 65
4.2 *Skyfall* (Eon Productions et al. 2012) 67
4.3 *Skyfall* (Eon Productions et al. 2012) 70
5.1 *Casino Royale* (Eon Productions et al. 2006) 86
5.2 *Skyfall* (Eon Productions et al. 2012) 90
5.3 *Spectre* (Eon Productions et al. 2016) 92
6.1 *Skyfall* (Eon Productions et al. 2012) 107
6.2 *Spectre* (Eon Productions et al. 2016) 108
6.3 *No Time To Die* (Eon Productions et al. 2021) 110
7.1 *Quantum of Solace* (Eon Productions et al. 2008) 121
7.2 *Skyfall* (Eon Productions et al. 2012) 124
7.3 *Spectre* (Eon Productions et al. 2016) 126
8.1 *Skyfall* (Eon Productions et al. 2012) 135
8.2 *Casino Royale* (Eon Productions et al. 2006) 139
8.3 2012 Summer Olympics Opening Ceremony (BBC 2012) 145
9.1 *Casino Royale* (Eon Productions et al. 2006) 163
9.2 *Skyfall* (Eon Productions et al. 2012) 164
9.3 *Spectre* (Eon Productions et al. 2016) 168

Foreword

Bond is Dead. Long Live 007

Marwan M. Kraidy

No Time To Die perplexed me the first time I saw the film. When I watched it again a few weeks later, on a fourteen-hour flight from Doha to Chicago, I was hoping I would come to terms with my ambivalence, to no avail. After Christoph Lindner and I chatted briefly about the film over lunch in London sometime later, I began to understand why the film vexed me: it disconcerted me as a fan yet pleased me as critic. Reading the manuscript for *Resisting James Bond* helped me figure out the underlying elements contributing to this unique and unexpected sensation.

The editors of this book rightly identify the Daniel Craig era (2006–2021) as a time of social and geopolitical upheaval. Indeed, in 2006 Russia cut gas supplies to the Ukraine for the first time, the Iraq War escalated into a bloody sectarian conflict, the United Nations General Assembly voted the UN Human Rights Council into existence, Germany did not even make it to the final of the World Cup it hosted, Nintendo Wii was released and Israel and Hezbollah fought to an earth-scorching standstill. The ensuing fifteen years have witnessed Occupy Wall Street and the Arab Uprisings, the Gezi protests and Black Lives Matter, #MeToo and Trump, Brexit and Bolsonaro, and the list goes on and on. Change and uncertainty define the present and obscure the future, leading to a nostalgia for the 'certainties' of the past while overlooking the role that power, privilege and fear played in defining these 'simpler' times.

As I write this foreword, the North Atlantic sphere – James Bond's geographical, geopolitical and ideological home – is in upheaval: the United Kingdom and the United States are experiencing political instability and turmoil with high stakes. Once the self-proclaimed havens of liberal democracy and neoliberal economics, these two countries (now) have fractured political systems and unstable economies. Torn up by right-wing populism, both countries are in the throes of xenophobia, jingoism, nativism, racism and misogyny, revanchist reactions to the recent movements for justice, equality and dignity mentioned above. The Daniel Craig era ends in bleak times.

No Time To Die is disconcerting, of course, because James Bond dies. In their introduction to this timely and exciting volume, Funnell and Lindner tell us that James Bond is the longest-running franchise in film history. What was for decades a staple and stable source of colonial identity, geopolitical reimagining and cultural escapism has transformed into a national nightmare; the unthinkable has finally happened – James Bond is dead (at least, until the next 007 reboot). But when contextualized as the last instalment in the Daniel Craig era – *Casino Royale* (2006), *Quantum of Solace* (2008), *Skyfall* (2012) and *Spectre* (2016) – Bond's hitherto inconceivable demise makes sense. It is as if, in the time of #MeToo and #BlackLivesMatter, after rhetorical contortions of post-racial times under Obama, after 007 was almost emasculated during torture in *Casino Royale* and flirts with homoeroticism in *Skyfall*, James Bond's death on an island in the Bering sea, by 'friendly' missiles, is the self-immolation of a white man who has endured status reversal, professional demotion, physical disintegration and, eventually, annihilation by missile – an actual cancellation. The fact that his evil foe is a Russian renegade played by an Arab actor, while the new 007, Nomi, is a black woman, adds further poignancy to his tragic demise.

James Bond is dead. Long live 007.

But is the cinematic disarticulation of James Bond from 007 an effective dismantling of a coupling of power and privilege that extends from the geopolitical to the intimate? Ian Fleming himself was a child of privilege: the son of a merchant banker who became Member of Parliament, he was educated at Eton and Sandhurst. The franchise remained the playground of rich and powerful Western white men, until Judy Dench assumed the character of M. The Daniel Craig era is self-reflexive about the franchise's troublesome cultural politics. It recognizes problems, but it also reproduces them. Bond is surrounded by a cast that, over the course of the Daniel Craig era, has grown more diverse with black actors playing key figures like Felix Leiter (Jeffrey Wright), Eve Moneypenny (Naomie Harris) and even Agent 007 (Lashana Lynch). The Daniel Craig era confirms that Q is queer. After decades of Bond-girls-as-objects, Craig as Bond seems to forge genuine bonds with women-as-subjects, though they are all white and of European descent. Bond falls in love with two women – Vesper Lynd and Dr Madeleine Swann – and these relationships lead to a consistent focus on the internal struggles of Bond (rather than external geopolitical conflict) thereby reflecting the empire retreating to the boundaries of the nation, until things collapse in *No Time To Die*.

Nonetheless, as several contributors to this volume demonstrate, ambivalence – towards the environment, the previously colonized, women, people of colour – perfuses the last three James Bond films (ironically in the Jubilee era). Mallory's Foucauldian moment, in *No Time To Die*, when he makes the argument that the spy community must defend society against invisible (internal?) foes, echoes Foucault's 'Society Must be Defended', from enemies that may encompass all those groups, represented in recent James Bond casts, clamouring for rights and privileges alongside the sole province of elite white British men. With a bit of reckoning and some co-optation, the Daniel Craig era proceeded, one reticent opening at a time, dangling tantalizing prospects for how James Bond has evolved since 2006. This insightful collection is a fitting guide and offers a deep understanding of how power and privilege define and are defined by the Daniel Craig era.

Acknowledgements

Lisa: This book is dedicated to my dad, Lorne Funnell, who shared with me his love of James Bond and encouraged me to think critically about the world. I must also thank my mom Mary, as well as my brother Dave, sister-in-law Caren, and their three children Tailor, Harrison and Daniel for encouraging me to publish this book during a challenging time in our lives. I appreciate your never-ending support and belief in my work. Finally, I need to thank my sweet pup Justice for keeping me company as I edited multiple drafts of each chapter. I simply adore you, my Puppy Galore.

Christoph: Most of my work on this book was completed during pandemic lockdowns in London. I want to thank Hannah, Joseph and Rebecca for sharing space so generously and flexibly during that time. The academic community that has developed around James Bond is remarkably collaborative and I am grateful for the way in which everyone involved in this 007 project, from the authors to the publishers, has embraced and continued that approach.

We extend our deepest gratitude to our contributors whose thoughtful work features throughout this book. It was a privilege and pleasure to engage so actively with your research as you developed and refined your ideas. Thank you for contributing so thoughtfully to this project's shared dialogue and for being open to our comments and suggestions.

We also want to acknowledge a number of scholars who were interested in contributing work to this volume but ultimately could not. The pandemic has had a strong impact on the academic community and many people's ability to produce work under such difficult conditions. We support your decision to prioritize your physical, emotional and/or mental health, and look forward to engaging with you and your work in the future.

Introduction

Resisting James Bond in the Daniel Craig Era

Lisa Funnell and Christoph Lindner

Released between 2006 and 2021, the Daniel Craig era of James Bond films coincides with a time of increasing social and political unrest. This period is marked by the rise of various social justice movements challenging deeply entrenched systems of inequality and oppression. There have been local, regional and global movements targeting sexism, racism, immigration, religious oppression, pay and wealth inequality, corporate capitalism, reproductive justice, environmental justice and climate change, among others. Growing awareness of, and activism around, these issues has been matched within the academy by an increasing number of scholars producing thoughtful and engaging research exploring systems of oppression, their intersections and permutations, and their disproportionate and negative impact on marginal/minority groups.

While focus is often placed on individual actions and institutional policies and practices, it is important to recognize the role that culture plays within these systems. Mainstream blockbuster film, for example, is not simply 'mindless' entertainment but a key part of a global cultural industry that naturalizes and normalizes privilege. A comprehensive understanding of social *in*justice requires a detailed consideration of how culture shapes, maintains and rationalizes various forms of oppression (e.g. 'isms' such as racism and ableism) and produces fear (e.g. 'phobias' such as homophobia and xenophobia) in service of maintaining existing power structures.

It is against this backdrop that the #MeToo movement spread across digital platforms in 2017 and enabled sustained conversations about sexual violence in the workplace. The Hollywood film industry served as a microcosm for these broader discussions as women (although not exclusively) began speaking out about their experiences of sexual harassment, coercion and assault. Attention was drawn to the ways that the entertainment system has traditionally safeguarded predators – filmmakers, screenwriters, producers, actors – at the expense of survivors (Funnell and Beliveau 2022: 2). While the conduct of Harvey Weinstein was an 'open secret' in Hollywood (Garber 2017), actors who resisted and/or spoke out against him were often blacklisted in the industry (Saad 2018) prior to his public outing and criminal prosecution in 2020 (Andrews-Dryer 2022). While the conduct of predatory filmmakers continues to be highlighted, greater attention is also being placed on the depiction of sexual violence on screen – including in the James Bond films.

James Bond is the longest-running film franchise in history and over the years the series has been described by many critics and viewers as problematic in terms of its cultural politics and values. According to Bond scholar James Chapman, the films not only present 'sexist, heterosexist, jingoistic, xenophobic and racist' attitudes (2007: 12) but at times even celebrate these values and views. He notes that 'despite their political incorrectness – or perhaps even because of it – the Bond films have been enormously popular with cinema goers around the world', suggesting that some audiences pay less attention to these messages or that the pleasures garnered from watching a Bond film outweigh – or are sometimes even linked to – the discriminatory content (Chapman 2007: 12).

In the wake of the #MeToo movement, the Bond franchise has received renewed critical attention with a particular focus on the depiction of sexual violence in the 1960s. Similar to other films of the decade, sexual violence was problematically mobilized for a variety of narrative purposes, from justifying the violent and retaliatory actions of women (Honey Ryder in *Dr. No* [Young 1962]), to emphasizing feminine vulnerability and depicting threats against women (Tatiana Romanova in *From Russia With Love* [Young 1963]), to undermining and even attacking lesbian identity (Pussy Galore in *Goldfinger* [Hamilton 1964]). However, when Bond engages in violent and predatory conduct, it is often played off in the films as flirtatious (Patricia Fearing in *Thunderball* [Young 1965]) or even a necessary field tactic (woman in golden bikini in *Diamonds Are Forever* [Hamilton 1971]; see Funnell 2022). This conduct and its cinematic coding have not aged well and many viewers today struggle with watching these scenes, especially given the increasing importance of affirmative consent in social discourse and public consciousness in recent years.

An example of this dynamic occurred at the time of writing this introduction, when actor George Lazenby, who played James Bond in only one film, *On Her Majesty's Secret Service* (Hunt 1969), issued a public apology for making sexist and homophobic comments during an onstage interview for the Australian tour of 'The Music of James Bond' show. According to one source,

Introduction: Resisting James Bond in the Daniel Craig Era 3

It was absolutely unbelievable … At one point he named an Australian cricketer whose daughter he was chasing, and he said he dragged the daughter out of a pub and put her in a car in London, which again is, of course, horrific … It wasn't even charming, it wasn't even funny. It was creepy, it was offensive … He was disgusting, there's no two ways about it.

(qtd. in Romualdi 2022)

Whether this was an admission, exaggeration or fictitious tale, this bolstering of 'sexual prowess' and cavalier attitude towards sexual violence was considered inappropriate by the audience and Lazenby was jeered off stage. He has since been removed from the tour.

In addition to the actions of the assigned-male-at-birth (AMAB) characters featured on screen in the 1960s, the conduct of Bond filmmakers behind the scenes is now being questioned. In 2022, actor Marguerite LeWars stated that she was sexually assaulted by director Terence Young on her way to the wrap party for the inaugural *Dr. No* (1962). In her account, when she resisted his physical advances, he threatened to cut her out of the film exclaiming 'do you know who I am?!' (Binley 2022). While some fans have criticized LeWars for waiting sixty years before speaking out, what her account draws attention to is the way that power dynamics and intersectional privilege have historically operated by safeguarding and even bolstering white (cis-)men within the US and British film industries for decades. Moreover, LeWars' account opens up questions about the conduct of Young off-screen and how this may have influenced the depiction of sexual violence on screen, given his direction of the aforementioned *Dr. No*, *From Russia With Love* and *Thunderball*.

With the release of each new Bond film, the marketing team has to grapple with this contentious history and the legacies of privilege across the series. For instance, studio-supported promotional materials typically address the casting and characterization of each new leading woman, frequently seeking to distance the new actor from the series' history of sexual objectification (even as the pattern gets repeated). There are numerous interviews in which the actor describes herself as a new/different Bond girl (Stewart 2021; Zamlout 2021) or, in the case of Monica Bellucci, who plays the widow Lucia Sciarra in *Spectre* (Mendes 2015), contending that she is not a Bond girl but a Bond woman (Smith 2015). There is both a recognition and an admission in these stories about the problematic treatment of past women in the franchise and a desire to promote an alternative impression (regardless of whether the narrative actually supports it) in order to attract the widest possible audience to see the film.

This is most evident in the Daniel Craig era, where both the film narratives and promotional materials explicitly seek to position Craig as a new/different Bond for a new/different era. This is supported by the structuring of *Casino Royale* (Campbell 2006) as a prequel and origin story for Bond, which in turn opens up space for the revisioning of the figure, franchise and brand (Lindner 2009). And yet, many of the same problematic elements that have historically defined the series, such as sexual violence, still appear in the Craig-era films even though they have been superficially repackaged.

In *Skyfall* (Mendes 2012), for instance, Séverine tells Bond that she is a sex worker who is owned and abused by the villain Raoul Silva. She asks Bond to kill her captor so that she can be free. A few scenes later, Bond 'seals their deal with a kiss' by walking in on a naked Séverine in the shower and proceeding to have sex with her. While their encounter is intended to be steamy, it comes across as predatory and abusive given Séverine's vulnerable situation. When Silva finds out about the affair, he uses Séverine for target practice and she is killed midway through the film. The sheer disposability of Séverine renders her one of the most tragic and disempowered women across the entire series (see Funnell 2015). This is just one of many examples from the Craig era that undermines the assertion/assumption that the representation of women has substantively improved in the series.

Sexual violence is not only featured in the content of the Craig-era films but has recently been linked to those responsible for creating them as well. For instance, screenwriter Paul Haggis, who worked on *Casino Royale* and *Quantum of Solace* (Forster 2008), was arrested in 2022 on sexual assault charges in Italy. He had previously been accused of raping a publicist in 2017 and three additional women came forward with allegations in 2018 which are pending at the time of this publication (Hoffman 2022). Additionally, *No Time To Die* (2021) director, Cary Fukunaga, has been 'accused of inappropriate workplace behavior and abusing his power on set to engage in relationships with younger women' (Bergeson 2022). A number of women have accused the director of grooming them for sex, in addition to a consultant who claims that Fukunaga also groomed him to write scripts in his name (Bergeson 2022). Fukunaga made waves during the film's promotion, stating 'Sean Connery's character rapes women' as a way to suggest that his film, *No Time To Die*, moves Bond into a more progressive place than the earlier films in the series (Sharf 2021).

What these examples highlight are the complex interrelations between power, privilege and identity across long-running franchises such as the James Bond films. In particular, they prompt us to question whether sexual violence is permanently engrained in the figure of Bond and the spy genre more broadly. Not only are most Bond/spy film creators privileged in terms of their gender, race, class, sexual orientation, ability and/or nationality, but some have reportedly engaged in sexual harassment, coercion and assault – conduct that, at the very least, influences our perception of their films and the conditions of their creation. This connection between film content and the conditions of film production, alongside broader social, ideological and cultural issues, cannot be overlooked.

While the Craig era has been described as more progressive due to the interventions of women creators – with Barbara Broccoli serving as co-producer across all the films and Phoebe Waller-Bridge providing script support for *No Time To Die* – it is important to remember that these women are still in the minority of creative positions and operate in a profit-driven space that promotes privilege. The assumption that a woman filmmaker will create inherently progressive and/or feminist texts also overlooks the economic and industry-based factors that dictate funding, production and profit.

What the #MeToo movement has accomplished, by influencing social consciousness and creating an environment for people to speak up about sexual misconduct, is to call much closer attention to the ongoing imbalances of privilege and abuses of power (within the cultural industries and beyond), which the Bond series so frequently and diegetically reflects, represents and upholds. Moreover, while the #MeToo movement encourages cultural critique, it also challenges us to think more expansively and intersectionally about systems of power and how they interrelate with and rely upon inequalities of gender, race, class, ability, nationality/coloniality and sexual orientation. As such, the #MeToo movement emerges at a particular cultural moment that is defined by challenges to and resistance against abuses of power that have historically been institutionalized, aestheticized, systematized and weaponized for the benefit of existing forms of privilege.

Building on this viewpoint while widening the scope of analysis beyond the #MeToo movement, *Resisting James Bond* brings together a multi-disciplinary collection of essays to offer new critiques of power, privilege and (in)justice across the Daniel Craig era of 007 films (2006–21). Covering a variety of topics from a range of critical and theoretical lenses, the chapters are organized thematically around embodiments *and* disembodiments of power and privilege, and look across the formal, narrative, cultural and geopolitical elements that define the revisionist-reversionist world of Daniel Craig's Bond (Funnell 2018).

In Part One, 'Embodiment', Tatiana Konrad explores the depiction of environmental injustice and 'slow violence' in the Craig-era films. Focusing on the Global South and specifically postcolonial nations and environments, Konrad argues that the Craig-era films can be read as ecocinema and portray environmental injustice in such a way that both calls for and simultaneously sabotages environmental action. Ron E. Hassner examines the depiction of state-sponsored torture across the Craig era and the conflicting messages conveyed through its cinematic presentation and apparent condemnation. He argues that a shift towards emotional and psychological torture in *No Time To Die* ultimately results in Bond's undoing. Colin Burnett considers how the classic image of Moneypenny is being challenged from within the series during the Craig era as well as by writers and artists developing texts outside the film canon. He argues that the revisionings of Moneypenny – from a secondary character to a primary figure – can be understood as means of resistance against a franchise known for its sexualization, denigration and subjugation of women. Mary M. Burke examines Bond's physical and psychological disintegration in *Skyfall* in relation to Alexander McQueen's autumn 1995 fashion collection 'Highland Rape', which critiqued British culture's subjugation of its own margins. She argues that Bond's reassembly as a fighting-fit, loyal Englishman by the film's close denotes its ultimate evasion of the questions of both Scottish independence and the cultural evisceration of the Highlands. Bridget E. Keown analyses the ways in which gender, power and subjectivity inform the various depictions of trauma across the Craig-era films. She argues that while these different manifestations of trauma emphasize the humanity of certain (privileged) characters and encourage audience empathy, this often happens at the expense of the agency and potential of marginalized others.

In Part Two, 'Disembodiment', Kathryn Hendrickson and John Brick discuss how the Craig-era films position James Bond in a changing world of technology, cyberterrorist threats and shifting global tensions. They argue that the Craig films rationalize information as a privileged resource and justify the exercise of extraordinary state violence and surveillance in the pursuit of maintaining its control and upholding traditional (nationalistic) hierarchies. Milo Sweedler considers how the Craig-era films synthesize and fictionalize contemporaneous macroeconomic and socio-political developments thereby providing an audio-visual narrative that traces the evolving spectre of capitalism haunting the world. Harshad Keval explores contested spaces of belonging through the transversal raciality of classed, gendered and sexualized representations contained within the 007 film narratives, and unpacks how racialized 'others' appear and disappear across the Craig-era films. Focusing on the place and significance of cities in the 007 cinematic imaginary, Fernando Gabriel Pagnoni Berns discusses how warfare and international terrorism have become highly urbanized across the Craig-era films, which show a notable disinterest in the safety of everyday citizens.

This book's discussion of the dis/embodiments of power and privilege in the James Bond films takes place at a critical moment in the history of the 007 series: James Bond is dead. His on-screen demise in *No Time To Die* not only signifies the end of Daniel Craig's tenure as 007 but also, more importantly, creates a unique opportunity to radically reimagine the world of James Bond moving forward. At the time of publication, the Bond franchise is preparing to cast a new actor in the title role and to reinvent the series once again. 'James Bond will return', we have been promised, but what version of Bond will that be and to what extent will the next incarnation of the character adhere to – or break from – the established 007 formula?

References

Andrews-Dryer, H. (2022), 'Harvey Weinstein's Rape Conviction and Jail Sentence Upheld in New York', *The Washington Post*, 2 June. Available online: https://www.washingtonpost.com/arts-entertainment/2022/06/02/harvey-weinstein-conviction-upheld/.

Bergeson, S. (2022), 'Cary Fukunaga Accused of Inappropriate Behavior on Multiple Sets, "Grooming" Young Women – Report', *IndieWire*, 31 May. Available online: https://www.indiewire.com/2022/05/cary-fukunaga-accused-inappropriate-behavior-1234722624/.

Binley, A. (2022), 'James Bond Actor Breaks 60-Year Silence to Claim Dr No Director Sexually Assaulted Her', ITV.com, 13 July. Available online: https://www.itv.com/news/2022-07-13/bond-actor-breaks-60-year-silence-to-claim-dr-no-director-sexually-assaulted-her.

Chapman, J. (2007), *Licence to Thrill: A Cultural History of James Bond Films*, 2nd edn, London: I.B. Tauris.

Funnell, L. (2015), 'Objects of White Male Desire: (De)Volving Representations of Asian Women in Bond Films', in L. Funnell (ed.), *For His Eyes Only: The Women of James Bond*, 79–87, New York: Wallflower Press.

Funnell, L. (2018), 'Reworking the Bond Girl Concept in the Craig Era', *Journal of Popular Film and Television* 46: 11–21.

Funnell, L. (2022), 'Delightful Duties?: Sexual Violence in the Connery-Era James Bond Films (1962–1971)', in L. Funnell and R. Beliveau (eds), *Screening #MeToo: Rape Culture in Hollywood*, 11–28, Albany: SUNY Press.

Funnell, L. and R. Beliveau (2022), 'Introduction: The Promise of #MeToo as a Theoretical Lens', in L. Funnell and R. Beliveau (eds), *Screening #MeToo: Rape Culture in Hollywood*, 1–9, Albany: SUNY Press.

Garber, M. (2017), 'In the Valley of the Open Secret: From Thomas Carlyle to Harvey Weinstein, A Brief History of a Pernicious Term', *The Atlantic*, 11 October. Available online: https://www.theatlantic.com/entertainment/archive/2017/10/harvey-weinstein-latest-allegations/542508/.

Hoffman, J. (2022), 'Paul Haggis, Oscar-Winning Filmmaker, Arrested in Italy on Sexual Assault Charges', *Vanity Fair*, 20 June. Available online: https://www.vanityfair.com/hollywood/2022/06/paul-haggis-arrested-in-italy-on-sexual-assault-charges.

Lindner, C. ed. (2009), *Revisioning James Bond: James Bond and Casino Royale*, New York: Wallflower.

Romualdi, M. (2022), 'Former James Bond Star George Lazenby Accused of "Homophobic" Comments Issues Apology', *Entertainment Canada*, 12 September. Available online: https://etcanada.com/news/927958/former-james-bond-star-george-lazenby-accused-of-homophobic-comments-issues-apology/.

Saad, N. (2018), 'Harvey Weinstein's Accusers: List Includes Fledging Actresses and Hollywood Royalty', *Los Angeles Times*, 25 May. Available online: https://www.latimes.com/entertainment/la-et-weinstein-accusers-list-20171011-htmlstory.html.

Sharf, Z. (2021), 'Cary Fukunaga Says Sean Connery's Bond Is "Basically" a Rapist: "That Wouldn't Fly Today"', *IndieWire*, 23 September. Available online: https://www.indiewire.com/2021/09/cary-fukunaga-sean-connery-bond-rapist-1234666901/.

Smith, N. M. (2015), 'Monica Bellucci: "I'm Not a Bond Girl, I'm a Bond Woman"', *Guardian*, 17 September. Available online: https://www.theguardian.com/film/2015/sep/17/monica-bellucci-james-bond-spectre-bond-woman.

Stewart, S. (2021), 'Ana de Armas Redefines the "Bond Girl" in "No Time To Die"', *New York Post*, 7 October. Available online: https://nypost.com/2021/10/07/how-ana-de-armas-redefines-the-bond-girl-in-no-time-to-die/.

Zamlout, N. (2021), 'Halle Berry Reveals Why She Accepted the Role of Jinx in "Die Another Day"', *Collider*, 3 December. Available online: https://collider.com/halle-berry-die-another-day-jinx-role-comments/.

Part One

Embodiment

1

James Bond, Environmental Injustice and 'Slow Violence' in the Craig Era

Tatiana Konrad

In the age of environmental degradation and global climate change, nations are continuously viewed through the lens of wealth and political power. The Global North that through industrialization triggered anthropogenic climate change fails to take adequate and radical measures that would help minimize the effects of the ongoing environmental crisis, perpetuating false hopes that humanity can go on living the way it is now (see Pardikar 2020). In turn, the Global South is especially strongly experiencing climate change through such phenomena as rising sea levels, flooding and droughts. One way to perceive inequality today is through the perspective of the environment. The postcolonial and environmental studies scholar Rob Nixon has coined the term 'slow violence' to explain environmental inequality experienced by postcolonial nations (see Nixon 2011). While the Global North still remains in a privileged position when it comes to living in a world that is being transformed by climate change, the Global South, and especially postcolonial nations, has been struggling to survive on the planet transformed by pollution, climate change and other environmental issues.

The stark difference in the ways climate change and environmental degradation impact the Global North and Global South is overt in James Bond films created during the Daniel Craig era. Slum living in Uganda, as portrayed in *Casino Royale* (Campbell 2006); privatization of natural resources and lack of access to clean water in Bolivia, as depicted in *Quantum of Solace* (Forster 2008); desert landscapes in *Spectre* (Mendes 2015); and impoverished urban images of Cuba in *No Time To Die* (Fukunaga 2021) are all impactful images of this 'slow violence'. These films recognize environmental injustice as a way to oppress individuals and nations. As such, they not only dramatically influence the identity of James Bond as a white saviour (impacting his masculinity and heroism), but

12   *Resisting James Bond: Power and Privilege in the Daniel Craig Era*

also foreground environmental injustice, particularly in the Global South, where people and the environment have continuously been exploited and abused through systematic 'slow violence'. This essay argues that while the images of 'slow violence' that affects the postcolonial world serve as a background in every Bond film in the Craig era, their omnipresence makes 'slow violence' conspicuous, and the devastation of the Global South ultimately comes to the fore in each of these films. This 'slow violence' becomes necessary for the plots of the films, being in service to colonial pursuits. It is also conspicuously characteristic of the Global South, for attacks on the homeland are framed differently (in *Skyfall*) than the destruction of places, spaces, people and their livelihoods in the Global South. James Bond fights against evil in a world dramatically altered by 'slow violence', frequently committing or contributing to 'slow violence' himself.

The essay explores the role of the Global South, and postcolonial nations and environments in particular, in the recent Bond films and re-envisions these films as examples of what Scott MacDonald has termed 'ecocinema' (2004: 107–32). Paula Willoquet-Maricondi defines ecocinema as films that 'actively seek to inform viewers about, as well as engage their participation in, addressing issues of ecological import' (2010a: 10). The scholar elaborates on this definition, arguing that ecocinema has

> consciousness-raising and activist intentions, as well as responsibility to heighten awareness about contemporary issues and practices affecting planetary health. Ecocinema overtly strives to inspire personal and political action on the part of viewers, stimulating our thinking so as to bring about concrete changes in the choices we make, daily and in the long run, as individuals and as societies, locally and globally.
>
> (2010b: 45)

This essay views the Craig-era films as ecocinema that displays environmental injustice and both calls for and sabotages pro-environmental action.

Ruined environments and the visibility of 'slow violence'

Depictions of environments, landscapes, places and spaces in James Bond cinema are rich and multiple. They vary from easily recognizable Western cities that convey the aesthetics through coded images, like Big Ben in London or the narrow channels that connect streets in Venice, to more opaque places whose location is introduced in the film through captions that indicate the geographic place or setting (i.e. hotels, bars, etc.) thereby helping to situate the viewer. According to Lisa Funnell and Klaus Dodds, James Bond is 'strongly defined by political and physical geography—the places, spaces, and very material contexts within which he operates including air, rock, snow, wind, and water' (2017: 2). Geography not only drives the plot, creating action through quickly changing, fascinating images of buildings, monuments and natural landscapes, but also helps shape the character of James Bond, telling the viewer much about his choices and priorities, as well as about Great Britain that he represents. As noted by Funnell and Dodds,

> film geography and popular geopolitics offer critical lenses through which scholars can examine the ways in which physical and human environments are conceptualized; often gendered but also intersected by age, race, class, and sexuality amongst other social locations; and depicted in mainstream culture, which in turn influences social-spatial discourses and practices.
>
> (2017: 2–3)

While the portrayals of both the Global North and Global South successfully convey these problematic intersectionalities, this essay explores specifically how the depictions of postcolonial nations communicate environmental issues that are the result of global environmental degradation yet have a particularly devastating effect on postcolonial territories, including humans and nonhumans that inhabit them.

The concept of 'slow violence' helps us better understand how environmental inequality and environmental racism consistently serve as backdrops to action plots that reinforce the power of white Western characters while reflecting ongoing environmental decline. Bringing together the environmental humanities and postcolonial studies, Rob Nixon describes 'slow violence' as 'a violence that occurs gradually and out of sight, a violence of delayed destruction that is dispersed across time and space, an attritional violence that is typically not viewed as violence at all' (2011: 2). Focusing his attention on environmental degradation in the postcolonial world, Nixon writes:

> Violence is customarily conceived as an event or action that is immediate in time, explosive and spectacular in space, and as erupting into instant sensational visibility. We need ... to engage a different kind of violence, a violence that is neither spectacular nor instantaneous, but rather incremental and accretive, its calamitous repercussions playing out across a range of temporal scales. In so doing, we also need to engage the representational, narrative, and strategic challenges posed by the relative invisibility of slow violence.
>
> (2011: 2)

Despite this unspectacular and non-immediate nature of 'slow violence', its images are very powerful. The postcolonial world depicted in *Casino Royale*, *Quantum of Solace*, *Spectre* and *No Time To Die* is used as a visual device to reinforce difference and emphasize the environmental/ecological otherness of those regions and their human and nonhuman inhabitants. In an Orientalist manner, the films other these locations in order to fulfil the exotic geography part of the 007 formula, but in doing so, they call attention to how Western systems of othering have created the very conditions leading to slow violence. Thus, the Craig-era films both critique and perpetuate slow violence.

It is also imperative to draw a distinction between the term 'an ecological other' dubbed by Sarah Jaquette Ray (2013) and my own usage of 'environmental/ ecological otherness' throughout this essay. For Ray, 'ecological others are often those from whose poor decisions and reckless activities the world ostensibly needs to be saved'; these individuals are contrasted to 'ecological subjects' whose goal is 'to save the world' (2013: 5). The two – i.e. 'ecological others' and 'ecological subjects' – form a binary opposition, which, in turn, generates difference and inequality in the issues related to the environment. The environmental/ecological otherness in the recent Bond films creates a similar effect as described by Ray, but it also reinforces the doomed nature of postcolonial nations. These nations do not make anti-environmental decisions; they are unable to make *any* decisions at all, as depicted in the films. This happens, for the most part, because nothing and no one (including James Bond) can save these nations but also because these nations are allegedly passive (which is particularly effectively illustrated in *Quantum of Solace*). This creates a form of disposability and thereby a good backdrop for Bond to be destructive without having to worry about the consequences. The very nature of Bond cinema becomes disrupted through environmental/ecological otherness that has become possible through 'slow violence': James Bond can only eliminate certain individuals, the bad guys, but he cannot save *the world* because a larger part of the world is dramatically affected by environmental degradation that is beyond Bond's power to fix.

Postcolonial nations, as sites of 'slow violence', serve as a background in every recent Bond film. Uganda, the Bahamas, Madagascar, Bolivia, Mexico, Morocco and Cuba are some of the silenced landscapes that turn into a playground for the white Western hero. These former colonies appear disposable, having been depleted of their resources and intrinsic value. The nations and the environmental issues that affect them (and, consequently, the planet), in turn, are either neglected (they function as a cinematic decoration) or muted. Such representations directly reflect what Nixon identifies as '[c]asualties of slow violence' (both 'human and environmental') that are 'most likely not to be seen, not to be counted', and therefore are 'light-weight, disposable casualties, with dire consequences for the ways wars are remembered, which in turn has dire consequences for the projected casualties from future wars' (2011: 13). People that become casualties as a result of James Bond's hunt for villains and the environments (both natural and physical) which are brutally destroyed through fighting and the use of military weapons remind the viewer about the ongoing inequality used to subjugate postcolonial nations and empower the Global North, specifically, hegemonic white masculinity embodied by James Bond.

Transformation of postcolonial environments began in the times of colonization. Alfred W. Crosby's idea of 'ecological imperialism' aptly describes the detrimental impact that colonization has had on the environment, forever changing environments and ecologies (Ashcroft, Griffiths and Tiffin 1998: 76). There are a variety of ways in which ecological imperialism manifests itself:

(a) the geographical introduction of non-native organisms such as disease pathogens, crops, and livestock and, during recent years, the transfer of toxic waste, nuclear contaminants, and other hazardous materials; (b) the ecological interaction of the introduced organisms and materials with human activities that incur environmental changes, often degradation; (c) the environmental role of imperial institutions, historically often those belonging to colonialism; (d) the work of the environmental sciences in the context of imperialism, in some cases for the goal of conservation; and (e) the use and ideas of the environment by persons and groups that resist the rule of empire.

(Zimmerer 2001: 4026)

Colonialist views of the world and the environment are dangerous and harmful on their own; yet the current climate crisis and ongoing environmental decline only further intensify the deadly nature of colonialist ideas that continue to permeate politics and impact decisions today.

Judith Butler's concept of 'global responsibility' that the scholar advances in the context of recent wars provides insight into discussions of global environmental crisis and, specifically here, into the imagery that the recent Bond films supply (2009: 36). It seems that in the times of a global crisis, there should indeed be a global response to the problem that might appear to be local yet will inevitably have a global impact. Butler reasons: 'one way of posing the question of who "we" are in these times of war is by asking whose lives are considered valuable, whose lives are mourned, and whose lives are considered ungrievable' (38). Susan Sontag has addressed a similar problem earlier, examining what happens 'when the subject is looking at other people's pain' depicted in photographs (2003: 7). According to Sontag,

> that 'we' would include not just the sympathizers of a smallish nation or a stateless people fighting for its life, but—a far larger constituency those only nominally concerned about some nasty war taking place in another country. The photographs are a means of making 'real' (or 'more real') matters that the privileged and the merely safe might prefer to ignore.
>
> (2003: 7)

Casino Royale, Quantum of Solace, Spectre and *No Time To Die* transmit the impact of 'slow violence' and colonial exploitation on selected postcolonial nations. Yet these cinematic representations persistently oscillate between the West and East, the Global North and Global South, privileged environments and destroyed/impoverished ones, white people and people of colour (and often unnamed secondary characters), insistently moving away from the idea of 'us' and toward the everyone-for-themselves approach. All this happens against the background of the world that has been violently transformed to create better conditions for white people through the siphoning and displacement of (natural) resources, leaving people of colour in environmentally precarious and hazardous conditions.

Postcolonial regions depicted in *Casino Royale, Quantum of Solace, Spectre* and *No Time To Die* can be roughly divided into two categories: tourist resorts and criminal places. The two also often overlap, with tourist locations swiftly turning into places full of criminal activity, and vice versa. In *Casino Royale*, there are several locations through which 'slow violence' is visualized. The film opens with the scenes in Uganda, where Le Chiffre and Steven Obanno make a financial deal (see Figure 1.1). Le Chiffre will be able to make a profit if a terrorist attack takes place. Yet James Bond intervenes and in the breathtaking scene that follows, the viewer is transmitted to Madagascar, where Bond is chasing the bomb-maker Mollaka. In the end, Bond kills the man as well as destroys via explosion the embassy that he ran into. And immediately, having discovered that Alex Dimitrios is involved in the matter, Bond travels

Figure 1.1 *Casino Royale* (Eon Productions et al. 2006).

to the Bahamas to find him. Uganda and Madagascar are portrayed in rather stereotypical, Hollywood-style ways to be recognized as 'Africa' (see also Mafe 2011). Through the armed men in Uganda who are part of a resistance movement and the bomber in Madagascar, 'Africa' is depicted as a vitally dangerous place. In turn, the environments in both scenes distinctly communicate the impact of colonial exploitation of these territories: impoverished, without a sufficient infrastructure, Uganda and Madagascar reflect environmental and ecological otherness, backgrounding the role of imperialism in the destruction of these places and foregrounding the present state in which these countries find themselves as sights of 'slow violence'.

The images of the Bahamas, in turn, are rather deceptive. Introduced as an expensive resort with stunning nature, the islands are a place of criminal activity. The intrigues and brutal murders that take place there reconstruct the Bahamas as a distinctly 'other' place: there, rich and predominantly white people spend holidays (due to its warm climate and beautiful, exotic nature), spend their money and perform various kinds of criminal acts. Environmental/ecological otherness of Uganda, Madagascar and the Bahamas communicated through slum living, impoverished houses and streets, and exotic nature code these places as the environment of the Global South, distinctly separating them from the rich parts of the world. Yet *Casino Royale* reminds the viewer how wrong it is to think about environments of places as disconnected units that can be artificially controlled by a (white) (hu)man. Toward the end of the film, the building collapse in Venice, Italy, relates directly to the impact of climate change on this place. This illustrates that while 'slow violence' is directed toward selected nations, it inevitably has a global impact, causing global environmental degradation. The image of Vesper Lynd, drowning in a locked elevator inside the collapsed building, illuminates the global impact of environmental crisis that will destroy the Western world, too, if no sufficient measures are taken.

Very similar portrayals occur in *Spectre* and *No Time To Die*. In one scene in *Spectre*, James Bond and Dr Madeleine Swann are on a train driving through the desert landscape of Morocco. The emptiness created through the absence of any other human characters helps to both emphasize the presence of nature in the scene and reinforce the state of the depicted nature. The uninhabited territory of the Sahara, albeit the desert's vastness, foregrounds the limited nature of the planet as a place that can be inhabited. The only two characters depicted in the scene, Bond and Swann, appear wearing expensive, fashionable clothes and accessories – all that against the background of a desert raises the questions of consumption, the priorities that the West (portrayed through the two characters) has set for itself and the danger of the world that the West has created at the expense of the planet's health. The scene also effectively contrasts the postcolonial environment as poor, scarce, uninhabitable and dangerous (as conveyed through the images of the desert) with the West, i.e. Bond and Swann, who care about the way they look (expensive, clean, ironed clothes, fine accessories, good haircuts, etc.) and whether they can be picked up by a driver on time (see Figure 1.2). Similarly, in *Quantum of Solace*, Bond and Montes are depicted walking away from the plane crash through the desert in fancy clothes. They look dirty but still they are a contrast to the locals around them.

Figure 1.2 *Spectre* (Eon Productions et al. 2016).

Bond, Environmental Injustice and 'Slow Violence'   19

In *No Time To Die*, Cuba is portrayed similarly to the Bahamas in *Casino Royale*: it is both a tourist resort and a place of criminal activity. James Bond is depicted there in his 'retirement' times, fishing, drinking in the local bars and leading a rather relaxed life. His experiences in Cuba are contrasted to impoverished urban images of the country. Bond's alleged retirement is portrayed in a similar fashion in *Skyfall*. After having been accidentally shot by Moneypenny, Bond survives, yet decides to retire and goes to Turkey. He is depicted having sex with a woman, then walking along the beach and later participating in a scorpion drinking game in a bar, where literally everyone is rooting for him. Expectedly, Bond wins the game. The scene concludes with the images of Bond in that same bar, learning from a TV report about a terrorist attack on MI6. This event makes Bond reconsider his decision to retire so soon, and the agent returns to London. The scene from *Skyfall*, however, is technically incomparable to the depictions of postcolonial places in *Casino Royale* and *No Time To Die* because unlike Cuba and the Bahamas, Turkey has never been a colony. Yet, the images of Turkey convey very similar messages as Cuba and the Bahamas: this is a resort that is popular among Europeans; Turkey is also a gateway that connects the West and East, North and South, and yet it is depicted as being far less developed. The superior role of Bond is reinforced through the dangerous game that only he dares play and ultimately wins. Moreover, just as many postcolonial countries in Bond cinema, Turkey is only an exotic place where the agent can relax but that he has to leave to protect a culturally, politically and economically more important country, Britain.

When it comes to ruined environments, *Skyfall* is a very curious example of Bond cinema created in the Craig era. Colonial nostalgia is evoked through the images of Shanghai, China, yet the film is scarce in images of the Global South. Instead, it uses other locations to communicate the idea of environmental degradation, specifically, denuded Scottish Highlands that Bond and M contemplate when Bond brings M to his childhood house (see Figure1.3). Additionally, Silva's island, located between the techno-orientalism of Shanghai and the various professional spaces of London, represents a crumbling city that is filled with wiring to facilitate Silva's plan. In *Skyfall*, the images of Great Britain, former British Empire, reflect the state's current vulnerability: explosions in the MI6, attacks on the London Underground and the Parliament and, finally, the images of poorly vegetated land around the house in the Scottish Highlands. Such vulnerability and instability echo the situation in the formerly colonized nations depicted in *Casino Royale*, *Quantum of Solace*, *Spectre* and *No Time to*

Figure 1.3 *Skyfall* (Eon Productions et al. 2012).

Die. In *Skyfall*, Great Britain functions as a site through which ruination can be contemplated. In doing so, and specifically by excluding the Global South and focusing on Great Britain, *Skyfall*, in a rather colonialist manner, foregrounds the only truly important location for Bond and his team – when Britain is in danger, all forces should be attracted to help the heartland, as Funnell and Dodds term Great Britain and its meaning for Bond (2017: 199–218).

Most overtly, the problem of 'slow violence' and environmental ruination is, however, addressed in *Quantum of Solace*. Through its focus on the water supply problem in Bolivia, the film depicts how access to clean water has been shaped by various political and cultural practices and choices as a form of privilege. *Quantum of Solace* portrays water as a natural resource that can be bought and sold and thus explores the complex cultural meanings of water privatization. The story plotted in *Quantum of Solace* is based on a true story of water privatization in Bolivia in 1997 and 1999. Cultural and environmental studies scholars Gay Hawkins, Emily Potter and Kane Race emphasize that even bottled water 'threaten[s] the universal human right to water' (2015: 133). Raising the problem of water privatization and seeing it as major evil, *Quantum of Solace* makes an important and timely contribution to environmental debates.

Ellen E. Moore, whom I draw on in my analysis of the film, provides a detailed reading of *Quantum of Solace* and its (anti-)environmental messages. While recognizing the potential of the film to deal with environmental (in)justice globally, reinforcing unequal power relationships among nations and within nations, Moore is concerned with the way the Bolivian people are portrayed in the film (2017: 78). Specifically, Moore draws attention to the inability of these characters to estimate the problem, enquire why it could have happened and ultimately find a way to solve it (78). *Quantum of Solace* 'depicts them [Bolivians] as passive—things happen *to* them and they have no ability or (perhaps) desire to control their fate—and also ignorant of the cause of the woes facing them' (78–9, italics in original). They need a 'White Savior', i.e. James Bond, who comes and solves the situation for them (79). 'Slow violence' is thus exercised by white people, and specifically Dominic Greene, toward Bolivians, and can be stopped by white people, and specifically James Bond. Even the fact that the film includes scenes where Bolivians speak yet the viewer is not provided with subtitles emphasizes the alleged insignificance of these characters, whose words function merely as background chatter.

Moore also criticizes the way environmentalism is communicated in *Quantum of Solace*. First, Greene as a 'pathological, homicidal, and elitist' individual is more of a profit-driven white capitalist than a true 'green' person, as his name suggests (2017: 80). Similarly, everyone whom the audience can observe at the fundraising party are just rich people who care more for their reputation than for the planet (80). Finally, Bond himself does not care for the environment, which can be observed through both his consumerist way of life (abundance of clothes, accessories, reliance on his car, to name just a few) and his attitude toward the clean water problem in Bolivia that he does not address at all (80). Environmentalism in the film is just another way to sustain the power imbalance between the rich and the poor, white people and people of colour, the Global North and the Global South. One iconic scene that vividly illustrates this imbalance achieved, in part, through access to natural resources, is the death of Strawberry Fields. *Quantum of Solace* remakes the famous Gold-painted dead woman from *Goldfinger* (Hamilton 1964), except here it is a woman covered in black oil, dying from total bodily immersion in fossil fuels in Bond's bed. Moreover, the film fully erases postcolonial nations, and Bolivians in particular, from the map of geopolitical control, illustrating and promoting 'slow violence'. Moore observes:

> *Quantum of Solace* implicitly identifies who should be in charge of a precious natural resource like water: it can't be Bolivians, who are portrayed as either too immoral (the General) or too ignorant (the people) to protect it or use it sustainably. In this respect, the film presents postcolonial fantasies about the need for the British Empire to act decisively on the world stage to protect natural resources on behalf of other countries who are too poor, disorganized, or corrupt to do it themselves.
>
> (2017: 80–1)

The film problematically reduces environmental degradation and ruination to an issue that can be solved by one person only, and specifically by a white powerful man whom James Bond stands for. Avi Brisman notes that *Quantum of Solace* belongs to the cinema with which, 'we either overlook or become desensitised to a particular environmental problem … and come to believe that the perpetrator of a given environment-related conflict has been thwarted or that whatever harm that has occurred has been repaired or could be repaired—just as in "crime fiction" where the "bad guys" are caught and justice is served' (2016: 294). The film not only belittles the ramifications of 'slow violence' but also caters the problem of environmental degradation to the viewer as an insignificant issue that can be easily fixed. Just as other Bond films that belong to the Craig era, *Quantum of Solace* perpetuates dangerous imperialist ideas and ideals, reflecting the real-existing environmental injustice but also promoting it.

Imperialism and environmental crisis

Bond's character is shaped by the images of ruined postcolonial environments and environmental injustice that feature in selected locations where he travels. The reasons Bond travels to these places, the way he interacts (or not) with the locals, the decisions he makes as he hunts criminals and, finally, the legacy he leaves there as he moves to another place impact the way the viewer understands Bond in the context of environmentalism, and imperialism.

Scholars argue that Bond cinema is 'a way of celebrating the continued relevance—and implied superiority—of (post)colonial ways of governing societies in the battles that have to be fought against terrorism' (Hasian qtd. in Moore 2017: 79). In a world that continues to operate through colonialist ideas and ideals, Bond, as a white British man in power, becomes a tool through which colonialism and imperialism can be realized. Moore notes that 'the "white savior" becomes directly—if inadvertently, or even supposedly unwillingly—identified as the protector of the environment and an agent for environmental justice' (2017: 79). Timo Müller's reading of the Bond character helps outline not only the known colonialist patterns communicated through Bond but also the way they reflect and shape neocolonialism today: 'His [Bond's] appeal as a spectacular saviour sustains not just nostalgia for the old Empire but also a neo-imperial mind-set, for which he performs the old imperial strategy of camouflaging political, economic, and discursive appropriation' (2015: 311). Such ongoing imperialist domination exercised through Bond, who intervenes in literally every geopolitical space that he wants to on behalf of Britain, fosters a problematic power dynamic in the era of environmental crisis, perpetuating environmental injustice that Nixon succinctly describes as 'slow violence'. Namely, the white West/Global North is depicted as the only entity that has power and resources to make a change, and even if the means and ways through which that change is achieved are conspicuously anti-environmental, this allegedly does not contribute to environmental degradation.

In the world of James Bond, environmental crisis is a distant danger that can never reach the West/Global North; it affects only the Global South that is already depicted through an environmental/ecological otherness. There is an astounding form of parallax in the recent Bond films, with one man allegedly being able to solve an environmental crisis on a global scale through local communities; yet these very communities remain affected by environmental injustice that seems to be a normality in the eyes of the West. The kind of '[i]mperialist nostalgia' that Moore describes in the context of *Quantum of Solace* permeates all other examples of films from the Craig era that either depict former British colonies, like Uganda, the Bahamas and Shanghai, or focus on the countries that have colonial history, including Madagascar, Bolivia, Mexico, Morocco and Cuba (2017: 79). Because there is no logically expected conclusion that would celebrate the people of Bolivia who have got access to water, it becomes clear that the chief problem in *Quantum of Solace* is not the fact that a whole nation could die due to an act of environmental injustice but a specific person, Greene, who is dangerous for Britain, and happens to be in Bolivia (Moore 2017: 79). There was disappointment that the fight was not over oil. As a result, the resource conflict does not directly impact Britain and therefore its resolution does not register in the film. Bolivians are thus not only entirely neglected in the film but also, just as all other postcolonial nations in the recent examples of Bond cinema, are 'marginalize[d]' and fully misinterpreted as individuals who cannot restore environmental justice (Moore 2017: 81).

The environmental impotency that is characteristic of postcolonial nations in the recent Bond films serves to strengthen the hegemony of James Bond and, through him, the West. Bond is the only character who can exercise control over the environment and environmental issues. Funnell and Dodds make a crucial observation, connecting colonialism/imperialism and environmentalism through the character of Bond: 'Bond's colonial masculinity remains a consistent and dominant force that is needed to maintain global order and that authority is quite literally elemental. As the embodiment of a country with extraterritorial reach and global authority, Bond's feeling and understanding of ice, water, fire, and the earth strengthens his and Britain's virility and vitality' (2017: 160). In turn, postcolonial nations are reduced to less-than-humans who become part of the environment dramatically transformed by 'slow violence' and can be destroyed together with that environment, as collateral damage. And Bond actively supports this kind of politics himself. For example, as Müller notes in the context of *Casino Royale*, 'Daniel Craig's Bond has no second thoughts about starting gun-fights in African embassies and shooting unarmed black suspects' (2015: 312). André J. Millard reminds us that in every Bond film 'a weapon of mass destruction falls into the wrong hands and threatens global destruction' (2020: 4). While this observation is true for the pre-Craig era, it cannot be straightforwardly applied to the recent films. The enemy has become more complex and harder to find and eliminate. But what is even more important is that the very idea of 'global destruction' has been transformed. The ongoing environmental crisis poses a threat to the whole planet; yet in the world of James Bond, this issue is relevant only in the context of postcolonial geographies. Misinterpreting the global threat as a local issue, the recent Bond films sustain colonialist views through which protection of the West becomes the priority, while the postcolonial world continues to be oppressed through, among other means, 'slow violence'.

Conclusion: Bond cinema as ecocinema?

Can one classify *Casino Royale*, *Quantum of Solace*, *Skyfall*, *Spectre* and *No Time To Die* as ecocinema? This depends on how one reads the films and, in the end, how one interprets ecocinema. Environmental injustice is an important part of all these films about James Bond. But whether the films actively seek to communicate environmental injustice as such to the viewer and fight for environmental justice is questionable. Environmental injustice is not framed as an issue directly impacting Britain and is thus not priority in the films. In a globally connected world where climate crisis crosses national borders and hemispheres, the Bond films show connection but not collaboration and cooperation. Helen Hughes claims that 'activist films are concerned to make visible the necessity for human cooperation in the protection of endangered species' (2011: 735). This is, of course, only one way to understand activist films, but it foregrounds the crucial aspect that advertently lacks in the recent Bond films – *cooperation*. To be sure, there is no cooperation in these films at all: the world is conspicuously divided into those who live in environmentally privileged places and postcolonial nations that are slowly but steadily being ruined by the privileged.

The disjunction of the world in the era of environmental crisis, and the unwillingness of the West to see 'slow violence' and environmental injustice (or, essentially, the choice to view it as something that is happening to 'them' and not to 'us') and fight both, depicted in these films, is especially problematic considering the genre of Bond cinema. According to Moore, traditionally, in spy films, 'white men [are portrayed] as those who save the day and people of color as either corrupt or inept' (2017: 91). Developing a sophisticated environmental plot is rather difficult in this context: 'Including environmental degradation in this particular generic form leads to a kind of awkwardness in portrayal. There's not much room for level-headed, rational thinking about environmental issues in the fantastical plots of spy films' (2017: 91). Yet, I would argue that these are exactly 'the fantastical plots' that could be effectively used to re-envision the world and its power dynamics and offer scenarios, according to which, cooperation is restored and the world works together toward environmental justice.

No Time To Die has shown the viewer that James Bond cinema is ready for change; the film embraces the reality of the twenty-first century through the black woman agent who replaces 007 (although this portrayal is not unproblematic either, considering that the number is reassigned multiple times throughout the film). Moving toward environmentalist and activist images that replace colonialist/imperialist visions of the world dramatically transformed by environmental degradation could be another important way for James Bond cinema to progress. Pat Brereton argues that 'the development of a deeper form of ecological media thinking, while recognizing all aspects of environmental justice, alongside promoting increased levels of critical literacy, is essential in creating a robust, sustainable environmental citizenship and embedding a comprehensive strategy for activating effective solutions into the future' (2019: 1). The recent Bond films are not successful ecocinema; but the fact that they make attempts to entwine environmental issues in the plots reveals the series' recognition of the changing world and the important role that environmental justice plays in it. This leaves hope that in the future James Bond films will recognize environmental crisis as the true threat to the global population, and James Bond will become a global hero, protecting not only the Crown but also the rest of the world.

References

Ashcroft, B. et al. (1998), *Key Concepts in Post-Colonial Studies*, London: Routledge.

Brereton, P. (2019), *Environmental Literacy and New Digital Audiences*, New York: Routledge.

Brisman, A. (2016), 'Environment and Conflict: A Typology of Representations', in A. Brisman et al. (eds), *Environmental Crime and Social Conflict: Contemporary and Emerging Issues*, 285–312, London: Routledge.

Butler, J. (2009), *Frames of War: When Is Life Grievable?* London: Verso.

Funnell, L. and K. Dodds (2017), *Geographies, Genders and Geopolitics of James Bond*, London: Palgrave Macmillan.

Hawkins, G. et al. (2015), *Plastic Water: The Social and Material Life of Bottled Water*, Cambridge, MA: MIT Press.

Hughes, H. (2011), 'Humans, Sharks and the Shared Environment in the Contemporary Eco-Doc', *Environmental Education Research* 17 (6): 735–49.

MacDonald, S. (2004), 'Toward an Eco-Cinema', *Interdisciplinary Studies in Literature and Environment* 11 (2): 107–32.

Mafe, D. A. (2011), '(Mis)Imagining Africa in the New Millennium: *The Constant Gardener* and *Blood Diamond*', *Camera Obscura* 25 (3 75): 68–99.

Millard, A. J. (2020), 'James Bond and the End of the World', *The International Journal of James Bond Studies* 4 (1): 1–13.

Moore, E. E. (2017), *Landscape and the Environment in Hollywood Film: The Green Machine*, Cham: Palgrave Macmillan.

Müller, T. (2015), 'The Bonds of Empire: (Post-)Imperial Negotiations in the 007 Film Series', in B. Buchenau and V. Richter (eds), *Post-Empire Imaginaries? Anglophone Literature, History, and the Demise of Empires*, 305–26, Leiden: Brill.

Nixon, R. (2011), *Slow Violence and the Environmentalism of the Poor*, Cambridge, MA: Harvard University Press.

Pardikar, R. (2020), 'Global North Is Responsible for 92% of Excess Emissions', *Eos*, 101. Available online: https://doi.org/10.1029/2020EO150969.

Ray, S. J. (2013), *The Ecological Other: Environmental Exclusion in American Culture*, Tucson: University of Arizona Press.

Sontag, S. (2003), *Regarding the Pain of Others*, New York: Picador.

Willoquet-Maricondi, P. (2010a), 'Introduction: From Literary to Cinematic Ecocriticism', in P. Willoquet-Maricondi (ed.), *Framing the World: Explorations in Ecocriticism and Film*, 1–22, Charlottesville: University of Virginia Press.

Willoquet-Maricondi, P. (2010b), 'Shifting Paradigms: From Environmentalist Films to Ecocinema', in P. Willoquet-Maricondi (ed.), *Framing the World: Explorations in Ecocriticism and Film*, 43–61, Charlottesville: University of Virginia Press.

Zimmerer, K. S. (2001), 'Ecological Imperialism', in N. J. Smelser and P. B. Baltes (eds), *International Encyclopedia of the Social & Behavioral Sciences*, 4026–7, Amsterdam: Elsevier Science.

2

'Do You Expect Me to Talk?'

Bond the Torture Critic

Ron E. Hassner

The Bond films are designed to entertain, not to break new moral ground. Their stance on violence is consistently hawkish: Violence is portrayed as effective as long as it is carried out on behalf of the state. Thus state-sanctioned assassination, special operations, conventional armed forces and sophisticated weaponry are all showcased as legitimate forms of violence that play an important role in securing state goals. On the other hand, the violence committed by non-state actors is framed as deplorable. It takes the form of terrorism, guerrilla warfare and weapons of mass destruction, all breaches of the laws of armed combat.

The glaring exception to this logic is the Bond franchise's position on torture. Torture is a frequent trope in both the Ian Fleming novels and the Bond movies. Recent surveys suggest that viewers, Western and non-Western alike, are split in their opinions on torture. Between one-third and half of those surveyed after 2001 tend to view torture as both an effective and necessary counter-terrorism tool (Gronke et al. 2010; Jordan 2014; Pew 2015; Blauwkamp, Rowling and Pettit 2018). The films step into this controversial area of public debate and take a bold and surprising stance: they consistently critique torture. The movies represent torture as an illegitimate and ineffective form of violence thereby rendering James Bond as an anti-torture franchise. Remarkably, even the Craig-era films, which exhibit a clear break from their formulaic predecessors, are consistent with the rest of the franchise on this front. Craig's Bond is as much a torture critic as are his predecessors. In these recent films, the disdain for torture is presented in an even starker form until, in *No Time To Die* (Fukunaga 2021), physical torture is absent altogether.

Throughout the franchise, this disdain for torture takes four forms. First, torture is sadistic, not pragmatic. Torturers take joy in the pain they cause, and they blur the line between interrogation, sexual assault and execution. Second, torture is evil.

It is not just performed by criminals, it constitutes them. These villains engage in lengthy discourses on torture that serve to mutually reinforce their evil and the evil of torture. Third, torture is ineffective. Bond does not yield to torture. Instead, he mocks it because it is a disreputable form of espionage, ineffective and dishonourable. It causes lasting psychological and physical damage and, in so doing, produces new villains. Fourth and finally, in the rare instances in which Bond engages in torture, these three logics are reversed. Bond uses force to extract information, but he does so rarely, quickly, superficially and effectively. He may (literally) twist an arm to extract information with no apparent effect on their subsequent relationship.

I explore these four themes in succession and conclude this chapter with a closer look at torture scenes in two closely related films (Funnell 2011) that appeared after 9/11: the opening sequence in *Die Another Day* (Tamahori 2002), the first Bond movie released after the events of 2001, and the infamous torture scene in *Casino Royale* (Campbell 2006), the first film in the Bond reboot starring Daniel Craig. My focus in this chapter is on the Bond films, not the Fleming books. Though the movies were not created as a coherent body of work, and vary in multiple and important ways, I propose here that the anti-torture sentiment in these films is a consistent motif across sixty years of Bond filmmaking, very much in contrast to the treatment of torture in cinema more broadly (Flynn and Salek 2012; Schlag 2019; Delehanty and Kearn 2020).

In the new Craig era, with the topic of state-sponsored torture hotly debated in the United States and Europe, torture assumes an even more important role in Bond narratives than it did during the formulaic period (1962–2002). The Bond films starring Daniel Craig don't merely reject torture, they condemn it outright, using the most shocking tools at the filmmakers' discretion to evoke disgust about torture. *No Time To Die* takes that condemnation to its logical conclusion: The physical torture trope, a fixture in the formulaic period, is absent from this film. There, the villain hopes to torture Bond emotionally: He can never be in contact with his family again, lest he kill them. Bond would rather end his own life than endure such psychological torture.

Torture is sadism

Why do villains consistently fail to shoot Bond on sight? Surely, there is no greater puzzle about Bond than this. Why do they devise elaborate means of executing Bond that are cumbersome, outlandish, slow and always unsuccessful? The simple answer is that these complex and convoluted executions can provide Bond with the time and opportunity that he needs to escape. The more nuanced answer is that killing Bond quickly would deprive villains of joy. Bond takes no pleasure in killing or torturing, but his arch rivals are his antitheses. They *only* take pleasure in killing if it is accompanied by their victims' severe and prolonged suffering. The trope of the torturous execution sends a message about the sadistic nature of Bond villains, but it also conveys ideas about the sadistic nature of torture. Only villains take joy in the pain of others. Physical torture, psychological torture, sexual assault and the killing of innocents are variations on the same obscene theme.

This blurring of sadistic categories is crisply displayed in one of the most famous torture scenes in any Bond movie, the laser scene in *Goldfinger* (Hamilton 1964). But is it a torture scene? Bond is as confused as the audience. The industrial laser gradually threatening to slice Bond in half, and the table to which he is strapped, surely look like torture devices (see Figure 2.1). But Auric Goldfinger asks no questions and seems disinterested in the proceedings. As the laser inches towards Bond, Goldfinger turns to leave the room:

> **Bond:** I think you've made your point, Goldfinger. Thank you for the demonstration.
> **Goldfinger:** Choose your next witticism carefully Mr Bond, it may be your last. The purpose of our two previous encounters is now very clear to me. I do not intend to be distracted by another. Good night, Mr Bond.
> **Bond:** Do you expect me to talk?
> **Goldfinger:** No, Mr Bond, I expect you to die. There is nothing you can talk to me about that I don't already know.

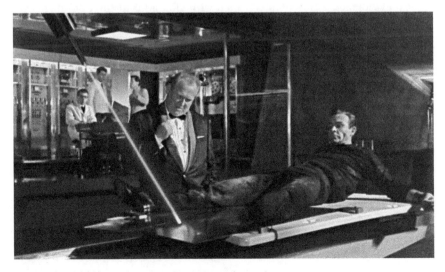

Figure 2.1 *Goldfinger* (Eon Productions et al. 1964).

Goldfinger's warning about witticisms might be an invitation for a confession. Or it might be an announcement of Bond's looming death. This distinction is clearer in the novel, where Goldfinger wants Bond to confess (Fleming 2012a: 185–7). In neither the film nor the novel does Bond collaborate. Is the film depicting torture, or a painful and complicated execution?

Bond villains frequently sow this confusion. Why does *Dr. No* (Young 1962) urge his troops to 'soften him up, I haven't finished with him yet'? We hear Bond being beaten off-screen, but the film provides no further clues about the purpose or results of this brutality, perhaps due to the constraints of the Hollywood Production Code. In *Live and Let Die* (Hamilton 1973), Mr Big threatens to have Bond's little finger (and more) snipped off if Solitaire fails in her prediction. His threats cannot motivate Bond, who is not under interrogation, or Solitaire, who has no access to information. In all these instances, torture seems to be the ends, not the means.

Because torture is equivalent to sadism in the Bond films, providing perpetrators with cruel pleasure, its primary use is not to extract information but to kill in a manner pleasing to villains. *Thunderball* (Young 1965), *Diamonds Are Forever* (Hamilton 1971), *Moonraker* (Gilbert 1979), *For Your Eyes Only* (Glen 1981) and *Licence To Kill* (Glen 1989) involve attempts to stretch, spin, crash, drown and shred Bond to death. In all these instances it is not clear whether the villain's primary goal is Bond's suffering or death. Perhaps they are disinterested in the distinction between the two. In the minds of villains, physical torture and psychological torture go hand in hand.

Sexual violence is closely intertwined with villainous torture. Bond engages in sexual aggression throughout the franchise (Funnell 2022). But in these torture scenes, he is often the target of sexualized violence. Goldfinger's laser is aimed at Bond's groin. Xenia Onatopp tries to kill Bond by squeezing him to death with her thighs while they are having sex in *GoldenEye* (Campbell 1995). Bond's moans of pleasure morph into moans of pain but for Onatopp, the two activities, sex and torture, provide equal pleasure. In *Tomorrow Never Dies* (Spottiswoode 1997), the villain threatens to use torture tools to 'probe' Bond's genitals. Le Chiffre's torture of Bond in *Casino Royale*, further explored later, is focused entirely on Bond's genitals. But Chiffre is also attracted to Bond, commenting on how well he has taken care of his body. Similarly, in *Skyfall* (Mendes 2012), the villain Raoul Silva slips easily from a monologue about the torture of rats to homoerotic overtures towards Bond. As he caresses

Figure 2.2 *The World Is Not Enough* (Eon Productions et al. 1999).

Bond, who is tied to a chair, their conversation blends all these themes together: death, torture, espionage, discipline, bondage, sex.

In *The World Is Not Enough* (Apted 1999), Elektra King straps Bond to a garrotte, a device for torturing or executing by strangulation (see Figure 2.2). She threatens Bond using the type of statement that would usually precede an interrogation: 'Five more turns and your neck will break'. Yet, though she continuously tightens the garrotte around his neck, she asks for no information. Indeed, in an overturning of the logic of torture, it is Bond, immobilized and tormented, who asks the questions and King, the torturer, who provides the information. King then straddles Bond, adding a sexual dimension to the torture ('You know what happens when a man is strangled?') as she throttles and kisses him simultaneously. Bond collapses the two themes – torture and sex – into one when he refers to both the garrotte and King as 'one last screw'. In bringing together all the elements of torture that characterize Bond's formulaic era – torture, sexual violence and death – and in blurring the distinction between the three, King and Bond remind us that torture is sadism.

Torture is evil

Torture is not merely a tool that Bond villains employ and take pleasure in. It is an action that identifies them as villains. Alongside their unique physical characteristics, megalomaniacal plans, dazzling lairs and muscular minions, torture is a primary building block of Bond's evil counterparts. We know that Franz Sanchez is the villain in *Licence To Kill* as soon as he is introduced: he surprises his girlfriend, Lupe Lamora, in bed with her lover and proceeds to whip her as she lies naked, crying. Lest the audience suspect that this torture serves any purpose other than his sadistic pleasure, Sanchez warns her: 'Not a word.' In the background, we can hear the last screams of Lamora's lover, as he is being mutilated to death.

Villains signal their obsession with torture not only by performing it, often personally and intimately, but by also talking about it at length. These discourses highlight the perversity of torture in two ways. First, the villains employ elaborate and nonsensical technical language, describing torture as a scientific process, a demented experiment of sorts. Darius Rejali has referred to this as 'torture talk' (Rejali 2008). The villains talk much but leave the 'hands on' physical work to their minions (Funnell and Dodds 2017).

Paradoxically, the villains' efforts to mask torture as science only serves to unmask the venal pleasure that is their true motive. For example, Emilio Largo's promise of torturing Domino Derval 'scientifically and slowly' in *Thunderball* is incongruous with his tools, a burning cigarette and a fistful of ice. Eliot Carver, the villain in *Tomorrow Never Dies*, supplements the usual 'torture talk' with a ridiculous 'theory of torture' that lays bare his sadistic purpose: the tools of torture (he refers to them as 'toys') will 'probe' Bond's 'chakra points', such as his heart and genitals, 'inflicting the maximum amount of pain while keeping the victim alive for as long as possible'. Carver's assistant, Stamper, hopes to break the previous torture record of 52 hours. Carver requests that Bond's heart be removed while it is still beating.

Second, 'torture talk' chillingly juxtaposes the lurid details of torture against the genteel demeanour of the villain. It tends to occur in the context of polite conversations between Bond and his nemeses. For example, in *Octopussy* (Glen 1983), Kamal Khan and Bond discuss the merits of various forms of torture and truth serums (sodium pentothal versus curare with psychedelic compounds) over the course of a dinner. Throughout the conversation, Bond conveys revulsion whereas Khan communicates delight. Bond may have a licence to kill but, as I argue below, prefers to kill quickly, and takes no delight in the suffering of his targets.

Usually, these monologues about torture make no reference to interrogation or information. Such is also the case in one of Bond's most recent, and very elaborate, torture scene in *Spectre* (Mendes 2015). As the most famous of Bond

'Do You Expect Me to Talk?': Bond the Torture Critic 35

villains, the appearance of villainous Blofeld here ties the Craig films to their formulaic predecessors. Blofeld straps Bond into a deviant medical device, a dentist's chair of sorts equipped with remote-controlled drills. He then explains the purpose of the machine and offers his own 'theory of torture':

> Torture is easy, on a superficial level. A man can watch himself being disemboweled and derive great horror from the experience, but it's still going on at a distance. It isn't taking place where he is. As you know all too well, dear Madeleine, a man lives inside his head. That's where the seed of his soul is … So James, I'm going to penetrate to where you are. To the inside of your head. Now the first probe will play with your sight, your hearing and your balance, just with the subtlest of manipulations … [A needle penetrates Bond's skull and he screams in agony] … If the needle finds the correct spot in the fusiform gyrus, you recognize no one … [A second needle penetrates Bond's skull, he convulses in pain]

The language Blofeld employs here evokes post 9/11 justifications for torture (Hassner 2019) with one notable exception: torture proponents argued that torture could yield information, but Blofeld is not interested in information. At no point does Blofeld make any effort to interrogate Bond. Torture serves no purpose other than to exemplify evil.

Torture is ineffective

Rudely juxtaposed with the villains' 'theory of torture' is the persistent failure of torture. Contrary to Blofeld's excursus, Bond does not go blind or deaf as result of the first drill and he does not lose his memory as result of the second drill. The movie does not even bother to explain why the torture has no lasting effect on Bond or how Blofeld could have erred so much in his prognosis. We must assume that Bond's heroism and superpower strength play some role in his physical immunity. More importantly, not once does a Bond villain succeed in extracting information from Bond, neither in the formulaic era nor under Craig. Their torture is as futile as their efforts to kill Bond or attempts at world domination. This serves to remind the audience that the primary purpose of torture is not pragmatic but sadistic.

Bond underscores the futility of torture not only by refusing to collaborate but by openly mocking his tormentors. In *You Only Live Twice* (Gilbert 1967), Bond tells his tormentor, Brandt, to 'enjoy herself', which earns him a slap across the face. When she threatens him with a scalpel, he proceeds to seduce her. Bond mocks the professional torturer in *Tomorrow Never Dies*, Dr Kaufman, inquiring whether his doctorate is in torture. Later in the same film, Bond mocks Carver's threats of torture ('I would have thought watching your TV shows was torture enough'), a sentiment he repeats in *Spectre* in response to Blofeld's 'torture talk'.

To counterbalance Bond's cavalier attitude towards threats of torture, the Bond franchise offers occasional reminders of the enduring psychological and physical impact of torture. These are no laughing matter. They underscore the futility of torture as an intelligence source by emphasizing what torture *does* produce: lasting physical and psychological scars. In *Thunderball*, Bond's partner in the Bahamas, the British secret service agent Paula Caplan, kills herself with a cyanide capsule rather than endure torture at the hands of Largo. In *Octopussy*, Khan notes that his preferred truth serum has the 'unfortunate side effect' of permanent brain damage, not unlike Blofeld's 'dentist chair' in *Spectre*.

Skyfall takes this logic to its natural conclusion: If torture damages the brain, and villains are depicted as 'insane', it stands to reason that torture produces villains just as villains produce torture. We learn that Bond's foe Raoul Silva was tortured for five months by the Chinese before he attempted suicide. Like Paula Caplan forty-seven years earlier, Silva tried to swallow a cyanide capsule to avoid torture, but his capsule served only to scar him inside and out. Indirectly, torture is responsible for his decaying gums, damaged jaw, sunken cheek, drooping eyelid and bloodshot eyes. He wears a prosthesis which he removes dramatically in front of M: 'Look upon your work ... mother.' Like Lyutsifer Safin in *No Time To Die*, the facial scars serve to identify Silva as 'evil'.

Silva's backstory provides a multi-pronged condemnation of torture. His is the 'ugly face' of torture and, more broadly, of the espionage business. It scars, emotionally and physically, and constructs villains. Torture is thus doubly ineffective. Not only does it fail to elicit information, it also generates villains who, in turn, engage in further torture. In this account, villains are epiphenomenal to torture. They are not the independent cause of torture, merely the medium through which torture reproduces itself.

Bond twists arms

To affirm and reaffirm this critique of torture, the Bond movies set up a stark contrast between the frequent, elaborate and futile torture that villains engage in and the brief, improvised and usually effective torture that Bond engages in. He

'Do You Expect Me to Talk?': Bond the Torture Critic   37

does so rarely and with decreasing frequency over the course of the franchise. Unlike his antagonists, who blend killing and torment, Bond takes no pleasure in torture, just as he takes none in killing. Nor does he intentionally introduce torture into the execution of opponents. Their brutal deaths occur by accident or necessity, usually because Bond is unarmed and has to improvise, or because the villains fall into a trap of their own devising.

Throughout the franchise, Bond is impatient when it comes to interrogating people. We learn in *Quantum of Solace* (Forster 2008) that he prefers to dispatch his opponents quickly rather than interrogate them, much to M's chagrin. When he does employ force to extract information, he uses no tools or machinery, only his hands. Whereas the torture engineered by villains can take up an entire scene, Bond's interrogations never last more than a couple of seconds. Indeed, some viewers might consider Bond's use of force to fall below the threshold of formal torture, what US intelligence officials post-9/11 would have called 'enhanced interrogation'.

Bond grabs Tatiana Romanova's arms and shakes her to extract information in *From Russia With Love* (Young 1963). He does not relent when she complains that he is hurting her, and he slaps her across the face when he perceives that she is lying. He twists Tracy di Vicenzo's arm in *On Her Majesty's Secret Service* (Hunt 1969), despite her protestations, and slaps her when she claims to know nothing. Curiously, neither show of force yields any information. It also seems to leave no lasting impression on the victims: Romanova becomes Bond's lover and di Vicenzo becomes his wife. When interrogating women protagonists, Bond's methods are particularly brief and never fatal. But they all entail sexual violence in one form or another (Funnell 2022).

Bond's spontaneous use torture is perfectly exhibited in the opening sequence of *Diamonds Are Forever* (Hamilton 1971). Here, Bond tortures three separate individuals at dizzying speed: Within the first fifty-six seconds of the film, he hurts, threatens and successfully interrogates all three. The first is a Japanese man, who Bond hurls across a room. 'Where is he? I shan't ask you politely next time. Where is Blofeld?' Having learned the answer ('Cairo') the camera pans to a casino, where Bond punches a man who is seated at a roulette table: 'One chance: Where can I find him?' Having gathered his information ('Marie, ask Marie') the camera pans to a scene at a beach, where Bond strangles Marie with her own bikini. The next shot shows Bond in Blofeld's lab. Marie must have provided its location. Three more women fall prey to Bond's violent questioning later in the same film.

As the films start to distance themselves from the early Sean Connery era and into the light-hearted Roger Moore era (Chapman 2008: 123–8), Bond's

38   *Resisting James Bond: Power and Privilege in the Daniel Craig Era*

aggressive interrogations decreased in frequency and then ceased altogether. In *The Spy Who Loved Me* (1977), Bond threatens to drop the assassin Sandor from a rooftop unless Sandor reveals the location of Aziz Fekkesh. Sandor cooperates but Bond, in a rare moment of intentional cruelty, drops him to his death regardless. That scene in the late 1970s is the last violent interrogation that Bond instigates.

This rooftop scene is parodied and inverted in *Quantum of Solace*, testifying to the ultimate futility of torture. Craig's Bond is even more reluctant to violently interrogate and takes even less pleasure at slowly dispatching his opponents than did prior Bonds. Here, Craig dangles his rival over an abyss, purportedly to find out who he is working for. But this Bond does not expect an answer and does not wait for a response. He drops the man without giving him a chance to speak. This new Bond does not believe in the efficacy of interrogation, let alone torture. The scene lasts all of five seconds. It is set on the roof of an opera house, with Puccini's opera *Tosca* playing in the background: a tale of violent torture in which all involved, the tormentor and his two victims, succumb to a tragic death.

Bond's torture post-2001

Bond ceased torturing others nearly half a century ago. Even his brief and pragmatic interrogations became unpalatable to a franchise that turned increasingly hostile to torture. At the same time, the tortures that Bond suffers at the hands of his rivals have come to assume an increasingly important role in the series' narratives. It is no coincidence that the first Bond of the post-9/11 era, *Die Another Day* (2002), features Bond's torment as a primary plot device.

The pre-credit sequence of the film sees Bond captured by North Korean officials. He is tortured in a concrete cell for more than a year. The torture continues through the opening title sequence and forms the backdrop for the title song. Instead of the customary stylized silhouettes, this title sequence shows Bond undergoing water torture. He is chained to the ceiling by his wrists and stabbed with red-hot irons. A jailor torments him with scorpions. Handcuffed on his knees, he is punched and beaten by two men. The water torture resumes. After fourteen months of torture, we see a haggard Bond, tired, dirty, thick-bearded and long-haired. He is subjected to a final round of psychological torture, a mock execution. General Moon makes one last

'Do You Expect Me to Talk?': Bond the Torture Critic 39

attempt to interrogate him: 'Your people have abandoned you. Your very existence denied. Why stay silent?'

What are we to learn from this elaborate torture scene, the longest and most detailed of the Bond franchise to that point? Two messages stand out. The first is a message about the brutality of torture. This scene has none of the fanciful elements of prior torture settings in which the focus is usually on the villain or the mechanical torture device, not on Bond's suffering. This torture, in contrast, is cold and stark, lacking any heroism or drama. It is crude and (perhaps with the exception of the scorpions) realistic. Contrasted with Goldfinger's laser, which never touches Bond, or Khan's and Carver's elaborate threats of outlandish torture, which are never realized, here Bond neither avoids nor escapes torture. He is victimized and brutalized at the pleasure of his captors.

The second message is that this torture is futile. Bond has stayed silent. This surprises General Moon as well as Bond's superior M, who rescinds Bond's 00 status under the assumption that he must have collaborated with the North Koreans. We conclude, then, that as far as high-ranking intelligence officials go, British or Korean, this is as extreme as torture gets. Yet it yields nothing. It is pure and inexcusable sadism that reduces even the great James Bond to a human shadow without providing a shred of intelligence.

Bold as this torture critique in *Die Another Day* may be, it is outdone in *Casino Royale*, the first film in the reboot of the franchise starring Daniel Craig. This iteration of Bond adheres more closely to the Fleming novels than prior movies and is correspondingly more ruthless, physical and brutal (Silberg 2006; Orr 2007; Arnett 2009). In *Casino Royale*, he is a vicious killer, lacking much of the grace, romance, humour or gadgetry that characterized him in prior films. Yet somehow the infamous torture scene in this film manages to exceed even the sadism of the torture depicted in Fleming's novel.

Bond's suffering is shocking. It lacks any masculine bravura. On the contrary, it is explicitly emasculating. It bears a closer similarity to a scene in a horror movie than it does to a commonplace torture scene in an action film. It may well be the most visceral depiction of torture in any modern action film, including films inspired by historical accounts of torture, such as *Battle of Algiers* (Pontecorvo 1966) or *Zero Dark Thirty* (Bigelow 2012). Le Chiffre's torture of Bond in *Casino Royale* is nauseating.

There are good reasons to believe that this excess was a conscious choice on the part of the filmmakers, who followed the Fleming novel in most other respects. In the film, as in the novel, the torture is the centrepiece of the plot, perhaps even the most memorable element of the narrative. In the book, however, it is set in a sunlit and furnished art nouveau-style room. In the film, it is a dark dungeon-like space containing only a broken chair. In the book, only Bond is tortured. In the film, Vesper Lynd, Bond's partner and lover, is tortured alongside Bond in a separate room and it seems as if her suffering may force him to collaborate. In the book, Le Chiffre hits Bond's groin with a carpet beater. In the film, Le Chiffre swings at Bond's sexual organs with the knotted end of a thick rope. The novel makes explicit that Bond recovers completely and 'none of the functions of [his] body will be impaired' (Fleming 2012b: 125). The torture in the film lasts longer and, it is implied, disfigures Bond, perhaps permanently (see Figure 2.3).

This torture scene is the apex of the franchise's torture criticism, incorporating all the anti-torture elements from the prior films: the blurring of torture, sexual assault and execution, the focus on torture's psychological and physical scars, and, of course, the villainous 'torture talk'. Le Chiffre speaks:

> I've never understood all these elaborate tortures. It's the simple thing to cause more pain than a man can possibly endure. And, of course, it's not only the immediate agony, but the knowledge that if you do not yield soon enough there will be little left to identify you as a man. The only question remains: will you yield, in time?

Perfecting this condemnation of torture is Bond's silence. No viewer could imagine surviving such torture without capitulating, but Bond prevails. Even Le Chiffre, exasperated and exhausted from the physical demands of swinging the rope, recognizes that Bond will not speak. Rather than triumph over Bond, Le Chiffre dies in mid-torture, at Bond's side, on the floor of the torture chamber.

Figure 2.3 *Casino Royale* (Eon Productions et al. 2006).

'Do You Expect Me to Talk?': Bond the Torture Critic   41

We see echoes of this mutual failure of torture in *No Time To Die*. There is no formal torture here, only its outline. Bond and the villain Lyutsifer Safin wound one another. Safin, in echoes of Chiffre, seeks to deny Bond any hope of future love or sexual fulfilment by poisoning him so that Bond can never reunite with his loved ones. Safin seeks no information and the torture fulfils no logical function other than to torment. This is psychological rather than physical torture: Interestingly, the poison has no other physical effect on Bond beyond crippling his hopes for happiness. Bond kills the villain, then himself, rather than endure this emotional suffering. He ends his own torture before it has a chance to work its effects.

Conclusion

Why has a film franchise so notorious for its embrace of violence denounced this specific form of violence? It's tempting to offer a simple answer: torture must be repulsive, and torture must fail because Bond villains are repulsive, and Bond villains must fail. In this account, torture is maligned for the same reason that the films defame terrorism and weapons of mass destruction: they are, like torture, a signifier of evil and thus can never be allowed to achieve their purpose.

But this answer begs the question completely. Why affiliate torture with villains in the first place? Bond engages in all manner of immoral and violent behaviour: assassination, kidnapping, coercion and blackmail (not to mention dangerous driving and reckless endangerment). Why should he not employ the same type of protracted and elaborate torture that characterizes his opponents? Why did the creators of the Bond film series choose to place torture, to this day a pervasive and hotly debated intelligence-gathering practice, on the 'evil' side of the 'good vs. evil' divide, alongside terrorism and weapons of mass destruction? Bluntly put, both heroes and villains in Bond kill. Why do only villains torture?

The first Fleming novel appeared in 1953 and the first film in the Bond series aired in 1962, at the height of the Cold War. Perhaps the decision to depict torture as a villainous trait emerged out of an (erroneous) conviction that torture was more pervasive east of the Iron Curtain than among Western democracies (Rejali 2007)? Perhaps the filmmakers felt that torturing would undermine the image of Bond as a suave British gentleman-spy who accomplishes his missions through a mix of technical skill, seduction and sophistication? This answer, too, begs the question: Why are other series, such as the television action series *24*

(2001–14) and *Homeland* (2011–20), not to mention various police dramas, comfortable with having their protagonists torture (Greenhill 2007)? Why may Jack Bauer torture but not James Bond?

We may never know why this film series sided so comfortably with individually executed 'enhanced interrogation' while denouncing institutionalized and prolonged torture. Ironically, the franchise's depiction of torture is as misguided as its misrepresentation of all other aspects of espionage. Its depiction of recruitment, training, assassination, sabotage or interception is unrealistic, even comical. Its depiction of torture gets the story exactly wrong.

What little scholars know about torture suggests that it is precisely the type of torture that Bond and the franchise sanction that does not work at all. Instead, the type of torture that the franchise critiques the most, and dismisses as ineffective, is the very form of torture that is most likely to yield intelligence. Bond's opponents engage in prolonged, systematic, well-funded and sophisticated torture. In the past, that is the type of torture that has produced some accurate information (Einolf 2014: 51–8; 2022; Hassner 2020). Of all the torture scenes referenced above, the most realistic is Bond's fourteen-month suffering in a North Korean dungeon. In the real world, no agent could have expected to endure such prolonged torture in silence.

In contrast, Bond's improvised brutality, in the hope of extracting quick and crucial information, has the lowest chance of producing information (Hassner 2019). This so-called 'ticking bomb' torture is a figment of the imagination, and an unrealistic one at that. No spy has ever extracted the location of a terrorist by strangling an informant with their bikini.

References

Arnett, R. P. (2009), '"Casino Royale" and Franchise Remix: James Bond as Superhero', *Film Criticism* 33 (3): 1–16.

Blauwkamp, J. M. et al. (2018), 'Are Americans Really OK with Torture?', *Media, War and Conflict* 11 (4): 446–75.

Chapman, J. (2008), *Licence to Thrill: A Cultural History of the James Bond Films*, London: I.B. Tauris.

Delehanty, C. and E. M. Kearn (2020), 'Wait, There's Torture in Zootopia? Examining the Prevalence of Torture in Popular Movies', *Perspectives on Politics* 18 (3): 835–50.

Einolf, C. (2014), *America in the Philippines, 1899–1902: The First Torture Scandal*, New York: Palgrave Macmillan.

Einolf, C. (2022), 'How Torture Fails: Evidence of Misinformation from Torture-Induced Confessions in Iraq', *Journal of Global Security Studies* 7 (1).

Fleming, I. (2012a), *Goldfinger*, Las Vegas, CA: Thomas & Mercer.

Fleming, I. (2012b), *Casino Royale*, Las Vegas, CA: Thomas & Mercer.

Flynn, M. and F. F. Salek, eds (2012), *Screening Torture: Media Representations of State Terror and Political Domination*, New York: Columbia University Press.

Funnell, L. (2022), 'Delightful Duties?: Sexual Violence in Connery Era James Bond Films (1962–1971)', in L. Funnell and R. Beliveau (eds), *Screening #MeToo: Rape Culture in Hollywood*, 11–28, Albany: SUNY Press.

Funnell, L. (2011), '"I Know Where You Keep Your Gun": Daniel Craig as the Bond–Bond Girl Hybrid in Casino Royale', *Journal of Popular Culture* 44 (3): 455–72.

Funnell, L. and K. Dodds (2017), *Geographies, Genders and Geopolitics of James Bond*, London: Palgrave Macmillan.

Greenhill, K. M. (2007), '"24" on the Brain', *Los Angeles Times*, 28 May. Available online: http://articles.latimes.com/2007/may/28/opinion/oe-greenhill28.

Gronke, P. et al. (2010), 'US Public Opinion on Torture, 2001–2009', *PS: Political Science and Politics* 43 (3): 437–44.

Hassner, R. E. (2019), 'What Do We Know about Interrogational Torture?', *International Journal of Intelligence and Counter-Intelligence* 33 (1): 4–42.

Hassner, R. E. (2020), 'The Cost of Torture: Evidence from the Spanish Inquisition', *Security Studies* 29 (3): 457–92.

Jordan, W. (2014), 'Americans Find Some Tortures More Acceptable than Others', *YouGovAmerica*. Available online: https://today.yougov.com/topics/politics/articles-reports/2014/12/12/torture-report.

Orr, C. (2007), 'The Movie Review: "Casino Royale"', *The Atlantic*, 19 March.

Pew Research Center (2015), 'Global Publics Back U.S. on Fighting ISIS, but Are Critical of Post-9/11 Torture', 23 June. Available online: https://www.pewresearch.org/global/2015/06/23/global-publics-back-u-s-on-fighting-isis-but-are-critical-of-post-911-torture/.

Rejali, D. (2007), *Torture and Democracy*. Princeton, NJ: Princeton University Press.

Rejali, D. (2008), 'American Torture Debates', *Human Rights Review* 9: 393–400.

Schlag, G. (2019), 'Representing Torture in Zero Dark Thirty (2012): Popular Culture as a Site of Norm Contestation', *Media, War & Conflict* 14 (2): 174–90.

Silberg, J. (2006), 'Casino Royale, Shot by Phil Meheux, BSC, Attempts to Refashion the James Bond Franchise for a New Generation of Viewers', *American Society of Cinematographers*. Available online: https://web.archive.org/web/20070402131840/http://www.ascmag.com/magazine_dynamic/December2006/CasinoRoyale/page1.php.

3

The Thrusting Tip of the Spy Business

Discovering Resistance in the Modern Moneypennys

Colin Burnett

I particularly enjoy [007's] reports. They read more like adventure stories than terse explications of a mission, which I am sure is as much for my benefit as for 007's; he relies on me to edit out some of his more vivid descriptions before submitting them to M. I still derive immense satisfaction from the process of ciphering and deciphering. Setting the dials, keying in accurately what looks like a jumble of nonsense, then the moment of revelation as it's transformed into plain text. The thought that these ugly black boxes, so mechanically basic on the one hand, but so fantastically sophisticated on the other, tipped the balance of both wars in our favour—it's wonderful. The three years that I spent in Comms were never boring; we all worked hard, in an extraordinary atmosphere of camaraderie. I never lost the sense that we were the central pivot of the Firm—with the stations around the world and throughout the building forming the spinning spokes. So now, when a confidential signal is directed to M's eyes only, I attack it with relish.

For the time I am working on them, I am transported into the events they describe; it's probably the closest I will ever get to the thrusting tip of this business, active service.

– Miss Moneypenny, diary entry dated Tuesday, 7 August 1962,
The Moneypenny Diaries: Guardian Angel (Weinberg 2005: 161–2)

Who is Miss Moneypenny? What is her story? What lives has she lived both personally and professionally? In recent years, the James Bond franchise – by which I mean a network of licensed producers and their films, games, comics, novels and short stories – has been pursuing these questions in fictional form. Some franchise releases seek to nuance Moneypenny's traditional role within 007 fiction. Others set out to critique it. And this mix of storytelling strategies is promoting a fairly significant shift in the way Bond stories handle gender and race.

In previous decades, beginning with Ian Fleming's *Casino Royale* (1953), Moneypenny remained a relatively stable entity in Bond lore. Less a character than a serial 'figure' (Mayer 2014: 9), flat and seemingly unchanging, she was consistently deployed to lend an air of familiarity to each new story. Alongside the other furniture in Bond's world – his Walther PPK, his Aston Martin and the figures of M and Q – she contributed to a stock of relatively immutable objects and demi-characters which collectively fostered a sense of unity among the franchise's many series through a pleasurable (and dependable) formula. As a result, until roughly the mid-1990s, Bond fiction encouraged us to expect very little of Moneypenny. She was a 'secretary', little more. Dutifully filing reports and serving at M's side, her existence, we could assume, was subservient and unadventurous, a sub- or nonfiction that put into relief the sensational life – a man's life of risk and reward – in the field. She could taste that risk now and then in her fleeting exchanges, coquettish and warm-blooded, with 007. Yet we always knew that the thrusting tip of the spy business, for her, would forever remain out of reach.

This classic image of Moneypenny is being challenged in expected and unexpected ways. New Bond writers and artists are transforming Moneypenny into a more rounded persona within Bond fiction, with greater psychological depth, a fuller biography and a more compelling and indeed progressive commitment to self-determination. This fits with a current trend in media franchises, in which secondary characters who differ from the heroic status quo in terms of their gender, sexuality, race, ethnicity and ability, are being 'thickened' to address radical shifts in social attitudes. But this 'thickening' is generally permitted only within acceptable limits. By and large franchises restrict writers to changes which maintain the long-standing focus on cis male, white, heteronormative and non-disabled heroes. Recent Bond media offer scholars a prominent instance of this progressive thickening 'at the margins', not just with revisions to Moneypenny but with new versions of Q (Hines 2018), whose queer personal life is briefly explored in Eon Productions' *No Time To Die* (Fukunaga 2021), and M, who is depicted as a black father concerned for the safety of his daughter in Dynamite Entertainment's 'One-Shot' comic *Solstice*

(Moustafa 2017). The white cis male hero tends to retain his primacy in today's franchise stories even as secondary characters are given additional layers and (pardon the neologism) 'progressified'.

What makes the revisions we are seeing to the Moneypenny character so intriguing is that they extend well beyond the marginal 'thickening' of secondary characters as a means of displaying a franchise's social awareness. New writers and artists are boldly moving Moneypenny from the periphery of 007 fiction to its centre, developing tales which displace and resist Bond's status as hero. 007 is no longer the sole source of viewer or reader sympathy and fantasy within this storyworld. More than just another indicator of marginal change in franchise storytelling, Moneypenny is emerging as a genuine opportunity for writers seeking to perform a radical narrative pivot within franchise fiction – a means of resisting this franchise from within it, of opposing a property notorious for its sexualization, denigration and subjugation of all women.

One of the first to undertake this 'intra-franchise' resistance is writer Samantha Weinberg. Her novels and short stories, known collectively as *The Moneypenny Diaries*, turn the Moneypenny story – and by implication, the James Bond story – inside out (Weinberg 2005, 2006a, 2006b, 2006c, 2008). We re-experience the world of the original Fleming fiction from the perspective of Moneypenny (given name, Jane), who discovers a conspiracy within MI6. She witnesses it unfold but only she is empowered to expose it. This comes at great risk to herself and her niece, Kate Westbrook, who is presented on the novels' covers and in the stories themselves as the editor of a secret diary Moneypenny kept while under MI6's employ. As a form of tribute and a means of justice, Westbrook comes to the decision within the diegesis to publish the diary in increments in violation of the Official Secrets Act, a legal and personal gamble she takes in order to expose those forces responsible for her aunt's mysterious demise. Yet, the premise of the story, which reinvents Moneypenny and her niece as heroes within the Bond world, as rich women characters within a Cold War spy thriller where Agent 007, rather boldly, is pushed to the story's periphery, is only part of Weinberg's feminist subversion of the traditional Bond and classic Moneypenny.

As we read in the excerpt above, Weinberg feminizes the Bond world by employing what Rita Felski describes as a gender 'ambivalence' toward the everyday (2000: 94). Weinberg's novels utilize the diary form to ground the reader's experiences almost wholly through Moneypenny, in her mixed responses to the quotidian. Moneypenny's day is constituted as a flow of contrasting impressions – of repetition and rupture, regretful docility and excited participation, and solitude and community – impressions that are neither idealized nor demonized, a marker that the *Diaries* are inviting us to 'make peace with the ordinariness' of a service woman's daily life (94, 95). For the first time in Bond franchise history, we have a series which simultaneously demystifies *and* breathes new life into the Bond world by showing us the other side of what we thought we knew – the sensational, masculine-centred events of the Fleming novels – focusing instead on the flashes of excitement and disappointment which comprise Moneypenny's 'everyday'.

In this chapter, I examine two additional Moneypennys in contemporary Bond media, the black Moneypennys of the Daniel Craig films (2006–21) and the Dynamite Entertainment comics (2015–present). Franchise writers and artists aren't merely critiquing the thinly drawn Moneypennys of the past, they are using their stories to critique each other's depictions in the present. Today, comic producers in particular are seeking to reimagine Moneypenny by exploiting what I have called Bond's threaded, cross-media narrative structure (Burnett 2019). The franchise, comprehensively conceived, is configured to deliver to consumers multiple, mutually exclusive series running side by side one another in adjacent media. Each medium constructs its own 'James Bond', delivering sequences of stories which exist in diegetic isolation the one from the next, creating opportunities for intra-franchise competition over the character and his storyworld. Dynamite's writers and artists, as I intend to show, have taken this a step further. They have developed a distinct comic continuity which acts as a pointed form of representational opposition to the film series, exposing the limitations of Eon's black Moneypenny, played by Naomie Harris – *resisting* the Craig continuity with a comic-specific one. Dynamite, I claim, achieves this by combining all three strategies now available to Bond writers and artists: 1) a progressive 'thickening' of Moneypenny; 2) a centring of Moneypenny; and 3) a narrative and thematic emphasis on Moneypenny's gendered ambivalence toward the everyday, now inflected by her black experience.

From failed career girl to failed agent: The Eon Moneypennys (1962–2021)

Beginning with her film debut in *Dr. No* (Young 1962), Eon's Moneypenny, played by Lois Maxwell, is written primarily as an opportunity for serial 'play' (Higgins 2016: 10). A strict formula is adhered to, with the character restricted

Discovering Resistance in the Modern Moneypennys   49

to two fairly fixed narrative functions: she serves as a buffer between James Bond and MI6 authorities and as flirtatious comic relief. Early in a film, Moneypenny is shown at her post outside M's office, fulfilling her duties. When Bond passes her way, she steals a moment to gossip about office morale (M is often 'in a mood', so Bond should trespass lightly). She exchanges innuendos with 007, but her dream of a romance with the sexy superspy is inevitably dashed. After meeting with M, Bond sets out on a new mission and, as Moneypenny well knows, a string of new romances. She must remain behind. With its formula solidified, Eon introduces incremental variations for the returning viewer's delight as the series unfolds. In later movies, Moneypenny isn't stationed outside M's office but greets Bond in the field, in some unexpected and exotic locale (see for example *The Spy Who Loved Me* [Gilbert 1977]). New life is breathed into the basic scenario, but the character, you'll notice, is scarcely permitted to grow. At this stage in the series, Moneypenny isn't really a character at all. She's a dependable unifying device, one of many through which, every year or two, the film franchise renews its ritual with viewers.

So much is well known. But if viewed from a different perspective, that of a cross-media history, we gain a new appreciation of the Moneypenny formula and its gender politics. Based on Fleming's stories, Maxwell's Moneypenny is a loose caricature of the new woman depicted in the British Career Novel of the early 1950s through the mid-1960s. The Career Novel stressed a new reality in post-war Britain: more premarital women were seeking careers of their own. The educational system being too patriarchal and slow-moving to adapt to this rising trend, young women turned to mass produced fiction for guidance. The publisher Bodley Head, in particular, moved quickly to meet demand, producing a highly successful Careers for Girls series, including titles like *Sue Barton Staff Nurse* (Boylston 1952), *Pan Stevens Secretary* (Hawken 1954) and *Clare in Television* (Hawken 1955). As Stephanie Spencer explains, these novels were published in print runs of six thousand or so (2005: 108), a testament to their popularity, and though essentially didactic, their stories also romanticized the life of the career woman, depicting heroes embroiled in workplace melodramas. Not only did career women have to wrestle with the pressures of work and struggle for independence out of the home; they had to weigh these ambitions against the countervailing and, for these characters, attractive lures of full-time marriage and motherhood.

Maxwell's Moneypenny is based on what Spencer calls the 'heterosexy' Career Novel hero who construes the workplace as a site for 'responsible' coupling on the way to marriage (2005: 114). The heterosexy hero strives above all to 'get out before aging out', to avoid, in other words, the trap of the spinster. But in the virile world of the early Eon series, coupling is non-monogamous, *ir*responsible and principally favours men. In this context, plucked from a fictional realm where she might hope for success, the responsible young career woman cannot avoid the spinster's fate. This fate is made doubly insulting for Moneypenny when the normally promiscuous Bond decides to marry – not her, but the adventurous socialite Countess Tracy di Vincenzo in *On Her Majesty's Secret Service* (Hunt 1969). Bond's betrothal confirms that Moneypenny's prospects for marriage are forever lost. Once a heterosexy career woman, she is doomed to assume the role of the off-putting older single woman. *Octopussy* (Glen 1983) acknowledges this fate explicitly, when an ageing Moneypenny, still delighted to receive even a passing compliment from Bond, seems aware that she might soon be replaced by her young and voluptuous trainee, Miss Penelope Smallbone, who despite Moneypenny's motherly admonition that Bond will pay her little attention, gazes at him longingly.

In the 1990s, Eon abandons some aspects of the Moneypenny formula, and its Career Novel underpinnings, aligning itself with shifting gender norms. In *Goldeneye* (Campbell 1995), Samantha Bond's Moneypenny isn't dependent on the workplace for coupling; nor does she welcome Bond's flirtatious schtick. As Tara Brabazon writes, when *Goldeneye* shows Moneypenny in a black evening gown 'her clothes [...] signify a desiring and desirable woman who is able to demand rights in the workplace' (1998: 100). The whole scenario 'situates [Moneypenny's] body as the source of active desire *outside* the workplace' (Germanà 2017: n.p.). In the same scene, Moneypenny has a cutting reply for 007: 'I know you'll find this crushing, but I don't sit at home praying for an international incident so I can run down here all dressed up to impress James Bond. I was on a date with a gentleman.'

The Moneypenny of the 1990s and early 2000s nonetheless remains thinly drawn. It is only after the *Casino Royale* (Campbell 2006) reboot, and the release of the third Daniel Craig film *Skyfall* (Mendes 2012), that the series endeavours to 'thicken' the character with an origin story and a more rounded persona – a fuller psychology than the formulaic career girl caricature of the Maxwell films. This is coupled with another change; Moneypenny is reinvented, for the first time in *any* medium now, as a character of colour (played by Naomie Harris). Yet, for all of these changes, Harris's version also finds herself on a gendered career path beset by failure.

Discovering Resistance in the Modern Moneypennys

51

Throughout the Craig era, Harris's Moneypenny (given name, Eve) is written so as to climb higher in the MI6 ranks than any of her Eon Productions predecessors. She has more to do, and her role is more central in the films' plots. Her substantial failures along the way, however, make for a steeper fall. As Klaus Dodds quite rightly argues, fieldwork is the ultimate decider of character competence in this series (2015: 218).

In *Skyfall*, Moneypenny follows a fairly disjointed four-beat arc, each phase tied to fieldwork – what I will call, for simplicity's sake, *failure, reassignment, redemption* and *resignation*. The first beat comes in the pre-credit sequence. Moneypenny is presented as a dynamic field-agent-in-training who finds herself on a mission gone awry. This is a Moneypenny unlike any other in the Eon series – an essential partner to Bond on a mission much like Felix Leiter or a handful of other Bond girls/women. Tracking Bond in a high-speed chase, using the palm of her hand to bash away the blown-out windshield of her jeep, she's a contemporary woman of action. As the sequence comes to a head, Moneypenny is perched on a cliff, staring through the sight of her rifle, directly at Bond as he tussles atop a streaking train with the mercenary Patrice, who had stolen a hard drive containing a list of undercover agents. In a rare development in the Eon series (*Die Another Day* [Tamahori 2002] perhaps being the only other instance), subjective narration, in this case a POV shot, grants us access to Moneypenny's experience. We see what she sees, forming an allegiance with her as she anxiously ponders a dilemma, *her* dilemma: the man or the mission? Does she risk shooting Bond? M gives the order, but Moneypenny isn't in position to take a clean shot. Pressure mounts. She shoots. The blast sends Bond careening to a river hundreds of feet below. Patrice escapes, and Moneypenny is left to contemplate her failure.

Both in the pre-credit scene and elsewhere, *Skyfall* subjects Moneypenny to a disjointed 'yes, but' progression. *Yes*, she has been elevated to the status of field agent (she thus is given the opportunity to outgrow the limitations of Moneypennys past); *but* she is too inexperienced and too poor a marksperson to succeed in the role (she thus sinks to a status lower than Moneypennys past, who excel in professional spaces, however limiting they may be). The next we see her, she has been reassigned to serve under Sir Gareth Mallory, the chairperson of the Joint Intelligence Committee. Her reassignment again places her under Bond's control, only this time her past failure subjects her to his professional *and* sexual whim. Moneypenny is both 'disciplined and domesticated', as Kristen Shaw has put it (2015: 78). Sent to observe and assist Bond, Harris is the first screen Moneypenny to enjoy a romantic interlude with 007 (albeit only an implied one). But *Skyfall*'s Bond–Moneypenny liaison is doubly troubling, as Lisa Funnell and Travis L. Wagner have shown (Funnell 2015: 74–6; Wagner 2015: 58). In a narrative context where Harris's character is being punished for her inadequacy, the liaison, further inflected by the East Asian setting in which it takes place, renders her abject in gendered and racialized ways. Against the heavily orientalized backdrop of a Macau hotel room (Figure 3.1), the new black Moneypenny willingly takes to her knees to shave Bond, positioning her as an accomplice in the (re)colonization of her body by the British agent who commands her. In the colonial spaces of active service, Harris's Moneypenny, as if by some warped racial and gendered justice, must submit her body to the white man.

The 'yes, but' character progression can be seen in two additional beats in the film. *Skyfall* eventually sees Moneypenny achieve a moment of redemption. When villain Raoul Silva attempts to assassinate M during a ministerial deposition, Moneypenny matures, taking her place amongst a team of agents facing danger in the field. With gunfire raining on the deposition chamber, she glances off-screen at Bond, then down at a pistol at his feet. Without a moment's hesitation, Bond nudges the pistol her way and she takes it in hand. Now confident in Moneypenny's abilities, Bond – the scene's staging is both subtle and heavily symbolic – walks in front of her line of fire, certain that her bullets will find the target. The trust that had waned between the two as a result of the failed mission of the pre-credit sequence is restored. With Moneypenny's assistance, 007 turns the tide.

Figure 3.1 *Skyfall* (Eon Productions et al. 2012).

The character's newfound agency and sociality continue to grow in subsequent releases *Spectre* (Mendes 2015) and *No Time To Die*, as we will see. But whilst invested on some level in Moneypenny's redemption, *Skyfall* undermines the character's progressive potential within the continuity with a fourth beat: resignation. In the film's closing scene, Moneypenny opts for a desk job. She removes herself from fieldwork which, as she points out in an accepting tone, 'isn't for everybody'. The last we see her she is seated outside the office of Gareth Mallory, the new male M, her pleasure-filled off-screen glance directed at 007.

The heterosexy Moneypenny of yesteryear returns, though with slight revision. In *Spectre* we perceive her through a fresh array of socialities and intimacies, inhabiting a greater diversity of spaces than the Maxwell version was ever permitted to. Despite the impression we form at the end of *Skyfall*, Harris's Moneypenny isn't just an administrative assistant bolted to her chair awaiting M's orders and 007's flirtatious glances and quips. Midway through *Spectre*, we see her in her apartment, with – this is a crucial development in the character's history – a man and companion in her bed. Though fleeting, the moment puts a major crack in Eon's Moneypenny mould. Moneypenny isn't the single career girl setting all else aside in hopes that her workplace relationship with Bond will bud into a full romance. Harris's version already has her own intimacies – her own sex life – outside the workplace. Indeed, the sequence plays up the scandal of her independence. When Bond, on the other end of a phone call, is shocked to hear that Moneypenny has a man over at 'this time of night', she replies: 'Yes, Bond. It's called *life*. You should try it some time.' In this Bond continuity, the roles to some extent have been reversed; Moneypenny lives the life of romance while Bond is beholden to his 'sexless' duty.

With *Spectre* and its sequel, *No Time To Die*, Harris's Moneypenny inches ever closer to the centre of the drama. Though her screen time is limited, Bond depends on her now as a source of vital intelligence. Moneypenny has often been portrayed as a trader in information. In the recent novels, Moneypenny is positioned at the head of the notorious Powder Vine, described by Samantha Weinberg as an 'informal gossip network among secretaries and personal assistants, whose centre of power was the first-floor ladies' lavatory' (Weinberg 2005: 52). The screen version of Moneypenny is a variant on this, using her strategic access to assist Bond 'behind the scenes'. She never picks up the pistol again. The 'redeemed' action hero of *Skyfall* never returns. Moneypenny, rather, is redrawn as a figure whose closeness to M empowers her at opportune moments to open doors and lines of communication, the former often closed and the later often cut by stoic spy men like Bond and M, whose buried emotions and bruised egos hamper official and unofficial operations. When circumstances demand it, Moneypenny greases the proverbial wheels. In *Spectre*, Bond asks Moneypenny to his flat. The invitation contains a hint of innuendo, but Moneypenny senses that there's more to the request than an opportunity to resume their *Skyfall* romance. Later at the flat, it is to her that Bond confides the secret that Dench's M had left Bond a private message recommending that he hunt down one Marco Sciarra, later revealed to be a member of SPECTRE. She eases Bond's burden with a warm expression of sympathy: 'I think you've got a secret, and it's something you won't tell anyone. Because you don't *trust* anyone.' Bond *needs* Moneypenny in *Spectre*. His 'instinct' tells him to trust her. She's earned it, after all. In scenes that follow, she discretely accesses MI6 intelligence to support him on a rogue mission to hunt SPECTRE that both she and Bond know the new M would never sanction.

In *No Time To Die*, this relationship with Bond develops further. This time Moneypenny isn't *asked* to provide support. She volunteers it, her actions serving to steer Bond's fate and the film's plot. After an acrimonious exchange between M and the now-retired Bond – he demands a meeting with his incarcerated rival Ernst Blofeld but is told to leave MI6 premises when he questions the MI6's chief's handling of the stolen 'Heracles' nanobot bioweapon – the former 007 appears to be at a dead end in his quest for answers about the attempt on his life and the murder of SPECTRE's remaining leadership in Cuba. Moneypenny intervenes, surreptitiously. Glancing about to confirm no one is eavesdropping on their exchange, *she* relies on romantic innuendo now, asking Bond to dinner. Romance yet again is a mere cover. They convene at Q's flat where the comically frazzled MI6 armourer is perturbed that the pair deigned to intrude upon his carefully planned romantic *soirée*. The scene sees the old team reunited. Q deciphers the files on a secret flashdrive, discovering a list of future targets for the stolen bioweapon. Bond's need to interrogate Blofeld in his maximum-security hold now takes on extra urgency. Moneypenny had opened a crucial door for Bond when his investigation had ground to a halt.

For all these various attempts at thickening and centring, Moneypenny serves as a reminder of the limits of marginal 'progressifying' within the modern media franchise. Throughout the Craig era, Eon merely revises the figure of Moneypenny. Despite the additional layers she's given, she remains secondary and at times even abjectly subordinate within the narrative. *Spectre* may grant Harris's Moneypenny a romantic life 'beyond Bond', for instance, but this aspect of her existence is relegated to a passing subplot which serves, in the main, to reinforce the personal sacrifices Bond endures at this point in his life. We aren't given time to relish her romantic and sexual independence. And *No Time To Die* may grant her a degree of agency in the early stages of Bond's quest, but she never regains nor even appears to desire a field agent status that would entrust to her responsibilities in the higher-stakes *latter* stages of missions. Indeed, this possibility is displaced onto a new black woman character, Lashana Lynch's Nomi, but the results are equally mixed.

Nomi is herself subjected to a 'yes, but' form of characterization. Lashana Lynch's 007, in part written by Phoebe Waller-Bridge of the TV shows *Fleabag* (2016–19) and *Killing Eve* (2018–22), is authoritative, defiant and, unlike Moneypenny, totally immune to Bond's charms. In one scene, she skewers Bond's waning physical condition by threatening to remove him from her path: 'I'll put a bullet in your knee. The one that *works*.' Craig's body was once a chiselled ideal and an object of pleasure. Now, for this black superspy, it's a source of ridicule. In *No Time To Die*, space even opens up for sociality among black women when Nomi and Moneypenny share a moment of camaraderie over their frustrations with Bond. Nomi quips, 'I get why you shot him.' Yet, for Nomi, too, these potentially progressive qualities are soon undermined. The character isn't permitted to keep her '007' designation, relinquishing it to Bond for one last mission. And while Nomi plays an active role in the film's action, she is structurally 'decentred' in the film's climax. In the final act, she inexplicably agrees to lead Dr Madeleine Swann, revealed here to be able action hero in her own right, and Mathilde, Swann's and Bond's daughter, to safety, at just the moment when, presumably, her skills as a trained field agent would be crucial to the mission's success. Not so; for Bond, being the 'man that he is', needs no help. A solo display of masculine (and tragically self-sacrificial) prowess follows, with Bond impressively mowing down an army of thugs and confronting the film's villain, Lyutsifer Safin, in a mano-a-mano encounter, with no women in sight.

The thrusting tip: Dynamite's Moneypenny (2015–present)

Shaped by numerous factors like changes in social attitudes brought about over the decades by feminism and more recently the Black Lives Matter movement, as well as a film franchise which has 'cynically' appropriated liberation and social justice movements for years, mainly to reaffirm Bond's white, masculine dominance over this fictional world (Woollacott 2009: 130), the screen version of Moneypenny has only changed incrementally over the decades. Even during the Craig era, she can't seem to reach the business's thrusting tip. When Naomie Harris's Moneypenny gets too close to active service, the tip, as it were, impales her. Such is not the case for the Moneypenny of the recent Dynamite Entertainment comics. Written in a very different context, for a publisher that has cultivated a relatively strong roster of women editors (Molly Mahan), writers (Gail Simone, G. Willow Wilson, Nancy A. Collins, Amy Chu) and characters (Red Sonya, Vampirella, Xena: Warrior Princess), this version of Moneypenny claims her role as an active service agent with a mix of force and subtlety, encouraging us to rethink what is possible for women of colour within the Bond storyworld.

More than just a distinct version of the character, Dynamite's Moneypenny emerges as an oftentimes rather pointed critique of the limited representational forms we see in the Eon films. This is partially accomplished by *borrowing* from the Eon formula to subvert expectations and thereby emphasize the radical process of revision at work within the comic series. As we might expect from established convention, we are first introduced to Dynamite's Moneypenny (given name, Eve) in a panel which situates the character in her office (Figure 3.2). But this depiction, appearing in the first of the Dynamite series, *Vargr* (Ellis and Masters 2015), shows Moneypenny in an oddly lifeless workspace that calls attention to itself. It's a generic, unlived-in, defeminized space. There is no red lamp to add a splash of colour, as we find in *Dr. No* (Figure 3.3); there are no pictures of various flora on the wall; and there is no tea service for M atop the filing cabinet. Instead writer Warren Ellis and artist Jason Masters set the scene – and propose

Figure 3.2 *Vargr* (Dynamite Entertainment 2015).

Figure 3.3 *Dr. No* (Eon Productions et al. 1962).

a different set of assumptions about Moneypenny – with a panel which reveals her cleaning a pistol, with a row of rounds neatly lining her desk. Dynamite's black Moneypenny is no secretary. She's merely *posing* as one, and the room's lack of character shows it.

In subsequent comics, Dynamite relies on more than borrowings from the Eon formula to perform its fictional critique of the films. Its writers and artists construct an entirely distinct continuity for Moneypenny, one that imagines a black character who never experiences the lapses which lead to her namesake's reassignment at the beginning of *Skyfall*. In the Dynamite storyworld, Moneypenny is an accomplished agent, and has never been anything but. In fact, she is often placed on a par with Bond. In *Vargr*, M puts 007 in his place, remarking bluntly: 'I consider her job to be much more important than yours.' Freed from the traditional narratives of subordination, abjection and failure of the films, the Dynamite version of Moneypenny is strategically elevated within the MI6 hierarchy and given room to grow. Indeed, *Vargr* lays the foundations for subsequent storylines that position Moneypenny at the very centre of the Bond storyworld.

One such storyline, the forty-page 'One-Shot' comic entitled *Moneypenny* (Houser and Edgar 2017) – one of the few pieces of Bond fiction to be written by a woman, Jody Houser – serves the dual purpose of constructing Moneypenny as a black hero and character of relative depth and nuance. The comic follows an alternating structure to achieve this dual effect. We oscillate between timeframes – the past, which reveals her backstory, and the present, which follows a mission as it unfolds. This adds considerable weight to the character's personal and professional journey and to the thematic power of the story. *This* Moneypenny has early experiences and relationships to consider, ones never recounted in other Bond media. Shown as a young girl in what appears to be a diverse family home (her father is clearly black, while her mother is racially ambiguous, with lighter skin), she witnesses the horrors of an act of terror on TV at the side of her loving parents. Later, at school, she shows warmth to a Muslim girl who had been confronted by a mob of bigoted white students who associate her people with terrorism. A diverse home life alongside experiences of everyday racism and xenophobia, a traumatic encounter with mediated violence alongside the potential healing power of sociality among girls of colour – Houser, in weaving these details together, gives Moneypenny a fuller life. She is quite explicitly a character *of colour* whose early awareness of family, gender, race and their points of intersection shape the perceptive and indeed thoughtful ways she experiences those around her.

Houser's story goes on to reveal that shortly after Moneypenny is promoted to full field agent – whereupon she's awarded a pistol, the very same one she cleans in *Vargr* – M, who in this continuity is also of colour, elects, by *virtue* of her exemplary work in the field, to position her as his last line of defence. He tells her that this is 'one of the most essential jobs in MI6'. The 'admin' post outside his office is but a thin cover.

The new backstory creates additional opportunities for fictional critique. Like *Vargr, Moneypenny* periodically borrows from the Eon formula to call attention to its subversion of traditional gender roles within the franchise. James Bond makes a brief appearance in Dynamite's *Moneypenny*, in a five-panel vignette situated near the comic's end. At her desk, Moneypenny has a report in hand. On cue, Bond enters and launches a demeaning quip her way: 'Never thought I'd see you behind a desk, Moneypenny.' She fires back: 'Looks like they need the smarter agents to clean up your messes, James.' Crucially, the exchange is much chillier than in cinematic incarnations. Moneypenny appears genuinely irked by Bond's presence. She directs rather a biting glance at him out of the corner of her eye, and in the final panel, isolated in close-up (Figure 3.4), she stares off into the distance, her gaze canted, the inner corners of her eyebrows raised. Moneypenny had gained the verbal upper hand, but this all-too-familiar battle of the sexes, seemingly a commonplace in MI6 headquarters, strikes this version

Figure 3.4 *Moneypenny* (Dynamite Entertainment 2017).

of the character as futile, even troubling. In one instant, she is performing her duty, projecting confidence and professionalism. In the next, a white man and agent jabs her 'innocuously' as if her position outside M's office were a sign of sexual and professional punishment, drawing her into a juvenile give-and-take. The normally playful Moneypenny-in-the-office scene, typically showing Bond's charm, his sexualizing wit adding spice to Moneypenny's drab, office-bound existence, is rewritten to engender an abiding sense of ambivalence, in both Moneypenny and the reader.

Yet Dynamite's Moneypenny isn't overwhelmed by these gendered and racialized threats to her. She isn't shaken by the pangs of doubt which drive Harris's character from the field; she doesn't take to her knees at Bond's pleasure. Instead, she confidently assumes her post at the thrusting tip of the business. The comic culminates with an action set piece where M, now out in the field with Moneypenny serving as security, finds his life suddenly at risk. Much like the Bondian casino sequence in *Black Panther* (Coogler 2018), in which bodies-in-action express cross-gender communality among black characters, M and Moneypenny work in a choreographed display of bad-ass black heroism. Pulling their weapons, they rein in an assault by a group of predominantly white, domestic-American terrorists. But it's not M who leads; it's Moneypenny, thrusting to and fro in her polka-dotted summer dress and leather knee-highs as she works out a plan of action. She is revealed to have the eye of a keen marksperson. Artist Jacob Edgar uses embedded panels and colourist Dearbhla

Kelly a diffused green tint to articulate the character's extraordinary visual acuity (Edgar 2021: n.p.). Taking position, she zeroes in on her five targets. She takes aim and fires. Dynamic lines and a repeated action word – BLAM – take us through a rapid succession of kill-shots. Unlike her counterpart in *Skyfall*, this Moneypenny is resolute, precise, effective – and respected.

In its closing moments the comic continues to subvert expectations. Moneypenny doesn't retake her career girl perch outside M's office. Instead, the character remains on the move, strolling with the group – M and some dignitaries – she had rescued from peril moments earlier, accepting their kudos and exchanging witticisms. Formula dictates that a Bond story, particularly in the Eon films produced prior to the Daniel Craig era, will end with a sex joke (in *The World Is Not Enough* [Apted 1999], Bond lewdly observers to the woman he's romancing, named Christmas, 'I thought Christmas only comes once a year'). Houser de-sexualizes and inverts the gender dynamic, giving Moneypenny the edge in the story's departing quip. 'You were right sir,' she tells M. 'You do need a babysitter.'

Conclusion: The women of threaded media

Should Dynamite build on Houser's comic and give Moneypenny her own series? Undoubtedly. As I have argued elsewhere, series written by and featuring black women would be a crucial 'next step' in the decolonization of the Bond storyworld (Burnett 2021). For now, let us simply recognize that threaded, cross-media franchises such as Bond can do something that inflexibly unified franchises often cannot: they free their various writers and artists to openly play with and critique the official canon. This internal creative logic results in a contested canon – a *poly-canon* where continuities that present Moneypenny as a heroic black character are not mere aberrations, fanciful but 'unofficial' forays into speculative fiction. In Bond lore, the Moneypenny of *Skyfall* is no more canonical than the Moneypenny of the Dynamite comics. The comics emerge as a form of *critical* canonicity in this context, revising and resisting the official stories of the past and present.

In the modern Bond franchise, women authors are fundamentally rethinking Moneypenny, and through her, what's possible for women in the Bond storyworld. Jody Houser is one. Samantha Weinberg is another. Her novels, with which I began, interrogate Fleming's account of the character and invent

Discovering Resistance in the Modern Moneypennys

a world where both Moneypenny and her niece are placed at the centre of the action; new forms of sociality among women, in this case intergenerational, are explored. What's more, as readers of those novels will discover (major spoiler alert!), Weinberg's Moneypenny conquers *James Bond* – romantically, and not in the workplace but outside it. They live out their years together on a remote Scottish island. Moneypenny is now a rounded character, in other words, not the career girl caricature Fleming first imagined. To get to know her, her stories and her many lives, we must 'thread', following the franchise, comprehensively conceived, where it leads us – to the movies and the original novels, certainly, but also well beyond that.

References

Boylston, H. D. (1952), *Sue Barton Staff Nurse*, London: The Bodley Head.

Brabazon, T. (1998), 'Britain's Last Line of Defence: Miss Moneypenny and the Desperations of Filmic Feminism', *Hecate* 24 (1): 93–104.

Burnett, C. (2019), 'Theorizing Threaded Media; Or, Why James Bond Isn't Just a Failed Attempt at Star Wars', *Moving Patterns*, 2 September. Available online: https://colinatthemovies.wordpress.com/2019/09/02/video-lecture-theorizing-threaded-media-or-why-james-bond-isnt-just-a-failed-attempt-at-star-wars/.

Burnett, C. (2021), 'The Property of a Lady?: On Lashana Lynch—The First Black Female 007', *The Los Angeles Review of Books*, 27 September. Available online: https://lareviewofbooks.org/article/the-property-of-a-lady-on-lashana-lynch-the-first-black-female-007/.

Dodds, K. (2015), '"It's Not for Everyone": James Bond and Moneypenny in *Skyfall*', in L. Funnell (ed.), *For His Eyes Only: The Women of James Bond*, 214–23, New York: Wallflower Press.

Edgar, J. (2021), Email message to author, 4 January.

Ellis, W. and J. Masters (2015), *Vargr*, Mt. Laurel, NJ: Dynamite Entertainment.

Ellis, W. and J. Masters (2016), *Eidolon*, Mt. Laurel, NJ: Dynamite Entertainment.

Felski, R. (2000), *Doing Time: Feminist Theory and Postmodern Culture*, New York: New York University Press.

Fleming, I. (1953), *Casino Royale*, London: Jonathan Cape.

Funnell, L. (2015), 'Objects of White Male Desire: (D)Evolving Representations of Asian Women in Bond Films', in L. Funnell (ed.), *For His Eyes Only: The Women of James Bond*, 79–87, New York: Wallflower Press.

Germanà, M. (2017), 'What Would Moneypenny Do? Sexual Harassment, Desire and James Bond', *The Conversation*, 6 December.

Available online: https://theconversation.com/what-would-moneypenny-do-sexual-harassment-desire-and-james-bond-88410.

Hawken, P. (1954), *Pan Stevens Secretary*, London: The Bodley Head.

Hawken, P. (1955), *Clare in Television*, London: The Bodley Head.

Higgins, S. (2016), *Matinee Melodrama: Playing with Formula in the Sound Serial*, New Brunswick, NJ: Rutgers University Press.

Hines, C. (2018), "'Brave New World': The New Q, Masculinity, and the Craig Era Bond Films', *Journal of Popular Film and Television* 46 (1): 46–55.

Houser, J. and J. Edgar (2017), *Moneypenny*, Mt. Laurel, NJ: Dynamite Entertainment.

Mayer, R. (2014), *Serial Fu Manchu: The Chinese Supervillain and the Spread of Yellow Peril Ideology*, Philadelphia, PA: Temple University Press.

Moustafa, I. (2017), *Solstice*, Mt. Laurel, NJ: Dynamite Entertainment.

Shaw, K. (2015), 'The Politics of Representation: The Disciplining and Domesticating of Miss Moneypenny in *Skyfall*', in L. Funnell (ed.), *For His Eyes Only: The Women of James Bond*, 70–8, New York: Wallflower Press.

Spencer, S. (2005), *Gender, Work and Education in Britain in the 1950s*, New York: Palgrave Macmillan.

Wagner, T. L. (2015), "'The Old Ways Are the Best": The Colonization of Women of Color in Bond Films', in L. Funnell (ed.), *For His Eyes Only: The Women of James Bond*, 51–9, New York: Wallflower Press.

Weinberg, S. (2005), *The Moneypenny Diaries: Guardian Angel, by Kate Westbrook*, New York: St. Martin's Press.

Weinberg, S. (2006a), *The Moneypenny Diaries: Secret Servant, by Kate Westbrook*, London: John Murray.

Weinberg, S. (2006b), 'For Your Eyes Only, James', *Tatler*, November, 85–9.

Weinberg, S. (2006c), 'Moneypenny's First Date with Bond', *The Spectator*, 11 November.

Weinberg, S. (2008), *The Moneypenny Diaries: The Final Fling, by Kate Westbrook*, London: John Murray.

Woollacott, J. (2009), 'The James Bond Films: Conditions of Production', in C. Lindner (ed.), *The James Bond Phenomenon: A Critical Reader*, 2nd edn, 117–35, Manchester: Manchester University Press.

4

Highland Rape

Scotland's Traumatic Past in *Skyfall*

Mary M. Burke

As widely covered by men's fashion journalists and bloggers, in *No Time To Die* (Fukunaga 2021) James Bond (Daniel Craig) wears a sleek suit by Tom Ford, the designer who also outfitted Craig in *Quantum of Solace* (Forster 2008) and *Spectre* (Mendes 2015). According to Sarah Gilligan, slick, expensive and exquisitely tailored suiting is 'central to the construction and performance of Bond's hero persona, a means by which he is transformed from an ordinary to an extraordinary man' (2011: 77). She considers how 'Ford's fashions form one part of the fashioning of [the Craig] Bond' (80). However, one focus of this chapter will be the fabric the designer used for *No Time To Die*'s widely discussed black and white suit (as well as for the blue suit in *Spectre*), which was Prince of Wales check, a wool of Scottish origin with a traditionally muted woven twill design of small and large checks. This seemingly innocuous sartorial detail will be used presently to uncover the spectre of traumatic Scottish history in *Skyfall* (2012), Craig's third outing as Bond.

The Highlands: From political threat to aesthetic resource

After the defeat of the Highland insurrection by British government forces at the Battle of Culloden in 1746, the vanquished Scottish Gaelic Other of British identity became unfinished history. That ongoing past returns in *Skyfall*, as well as in the work of Anglo-Scottish couturier, Alexander McQueen. As emphasized by the latter's work (which will be examined presently), this traumatic history may be conjured up by paying attention to traditional and pseudo-traditional Highland clothing and fabric, in particular, since they were central to the transformation of Scottish Gaelic culture from political threat to aesthetic resource. In *Skyfall*, Bond, who has earlier failed a series of physical, medical and psychological examinations, takes his immediate supervisor, M (Judi Dench), and flees by road to Skyfall, his ancestral home in the Scottish Highlands, where the denouement is staged. The inner conflict that produces Bond's physical and mental breakdown will be linked to his northern Scottish origins, and the blasted, depopulated landscape into which he moves in the homeward flight evokes national as well as personal rupture. Indeed, the emphasis on this origin will be seen to be politically provocative, given the immediate context of the impending Scottish Independence referendum at the time of *Skyfall*'s release. However, to begin, the broad contours of Scottish Highland history as it pertains to this discussion are laid out.

Medieval Gaeldom spanned Ireland and Scotland's Highlands and Western Isles, linking these regions culturally and linguistically. However, after Culloden, Lowland Scottish culture dominated, not least because it increasingly identified as 'Anglo-Saxon' and 'constructed images of bifurcation and division' between itself and the inhabitants of 'Romantic [Highland] Scotland' (Pittock 2001: 7). The sequence of unifications within the British Isles is important to note at this juncture since the Scottish side at Culloden was 'strongly motivated' by opposition to the political Union between England and Scotland (Pittock 2021): The Act of Union between Ireland and Great Britain of 1800 that created the United Kingdom of Great Britain and Ireland (which became the United Kingdom of Great Britain and Northern Ireland in the 1920s after Irish Partition) was preceded by that of England and Scotland in 1707, which created the Kingdom of Great Britain. Nevertheless, that the other nations of the Union were subsumed by the more powerful England is evidenced by the commonplace use in everyday speech (and in sloppy writing about Bond) of 'British' and 'English' as interchangeable terms. In his 1760s lectures, Scottish Enlightenment economist and philosopher Adam Smith argued that tribal communities existed in an earlier cultural time, a belief that justified the abandonment of Scotland's 'barbaric' elements and the unambiguous embrace of Union, Britishness and development (Smith 2014: 14).

According to the linear Smithian model of entwined historical and economic progress, the 'backward' feudalism of the Highlands and of pre-Culloden Scotland in general had destined those spheres to obsolescence. However, that vanquished past is disinterred in the opening credits of *Skyfall*: in time to a majestically gloomy Adele theme song with the opening line 'This is the

Figure 4.1 *Skyfall* (Eon Productions et al. 2012).

end', Craig/Bond falls downward into the murky sea deep, patently suggestive of dissolution of self, loss of control and a journey into the 'barbaric' past (Figure 4.1). Scottish folklore is signalled by the selkie, a mythological seal-to-woman seen on the descent, and further down, guns are replaced by swords, a weapon with resonant links to the inaccurate cultural remembrance of Culloden as a doomed but heroic last stand in which English muskets outdid Scottish swords (Pittock 2021). Deeper still, a Celtic Cross emerges, suggestive of the submerged Gaelic culture shared across Ireland and the Scottish Highlands and Western Isles in the medieval period. Indeed, the house used as Bond's ancestral home in *Skyfall* is close to Glen Coe, a location that itself witnessed violent history, being the site of a notorious massacre in 1692 when about thirty men, women and children associated with the MacDonalds were killed by government forces, allegedly for that clan's failure to pledge allegiance to the new Protestant monarchs, William and Mary (Devine 2019: 43).

Queen Victoria's championing of Scottish sartorial traditions was central to the defanging of the old threat of the once recalcitrant Highlands. In 1851, the Queen, her seven children and her husband, Prince Albert, opened the Great Exhibition clad in the kilts and sporrans of Highland association (Weisbrod 2006: 243), co-opting an 'invented' signifier of Scottish Gaelic barbarism as a signifier of elite Britishness (Trevor-Roper 1988: 19). Victoria's adaptation of the kilt was, despite surface appearances, a celebration of victorious Lowland rather than vanquished Gaelic Scottish identity: after the putative victory of enlightenment and rationalism at Culloden, the Gael became an apolitically 'aesthetic' resource that was mined by nostalgic writers and balladeers for the English or Lowland Scottish reader (Scott 2004, I: cix–cx). Queen Victoria began visiting the Highlands in 1842, but the region's resultant transformation into a huntin'-shootin'-fishin' playground for the elite was significantly hastened by the potato blight that struck the Scottish Highlands at about the same time as Ireland in 1846, the dominant response to which was the coerced and voluntary emigration of tenant families to Canada and Australia. T. M. Devine frames this emigration upsurge as the second wave of the Highland Clearances, the first having been Culloden-period uprootings. After that defeat, Highland landlords had relocated the population to the coast in order to create extensive grazing lands for sheep. However, the new communities thus created were swept away in a second cycle of clearance during and after the 1840s food crisis. In comparison to Ireland, there were many fewer deaths in the Highlands as a result of the potato blight, but the subsequent mass emigration created the depopulated region that is today sometimes misleadingly marketed as a Western European 'wilderness' by Scottish heritage and tourism interests (Devine 2019: 306–12, 17).

The traumatized body in *Skyfall*

'Where are we going?' M asks in *Skyfall* as she and Bond begin the drive northward up Britain's spine from London to the Scottish Highlands. 'Back in time', is his laconic reply. Cinematographer Roger Deakins's framing of the flight as a journey into a bleak, overcast, treeless and depopulated Highlands creates an increasing atmosphere of desolation and abandonment that undermines the touristic image of that landscape. Viewed with historically informed eyes, this is not a pretty landscape, but a decimated and colonized one from which all evidence of human life and social and cultural activity has been extirpated. As Bond's Aston Martin pulls into the grounds of Skyfall, the camera focuses on a regal statue of a stag atop one of the estate's entrance pillars (Figure 4.2). This is a patent evocation of the *c.* 1851 painting of a proud stag in a sublime Highland setting, *The Monarch of the Glen*, one the best-known visual clichés of the reduction of the Highlands to a kind of proto-theme park for the huntin'-shootin'-fishin' aristocracy; the painter, Sir Edwin Landseer, was a favourite of Queen Victoria.

The recuperation of Queen Victoria's sartorial appropriation of Scottishness is apparent in the autumn 1995–96 collection, 'Highland Rape', by ferociously avant-garde designer Alexander McQueen (1969–2010), which critiques the role fabrics and garments signifying Scottishness have played in effacing darker

Figure 4.2 *Skyfall* (Eon Productions et al. 2012).

aspects of Scottish history. McQueen was of Isle of Skye descent on his father's side, part of the historically Gaelic-speaking Highlands and Islands, and his Scottish nationalist politics were so central to his persona that he was rumoured to have sewn profanities into the lining of jackets destined for the Prince of Wales, the heir to the British throne (Gleason 2017: 8). The 'Highland Rape' runway show mixed tartan wool with ripped lace dresses worn by blood-spattered models who staggered on a heather-strewn runway ('Dress' 2011), and McQueen reprised the looks and the politics in the Autumn/Winter 2006–07 collection, 'Widows of Culloden'. The latter show culminated with an eerie hologram of a spectral Kate Moss suspended in mid-air in a ragged, fluttering gown to the *Schindler's List* (Spielberg 1993) theme, a soundtrack evocative of genocide (Gleason 2017: 31–4, 147–54). Meeting with puzzlement and accusations of mere misogyny from critics regarding 'Highland Rape', McQueen's defence was that the collection was 'a shout against English designers [...] doing flamboyant Scottish clothes': 'My father's family originates from the Isle of Skye, and I'd studied the history of the Scottish upheavals and the Clearances. People were so unintelligent they thought this was about women being raped — yet Highland Rape was about England's rape of Scotland' (V 1997: 26).

To return to the fabric that Tom Ford used in suiting Craig for his *No Time To Die* performance: the Scottish Register of Tartans records that what is formally known as the Glenurquhart (or Glen Urquhart) Estate check was registered in 1840 and used soon after by Caroline Stuart, Countess of Seafield for the staff of her estate of that name in the Scottish Highlands (see 'Tartan details' n.d.). The authors of *From Tailors with Love: An Evolution of Menswear through the Bond Films* call the fabric a 'totem of Bond's style' as it was also used in suits for

Sean Connery in that role (Brooker and Spaiser 2021: 41, 29, 30, 70). (Indeed, their cover shows a close-up of a suit jacket in the traditional black and white Glenurquhart Estate check.) The Scottish Connery had reinforced the fabric's complex Anglo-Scottish associations and was central to its 1960s comeback in menswear when he wore a three-piece suit in the check in *Goldfinger* (Hamilton 1964). A waxwork of Connery sporting the suit was a popular attraction during the Barbican's *Designing 007: 50 Years of Bond Style* exhibition, which opened in 2012 and subsequently toured the world (Chilvers 2012). Although his father, Prince Albert, had initially sparked the fashion for Scottish tweeds and tartans among the sporting male elite with Scottish estates in the mid-nineteenth century (Harrison 1968: 22), the Glenurquhart Estate check gained wide cachet and became popularly known as 'Prince of Wales' check after it was adapted by the future King Edward VII (1841–1910). He was heir apparent for almost sixty years before taking the throne in 1901 after the death of his mother, Queen Victoria. As Prince of Wales, he established Glenurquhart Estate check as *the* sporting fabric for the Highlands (Woolnough 2008: 159, 267). Thus, the fabric speaks to the kind of cultural imperialism about which McQueen was so vocal, since it is, like the kilt, a trophy that celebrates not the Scottish Highlands, but its transformation into a depopulated playground for the pursuits of the landed elite. Fabrics of the Prince of Wales sort (or imitations of same) were used to make male leisure attire far beyond Britain. In *Tweed*, Fiona Anderson (2017) records that in the early decades of the twentieth century such were central to a globally circulated and widely adopted image of the huntin'-shootin'-fishin' English country gentleman. The Glenurquhart Estate check, which, as Anderson notes, was known as the 'Glen Check' in America, became particularly associated with such sporty tailoring. What Anderson names the 'sartorial Anglomania of the period' led one 1923 commentator to complain that fashionable young Italian civil servants dressed for the urban office as though heading for a weekend in Scotland (2017: 95).

The well-established co-option of Scottish signifiers by a style generally referred to as 'British' or 'English' informs Monica Germanà's examination of Bond's masquerade of Englishness in relation to his clothing. Although James Bond has been named 'an English cultural icon' (Groszewski 2019: 1), in the Ian Fleming Bond novels the hero's Scottish origins are occasionally referred to, and for Bond scholar James Chapman 'the question of national identity in the Bond novels and films is neither straightforward nor unproblematic' (2005: 130). In his seminal 1960s consideration of the Bond phenomenon, Kingsley

Amis declares: 'Clothes probably don't make the man, but they can tell us a lot about him' (1965: 6). Germanà's analysis of the hidden roots and associations of Bond's seemingly impeccably English tailoring develops this insight in probing the ambiguity and instability of his popular image as an unassailable icon of English masculinity. Bond's 'uneasiness' regarding the 'performance of upper-class Englishness' reflects 'anxiety about national identity and class', which may be traced to his Scottish origins and traumatized body (Germanà 2020: 26, 47, 59). That trauma is ultimately rooted in the fact that Bond is an instrument of those from whom he must take orders, regardless of any ethical quandaries or potential fear, a lack of true autonomy implicitly rooted in his origins in an internal colony of the kingdom.

Craig's first outing as Bond, *Casino Royale* (Campbell 2006), was adapted from Ian Fleming's 1953 novel of that title, and takes place at the beginning of Bond's career as a secret agent as he earns his 'licence to kill' status by, as Jeremy Black suggests, 'execut[ing] a defenseless British traitor' (Black 2017: 154). To a good degree, *Casino Royale* lays the groundwork for *Skyfall's* revelation of Bond as traumatized 'state-sponsored assassin' (Tedesco 2006: 114): before seeing off the second kill necessary to gain the '00' status in *Casino Royale*, Craig's Bond brutally kills an adversary in a grimy public restroom in an early scene. The filthy setting and the vicious, unrelenting nature of Bond's pummelling of the unindividuated target strips away every iota of the glamorous insouciance that generally adhered to the suave hero's violence in post-war Bond films. The international outrage at revelations of water torture of political prisoners at the United States Guantanamo Bay military detention camp in the years prior to *Skyfall's* release brought the previously obscure term 'waterboarding' into the public lexicon (Norton-Taylor and Goldenberg 2006; Rosenberg 2019). As such, Bond's attempt to drown his adversary by forcing his head into the water-filled sink of the restroom seems an explicit reference to such illegal but nonetheless state-sanctioned violence.

Interestingly, *Skyfall's* aura of a man hollowed out by the violence his employer requires of him is something of a return to Fleming's original conception of Bond, which appears to have been overtaken by the glamorization of the character on-screen. In 1962, the year in which the movie *Dr. No* (the first Bond novel to be adapted) appeared, Fleming told the *New Yorker* that 'When I wrote the first [Bond novel], in 1953, I wanted Bond to be an extremely dull, uninteresting man to whom things happened; I wanted him to be the blunt instrument [...] Now the dullest name in the world has become an exciting one' (quoted in Hellman 1962: 32). Philosopher Greg Forster unpacks exactly how Bond is, ultimately, a dehumanized marionette of the British authorities who 'does what he's told': 'Whatever friction may occur between Bond and his superiors [...] there is never a moment's doubt that Bond is an appendage of the liberal political system and that his actions, lechery excluded, are its actions' (Forster 2006: 126). Indeed, Fleming himself explored Bond's lack of autonomy in the 1960 short story 'For Your Eyes Only' (Fleming 1979), in which M, motivated by personal revenge, orders the secret agent to perform an unsanctioned assassination and is unquestioningly obeyed. (Incidentally, the issue of the actual existence of something akin to Bond's 'licence to kill' remains unclear: although Keith Jeffery's 2010 volume, *MI6: The History of the Secret Intelligence Service, 1909–1949*, supposedly 'lays to rest the idea that British secret agents had a "licence to kill"' [Press Association 2010], it is probably more accurate to state that the writer of this authorized history was not given access to any evidence that would confirm that this is or ever has been the case.)

The first scene of *Skyfall* that occurs in the Scottish Highlands opens with M and Bond standing near the parked Aston Martin in a rocky, treeless glen, obviously taking a break during the long drive northward (Figure 4.3). They are discussing how Bond had lost his parents as a child. 'How old were you when they died?' M asks. 'You know the answer to that', Bond replies, staring straight ahead. 'You know the whole story', he continues slowly. After a pause, M replies, 'orphans always make the best recruits'. The implication of the scene is that Bond believes himself to have been recruited when he was too young and too vulnerable. M's sardonic statement aligns Bond as a youth with the earlier years of *Skyfall*'s anti-heroine Séverine: both have been traumatized by

Figure 4.3 *Skyfall* (Eon Productions et al. 2012).

being trafficked into murky worlds while young. The story of Séverine's former enslavement, revealed by a tattoo that gives evidence that she had once been 'owned' by a Chinese sex-trafficking ring, is prefigured by the female selkie figure in the credits, since in Scottish lore human men force these mythological creatures into sexual bondage when their shed sealskin is confiscated (Westwood and Kingshill 2009: 404–5). Bond, meanwhile, recruited into the service as an 'orphan', evokes the boy soldier figure, an unprotected, vulnerable or orphaned child coerced into the adult world of violence and warfare. Altogether, *Skyfall* appears to nudge toward the increasingly uncovered history of children in a variety of twentieth- and twenty-first-century contexts who were passed off as orphans by those who would exploit them. (In response to estimates that 80 per cent of children living in the world's orphanages at present have at least one living parent and are placed therein because of the economic benefits of 'voluntourism', Australia recently became the first country in the world to recognize so-called 'orphanage trafficking' as a form of modern-day slavery in the Modern Slavery Act [No.153, 2018]). Altogether Bond and Séverine are indeed the 'best recruits' to the industries of sex and violence; dehumanized early, they can be all the better reconstituted as acquiescent adult marionettes.

Despite this similarity, however, the power differential between Bond and Séverine themselves means that true sexual consent is not possible in her case. McQueen's 1995 'Highland Rape' critiqued both Britain's subjugation of its own margins and invoked the vocabulary of Union: 'sexual tropes abound[ed]' in debates concerning unification of Scotland and England in 1707, represented both as a marriage of equals and the shameful coercion of a weak Scotland by England (Martin 2009: 18). Bond's unthinking personal replication of such structural power differentials is suggested by what some careless reviews of *Skyfall* referred to as his 'seduction' of Séverine. Played by Bérénice Lim Marlohe, who has Cambodian, Chinese and French roots, Séverine is a racialized sex slave who was trafficked while being 'rescued' (acquired) by the film's villain, Raoul Silva (Javier Bardem). The word 'seduction' implies some degree of consent, but Bond enters Séverine's shower uninvited *after* she has told him about her history of sexual violence. Thus, this slippery term cannot account in any meaningful way for the issues of money, power, control and commodification with which sex must be entangled for a woman of such traumatic experience. Moreover, Tim Hanley notes how the camera lingers on Séverine's cleavage in the scene in which she is executed after having been badly beaten, a death that draws only a callous quip from Bond, who never mentions her again. The 'loss of a sex slave', Hanley concludes, 'isn't worth a second thought' (2012). Altogether, as Lisa Funnell summarizes, Séverine is a 'disposable object of pleasure' who 'can be considered one of the most disempowered, pitiful, and tragic women in the Bond film franchise' (2015: 86). However, Human Rights Watch suggests that in the global context the girl sex slave and the boy soldier are linked phenomena that generally occur simultaneously in the same theatres of war or political instability or tyranny (see 'Child Soldiers' n.d.), so the implication is that Bond himself is ultimately expendable too, just as Silva had been. (A former MI6 agent, Silva went rogue after being sacrificed by his employer in exchange for captives.)

The traumatized body politic in *Skyfall*

It is increasingly apparent that beneath Bond's flawless suit what is left is not just 'the scarred body' of the man (Germanà 2020: 20), but the scarred body politic. The Craig-era Bond films have begun to acknowledge the fractured nature of British history and identity by acknowledging the fractured nature of Bond, as once popularly understood. The imminent threat to virtually all that remains of English power – the United Kingdom itself – of the era in which *Skyfall* was released marks that movie profoundly. On 15 October 2012, a mere twenty-five days before the release of *Skyfall*, and after long public discussion and debate, the Scottish Government and the United Kingdom Government agreed on terms for a Scottish Independence referendum (*Agreement* 2012). The referendum question was as follows: 'Should Scotland be an independent country?' The 'No' vote ultimately triumphed, but that outcome was far from certain in the tense lead-in to both the agreement to hold a referendum and the ballot itself. The referendum inspired sustained and widespread international coverage, not least because the Scottish-born Connery, who urged Scots to vote in favour of independence, made himself something of a global poster boy for the 'Yes' campaign (Frizell 2014). Now is a good juncture to remember that Bond has often been played by men whose roots speak to England's history of empire, annexation and colonization: George Lazenby was Australian, Pierce Brosnan was born in Ireland, Timothy Dalton was born in Wales.

Writing of the Bond created by Fleming and the movies of the post-war decades, Simon Winder's memoir-cum-love/hate letter to Bond, *The Man Who Saved Britain* (2006), theorizes that this confident, capable and all-conquering hero was a compensatory fantasy meant to assuage the wounds caused by the decades-long economic fallout of the Second World War and the loss of empire soon after. Cynthia Baron has similarly named the Bond phenomenon 'a nostalgic bandage for England's wounded pride in the "post-colonial" era' (2003: 153). Like the foot soldiers of the historical British Empire itself, the Bond of post-war fiction and film obeys orders to unleash his violence upon a series of non-white, foreign others, in Jacob M. Held's estimation (2006: 148–9, 150–1). For Winder, the pace at which Britain journeyed from being the world's largest empire in 1945 to being a 'shorn, flailing, International Monetary Fund beggar' by 1976 explains the need for the 'symptomatic' fantasy of Bond:

> Fundamentally the war, despite its being won, consisted for Britain of a ceaseless nightly Blitz of humiliations, compromises and setbacks, and these did not stop with 1945 but kept up a relentless battering until well into the 1970s. The country that reeled into the European Economic Community in 1973 was, with Ireland, the poorest member state, an ashen, provincial, polyester kind of country, no longer recognizable as the victor of 1945 and a million miles from the self-image British people had nurtured for themselves for generations.
>
> (2006: 5, 4)

Indeed, the genre of post-war British spy fiction as a whole 'sought to inform a reading public that the vast enterprise of British imperialism was, contrary to all apparent evidence, never more secure' (Goodman 2016: 2). The post-war appeal of an (only seemingly) unassailable Bond to an unreflective brand of male atavism that seems increasingly out of place in the twenty-first century is exemplified by fan Donald J. Trump: 'I think James Bond represents worldly omnipotence [...] What can be better than always winning? Absolutely nothing. That's why we like James Bond' (Cork and Scivally 2022: 288).

Non-binary British pop star Sam Smith's theme song for *Spectre* was widely interpreted as a challenge to the binaries of gender and sexuality upon which the masculinist post-war Bond phenomenon long relied (Manganas 2019: 436). The sense of emotional vulnerability and physical weariness that Craig brings to the role begins in *Casino Royale* with his response to the loss of lover Vesper Lynd (Eva Green), a story arc continued into *Quantum of Solace*. This sustained narrative of grief and hopelessness makes the shocking close of *No Time To Die* seem – with the benefit of hindsight – inevitable. Indeed, if *Skyfall* reckoned with the threat to the Union that was the 2014 Scottish Independence Referendum, then *No Time To Die*'s bleak ending might be read as a response to the existential crisis for the United Kingdom that is Brexit, its long-deferred withdrawal from the European Union in January 2020 as the result of a referendum in 2016. This has left the UK isolated from the clout and protection of the European Union, which looks all the more necessary after Russia invaded Ukraine in the spring of 2022. Moreover, and more threatening still, there has been much speculation in the Anglophone press and beyond that Brexit might be the catalyst for uniting the island of Ireland again and that Scotland may attempt a second referendum on independence, also as a result of Brexit (Peabody 2021). Within the latter context of ever-growing nationalism in Scotland, which seems bound up with the reclamation of long-ago co-opted signifiers of Scottishness, it is striking that in 2017 *The Monarch of the Glen*, which had originally been commissioned as part of a series to hang in the Houses of Parliament in London, was acquired by the National Galleries of Scotland in Edinburgh.

In a word-association exercise that he undergoes early in the action of *Skyfall* when his fitness for re-entering service is being assessed by MI6, Bond's bitter responses to the cues 'murder' and 'country' are 'employment' and 'England'. Bond's initial physical and psychological disintegration in *Skyfall* reflects the conflict created by his service to the former empire that had, to use McQueen's terms, raped his ancestral culture. By the close of *Skyfall*, he appears to have acquiesced after the ineffectual insurrection of the spitting out of those words. By then, a polished and fit-looking Bond stands with the Union Jack flag – representing the unified Scotland, Northern Ireland, Wales and England – fluttering behind him. Moreover, he happily receives a bequest from the by-now deceased M, a figurine of an English bulldog, a well-established symbol of English tenacity and strength (Baker 2001: 48–55), thereby symbolically accepting the effacement of his Scottishness. Bond's reassembly as a fighting-fit, loyal Englishman by *Skyfall*'s close denotes that despite all the questions it raised right from the opening credits, the movie ultimately evades the immediate question of Scottish independence and the longer vista of the cultural evisceration and depopulation of Britain's Highland Gaelic margins. The repeated rape of Scotland, like that of Séverine, has been repackaged as seduction.

References

Agreement between the United Kingdom Government and the Scottish Government on a Referendum on Independence for Scotland (2012), HM Government and The Scottish Government, 15 October. Available online: https://assets.publishing.service.gov. uk/government/uploads/system/uploads/attachment_data/file/313612/scottish_ referendum_agreement.pdf.

Amis, K. (1965), *The James Bond Dossier*, New York: New American Library.

Anderson, F. (2017), *Tweed*, London and New York: Bloomsbury Academic.

Baker, S. (2001), *Picturing the Beast: Animals, Identity, and Representation*, Urbana and Chicago, IL: University of Illinois Press.

Baron, C. (2003), '*Doctor No*: Bonding Britishness to Racial Sovereignty', in C. Lindner (ed.), *The James Bond Phenomenon: A Critical Reader*, 153–68, Manchester: Manchester University Press.

Black, J. (2017), *The World of James Bond: The Lives and Times of 007*, Lanham, MD: Rowman & Littlefield.

Brooker, P. and M. Spaiser (2021), *From Tailors with Love: An Evolution of Menswear through the Bond Films*, Orlando, FL: BearManor Media.

Chapman, J. (2005), 'Bond and Britishness', in E. P Comentale et al. (eds), *Ian Fleming & James Bond: The Cultural Politics of 007*, 129–43, Bloomington and Indianapolis: Indiana University Press.

'Child Soldiers' (n.d.), *Human Rights Watch*. Available online: https://www.hrw.org/topic/childrens-rights/child-soldiers.

Chilvers, S. (2012), 'Designing 007: James Bond's Style Celebrated in Barbican Exhibition', *Guardian*, 5 July. Available online: https://www.theguardian.com/film/2012/jul/05/james-bond-costumes-barbican-exhibition.

Cork, J. and B. Scivally (2002), *James Bond: The Legacy*, New York: Harry N. Abrams.

Devine, T. M. (2019), *The Scottish Clearances: A History of the Dispossessed, 1600–1900*, London: Penguin.

'Dress, *Highland Rape*, Autumn/Winter 1995–96' (2011), *Blog.metmuseum.org*. Available online: https://blog.metmuseum.org/alexandermcqueen/dress-highland-rape/.

Fleming, I. (1979), 'For Your Eyes Only', in *For Your Eyes Only: Five Secret Occasions in the Life of James Bond*, London: Jonathan Cape.

Forster, G. (2006), '"Just a Stupid Policeman": Bond and the Rule of Law', in J. M. Held and J. B. South (eds), *James Bond and Philosophy: Questions Are Forever*, 121–38, Chicago and La Salle, IL: Open Court.

Frizell, S. (2014), 'Sean Connery Wants Scottish Independence', *Time* magazine, 4 March. Available online: https://time.com/12430/sean-connery-wants-scottish-independence/.

Funnell, L. (2015), 'Objects of White Male Desire: (D)evolving Representations of Asian Women in Bond Films', in L. Funnell (ed.), *For His Eyes Only: The Women of James Bond*, 79–90, New York: Wallflower Press.

Germanà, M. (2020), *Bond Girls: Body, Fashion and Gender*, New York: Bloomsbury Visual Arts.

Gilligan, S. (2011), 'Branding the New Bond: Daniel Craig and Designer Fashion', in R. G. Weiner et al. (eds), *James Bond in World and Popular Culture: The Films Are Not Enough*, 76–87, Newcastle upon Tyne: Cambridge Scholars.

Gleason, K. (2017), *Alexander McQueen: Evolution*, New York: Race Point Publishing.

Goodman, S. (2016), *British Spy Fiction and the End of Empire*, New York and London: Routledge.

Groszewski, G. (2019), 'This SPECTREd Isle: James Bond, Alan Partridge, and Englishness', *International Journal of James Bond Studies* 2 (1): 1–10.

Hanley, T. (2012), 'Belated Skyfall Review OR Where It Went off the Rails OR Bond Girls Shouldn't Be a Thing Anymore', *Tim Hanley: Author and Historian*, 26 November. Available online: https://thanley.wordpress.com/2012/11/26/belated-skyfall-review-or-where-it-went-off-the-rails-or-bond-girls-shouldnt-be-a-thing-anymore/.

Harrison, E. S. (1968), *Our Scottish District Checks*, Edinburgh: The National Association of Scottish Woollen Manufacturers.

Held, J. M. (2006), '"Don't You Men Know Any Other Way?" Punishment beyond Retributivism and Deterrence', in J. M. Held and J. B. South (eds), *James Bond and Philosophy: Questions Are Forever*, 139–54, Chicago and La Salle, IL: Open Court.

Hellman, G. T. (1962), 'Bond's Creator', *New Yorker*, 13 April: 32.

Manganas, N. (2019), 'Real Men: Sam Smith's Emasculation of the James Bond Theme', *Celebrity Studies* 10 (3): 436–40.

Martin, M. M. (2009), *The Mighty Scot*, New York: State University of New York Press.

Norton-Taylor, R. and S. Goldenberg (2006), 'Judge's Anger at US Torture: Stinging Comments Come as America Dismisses UN Report on Guantánamo', *Guardian*, 16 February. Available online: https://www.theguardian.com/uk/2006/feb/17/politics.world.

Peabody, B. (2021), 'Brexit Is Probably the United Kingdom's Death Knell: An English-led Disaster Has Emboldened Others to Get Out', *Foreign Policy*, 3 February. Available online: https://foreignpolicy.com/2021/02/03/brexit-united-kingdom-death-knell/.

Pittock, M. (2001), *Scottish Nationality*, Basingstoke: Palgrave.

Pittock, M. (2021), 'Your Guide to the Battle of Culloden – Plus 7 Myths Busted', *BBC History Revealed Magazine*, 30 March. Available online: https://www.historyextra.com/period/georgian/myths-facts-battle-of-culloden-jacobites-bonnie-prince-charlie-stuarts/.

Press Association (2010), 'Spy Secrets Revealed in History of MI6', *Guardian*, 21 September. Available online: https://www.theguardian.com/world/2010/sep/21/spy-secrets-history-mi6.

Rosenberg, C. (2019), 'What the C.I.A.'s Torture Program Looked Like to the Tortured', *New York Times*, 4 December. Available online: https://www.nytimes.com/2019/12/04/us/politics/cia-torture-drawings.html.

Scott, W. (2004), *Minstrelsy of the Scottish Border*, 2 vols, Kelso: Ballantyne for Cadell and Davies.

Smith, A. (2014), in R. L. Meek et al. (eds), *The Glasgow Edition of the Works and Correspondence of Adam Smith: Vol. 5:* 'Lectures on Jurisprudence', Oxford: Clarendon Press.

'Tartan Details: Glenurquhart Estate Check' (n.d.), *The Scottish Register of Tartans.* Available online: https://www.tartanregister.gov.uk/tartanDetails?ref=1440.

Tedesco, M. (2006), 'The Moral Status of the Double-O Agent: Thinking about the License to Kill', in J. M. Held and J. B. South (eds), *James Bond and Philosophy: Questions Are Forever*, 111–20, Chicago and La Salle, IL: Open Court.

Trevor-Roper, H. (1988), 'The Invention of Tradition: The Highland Tradition of Scotland', in E. Hobsbawm and T. Ranger (eds), *The Invention of Tradition*, 15–42, Cambridge: Cambridge University Press.

V., L. (1997), 'All Hail McQueen', *Time Out*, 24 September–1 October: 26.

Weisbrod, B. (2006), 'Theatrical Monarchy: The Making of Victoria, the Modern Family Queen', in R. Schulte (ed.), *The Body of the Queen: Gender and Rule in the Courtly World, 1500–2000*, 238–53, New York and Oxford: Berghahn.

Westwood, J. and S. Kingshill (2009), *The Lore of Scotland: A Guide to Scottish Legends*, London: Random House Books.

Winder, S. (2006), *The Man Who Saved Britain: A Personal Journey into the Disturbing World of James Bond*, New York: Farrar, Straus and Giroux.

Woolnough, R. (2008), *The A to Z Book of Menswear*, Hamilton, Bermuda: Bespoke Solutions Limited.

5

'Do You Consider Your Employment to Be Psychologically Stressful?'

Gender, Trauma and Resilience in Daniel Craig's James Bond

Bridget E. Keown

At the 2015 opening of *Spectre* (Mendes), UK audience members saw a sixty-second public service announcement produced by Talking2Minds, a British charity focused on treating post-traumatic stress disorder (PTSD) among military veterans. The ad, designed by Tom Petch, shows several familiar domestic scenarios: a woman in a kitchen looking forlornly at a table, two children playing a game and a police officer knocking on the window of a stationary car. These scenes repeat: the empty seat at the table, a spot on the floor and the driver's seat of the car is filled by an automatic weapon. Audiences next see a patron at a local pub who accidentally bumps into a gun, positioned at a bar stool, which then transforms into a man, glaring at the person who bumped into him with unspoken malice. An off-screen narrator breaks the tension, reminding audiences that 'some weapons are harder to make safe' (Petch 2015).

In a blog post, Tom Petch noted that he hoped the ad would help destigmatize the condition, because James Bond himself 'has been on the frontline … and has shown several of the classic symptoms of suffering from Post-Traumatic Stress Disorder' (Petch 2015). Indeed, the Craig quintet highlights both Bond's PTSD-related symptoms because of the missions carried out in each film, and his experience of deep personal loss caused by the violent end of many relationships including his parents, his boss (and surrogate mother) M and his lover Vesper Lynd. With rates of PTSD among veterans in the public focus, largely due to the recent conflicts in Afghanistan (2001–21) and Iraq (2003–11), the focus on Bond's physical and mental wounds could be read as a progressive choice.

Allowing the full toll of Bond's years of service to show on his face, his body, his actions and reactions represents a significant departure from previous iterations of the character and ties Bond himself more closely with the realities of a society irrevocably changed by the War on Terror (Tremonte and Racioppi 2009; Dodds 2012; Murray 2017; Holliday 2018). However, as this chapter will demonstrate, the films also rely on outdated, deeply conservative ideas about trauma that perpetuate unsustainable notions of military masculinity. Ultimately, this antiquated notion of trauma ends up reinforcing some of the most conflicted and regressive aspects of the Bond franchise, especially as it relates to issues of gender and power.

This clichéd depiction of trauma stands out in particularly sharp relief because of the ways in which Craig's Bond attempts to incorporate a more nuanced, emotional form of trauma related to his deep emotional intimacy with women, and his suffering because of their loss. As a *New Yorker* review of *No Time To Die* (Fukunaga 2021) noted, 'Craig's distinctive persona suggests pathos that the series doesn't allow' (Brody 2021). Bond, we find, has a heart that can break as well as a body that can be bruised. It also challenges the essence of the character by showing the cracks in his masculine façade which lead to his ultimate demise. This chapter considers the multiple constructions of trauma across the Craig-era Bond films, recognizing how gender, power and notions of subjectivity are implicated in the portrayal of trauma. It does not consider the lived experience of trauma, or post-traumatic suffering, recognizing that the actual lived experience of trauma takes many different forms. The Bond films, however, provide an interesting framework for thinking about how trauma can render some characters empathetic and human, while diminishing the agency and potential of others.

'Relax, I'm not going to lose control': The gendering of PTSD

Thanks to advocacy by veterans of the conflict in Vietnam (1954–75) and the psychologists who treated them, post-traumatic stress disorder was added to the third edition of the *Diagnostic and Statistical Manual of Mental Disorders* (*DSM-III*) in 1980. The diagnostic criterion for PTSD continues to evolve as a more nuanced understanding of the brain and psyche emerge. Cinematic representations of PTSD, however, have changed little to reflect this understanding. Depictions of combat trauma frame the condition as one that overwhelmingly affects white men, whose 'cure' comes from a recommitment to their identity as a masculine warrior, with all the stereotypical rationality, stoicism and potential for controlled violence that implies. As a result, gender remains a critical category of analysis in these discussions, both because of the ways in which portrayals of combat trauma frame masculinity, and for the ways it erases or oversimplifies the experiences of women and racialized characters.

In a highly influential analysis, Elaine Showalter argued that the historic experience of battle 'feminized its conscripts by taking away their sense of control' (1985: 173). Essentially, men broke down when their individuality and ability to act aggressively was threatened or removed. While this metaphor has been challenged by trauma scholars, the idea that trauma represented a crisis of masculinity remains in film. As Duncan Shields explains, '[a]lthough the language differs, rather than offering a counterargument to the pervasive influence of military masculine norms, institutional psychiatry inadvertently reinforces these norms for men by gathering together the symptoms of PTSD into a regressive narrative and defining them as disordered, abnormal, and evidence of inadequacy' (2016: 71). The result is a representation of PTSD that pits a man's rational, stoic masculinity against his repressed emotions (coded as feminine) in a toxic battle that reduces the characters and their narrative arcs by representing emotional complexity or a lack of resilience in men as 'a fall from masculine grace' (Shields 2016: 66). Throughout his career as James Bond, Daniel Craig showed his character struggling with those repressed, feminine emotions, inviting discussion about the complex nature of Bond's experiences and his reactions to them. Although this Bond managed to emerge time and time again victorious from these struggles, in the end, it is that emotionality that results in his death.

Such a framework also invites discussion about the problematic nature of resilience in the Craig quintet. Traditionally, 'resilience' as a psychological concept is the learned ability to adapt positively in stressful situations. However, in a militaristic and highly masculine environment where hardship must be overcome at all costs, resilience becomes a kind of self-harming form of hopelessness, where carrying on is the only option (Chamorro-Premuzic and Lusk 2017). Bond's character is shown initially to be utterly opposed to introspection or discussion of his emotions, deflecting all reflective conversations with humour, sarcasm or violence. Early in the franchise, however, the self-harming aspect of this resiliency becomes evident as Bond forsakes medical care, professional assistance and emotional support rather than admit to being vulnerable or in pain. When asked if he needs more time to recover from Lynd's death, Bond responds, 'Why should I need more time? The job's done. The bitch is dead.' With these words, Amacker and Moore observe, he 'relegates everything he has just experienced to simply part of the mission … he pushes away any feelings or experiences that might threaten his hypermasculinity' (2011: 147). However, Bond says this after lingering over the seashell he finds in Lynd's personal effects, recalling the scene on the beach where he professed his love for her. He bobs erratically across the frame while talking to M, showing that he is profoundly destabilized and already suffering under expectations of resiliency that the franchise holds for him. The film hints that Bond has secured his identity by the next scene, as he arrives at Mr White's home in a suit and holding an automatic weapon. In fact, these accoutrements are a façade that allows the series, and the audience, to rest on the assumption that Bond has matured into the fully masculine hero they expected to see.

While fears of feminization reoccur consistently in narratives of PTSD, discussions or depictions of actual women are difficult to find. Cis-men remain representative of the nation, its strength and its ability to withstand threat, while women are the bodies – both human bodies and bodies of the nation – to be conquered and consumed. This threat is driven home in *Skyfall* (Mendes 2015), when the villain Silva begins flirtatiously touching Bond without his consent as a way of displaying his dominance over the space of his lair. Throughout the Craig quintet, feminization is coded as vulnerability, and woman characters who reject this premise by showing strength or stoicism are generally forcibly reduced to relying on Bond before they die. As Colleen M. Tremonte and Linda Racioppi note, 'even as women may break traditional gender roles by joining military and paramilitary forces, their service seldom results in a disruption of male power and control' (2009: 187). Powerful women within the world of both the Bond books and films are suspect, while villains are often feminized or effeminate, emphasizing the unnaturalness of their position, as well as foreshadowing their inevitable destruction (Bold 2009: 211; Funnell 2018: 14). The objectification and characterization of most of the women and villains in the Bond films emphasize that they are not wholly human in this story, especially in the complex, emotional way in which Bond is human. This trope has been so firmly established that when *Quantum of Solace* (Forster 2008) attempted a more nuanced woman character in Camille Montes, critics balked.

In describing Montes, Robert Ebert wrote, 'In this film, who do we get? Are you ready for this? Camille. That's it. Camille. Not even Camille Squeal. Or Cammy Miami' (2008).

Given this emphasis in Western society on masculine resilience and rationality, media that focus on men's service and suffering often provide narrative privilege to the hero's trauma in a way that denies his quest for closure or a deeper understanding of himself in the world. His suffering becomes the subject of whole plotlines; the camera fetishizes his psychic and physical wounds, while the plot hinges on his ability to overcome them. Ultimately, the very qualities that make such heroes capable of enduring and living up to their calling frequently render them incapable of returning to civilian life. To give in to stimuli like emotion, or to turn away from the next fight, is to surrender and admit personal weakness. Far too infrequently, media depictions of trauma and PTSD avoid the potential for healing in favour of showing warriors 'shrugging off what was regarded as the feminizing tendencies of disability' (Bourke 1999: 253). 'Resilience' becomes coded as the ability to bear all wounds until one is destroyed. Such rigid and unrealistic constructions of gender, health and victory offer little potential for agency or choice (Waling 2019: 363). What makes Craig's Bond interesting and compelling is that this Bond tries to find an alternative masculinity and a different version of success.

'Not bad James, for a physical wreck': Bond's many traumas

Taken as a whole, Daniel Craig's five outings as James Bond provide a complete, complex and conservative narrative of a traumatized warrior (Cunningham and Gabri 2009; Tremonte and Racioppi 2009; Amacker and Moore 2011; Funnell 2011; Cox 2014). From the earliest moments of *Casino Royale* (Campbell 2006), we see the trauma that Bond must endure in his job and the work he must do to maintain his stoicism and resiliency. Each subsequent film features various examples of Bond's ongoing suffering and resiliency in the defence of the nation and the geopolitical status quo.

The duality of the pre-title scenes of this film suggests that Bond is already engaged in a battle to suppress his reactions. Craig as Bond first appears in a scene reminiscent of classic film noir, intercut with a jarringly bright fight scene where Bond murders the associate of a double agent, a kind of flashback

84   *Resisting James Bond: Power and Privilege in the Daniel Craig Era*

in Bond's mind that plays out during his discussion with the double agent in question. The juxtaposition of these scenes offers visual and metaphorical insight into the contrasting sides of Bond's life, the suavity that must co-exist with the constant threat of brutal and lethal violence. Nevertheless, he emerges triumphant in both confrontations through his ability to demonstrate superior violence and rationality, two of the most valued qualities of a military man. Again, after he is poisoned by Valenka, the lover of Le Chiffre, the camera follows Bond's attempts to expel the poison from his body, hyper-focused on his increasing panic and realization of the gravity of his situation. In these moments, there is fear that Bond's body may betray him by succumbing to the poison. That Bond's own body has been rendered as both feminine and vulnerable by his enemies is a trauma that he will work to escape for the rest of the franchise.

That trauma is reinforced at the turning point of the *Casino Royale*, during the scene of Bond's genital torture at the hands of Le Chiffre. This scene of Bond's emotional, psychological and physical suffering is intimately intertwined with the series as a whole. We later come to understand this scene as the moment where Lynd betrays the British government to spare Bond's life, and as the first indication that Le Chiffre is part of a larger conspiracy (later revealed to be SPECTRE). It is also this trauma – both the physical harm to his manhood and the pain caused by Lynd's death – that will fuel the rest of his adventures, and justify his actions during their course. Bond returns from his revenge quest in *Quantum of Solace* (Forster 2008), again appearing as the independent and ruthless agent he is expected to be. He even drops Lynd's necklace in the snow at the end of the film, demonstrating that he is ready to leave her in the past. Here again, though, the film hints at a deeper, more complex battle going on beneath Bond's veneer. Lynd's theme music follows him off-screen, hinting his heart is still broken and his mind not yet healed.

Skyfall (Mendes 2012) further indicates that Bond's trauma is becoming an increasingly central part of his identity (Brown et al. 2010: 499). He is shown taking part in a wager in a beach-side bar, balancing a scorpion on the back of his hand while finishing a drink, behaviour which indicates an increasing recklessness that Sigmund Freud identified as a hallmark of PTSD. Indeed, Freudian trauma theory is present throughout *Skyfall*: many of the film's action scenes rely on underground architecture and penetration, from MI6's digital firewalls, to Bond's body (via a uranium-laced bullet), to the London

Underground, and the subterranean tunnels beneath Skyfall Lodge. As with the opening scene of *Casino Royale*, these settings are more than a riff on traditional Cold War spy narratives. They represent spaces of utter vulnerability and interiority, foreshadowing the emotionally fraught journey into Bond's psyche that the final three films will traverse. When these spaces are breached, Bond reacts with spectacular acts of destruction to avoid introspection. This is especially evident in the incineration of Skyfall, which represents 'everything Bond has to repress to be the stone-cold bastard we meet in the classic Bond films' (Daub and Kronengold 2015: 42).

An explosion in *Spectre*, however, hints that Bond's journey may be leading to a revelation, or at least a break from his cycle of traumatic repetition, thanks to the presence of Dr Madeleine Swann. Blofeld subjects Bond to another long, lingering torture session with a remote surgical device that will allegedly destroy Bond's long-term memory, emasculating him in front of the woman he loves. Unlike *Casino Royale*, Bond leaps from his restraints and lays siege to Blofeld's headquarters, destroying the space where he had to confront the trauma of Lynd's betrayal and death, relive his own tortured childhood with the Oberhauser family, and witness the death by suicide of Mr White.

In this act of retaliation, Bond's growing love for Dr Swann provides the strength he needs to be a hero, rather than hampering him, a shift that will be explored further. However, such a revelation also means that this Bond is no longer able, or no longer willing, to support the weight of unrealistic expectations of masculinity that he struggled to achieve up to this point, placing him in direct confrontation with the series' expectations of gender performance. This realization will come with the destruction of Safin's poison farm in *No Time To Die*, when Bond accepts that his love has made him both inhumanly strong (able to withstand being shot at point-blank range) and impossibly vulnerable. His death in an explosion is both a liberation and a moment when his emotions overpower him completely, emphasizing his unique complexity within the franchise. Yet it also forces us to realize that the women on whom Bond's character is built are not afforded the same complexity. With one notable exception, their trauma exists to support Bond's journey. Even while reviews touted the Craig Bond films as 'feminist' due to the inclusion of more women of diverse backgrounds and ages, the character arcs and emotional dimensionality afforded to these women remained reductive and unsympathetic (Palmer 2020).

'You're both damaged goods': Bond and women's trauma

The role that trauma plays in the narratives of women in the Craig quintet is deeply complex and deserves to be the focus of continuing thought and discussion. As we will explore, women are inherently dangerous to Bond because, as Christine Bold explains, they 'can destabilize the hierarchy of gender and race on which the Bond institution rests' (2009: 216). The Craig-era provided more screen time to its women characters than previous films; however, they do not meaningfully expand their emotional or psychological complexity, leaving these women generally incomplete characters. This is an issue present in Bond's individual interactions with women characters, as well as their treatment within the series.

Bond's work is to maintain global order and the gender hierarchy by vanquishing his enemies, and by co-opting and consuming the trauma of the women around him. By relieving these women of their trauma, Bond restores his authority as the hero of the films and of his relationships. It also removes the agency of the women characters by erasing their pasts, muting their emotional responses, and recentring Bond as the only character capable of feeling real pain. The first example of this comes in *Casino Royale*, when Bond comforts Vesper Lynd, who sits fully clothed in the shower, struggling to wash away the blood of a man she helped Bond kill (Figure 5.1). Craig himself worked with actor Eva Green and director Martin Campbell to emphasize the emotionality of the scene, including the moment shown here, when Bond tenderly sucks on Lynd's fingers to help remove the blood she thinks is still visible on her skin (Cotter 2021). While significant to the evolving romance between Bond and Lynd, the

Figure 5.1 *Casino Royale* (Eon Productions et al. 2006).

moment also represents how Bond literally and figuratively takes the trauma of women into himself. This moment also visually foreshadows Lynd's eventual drowning death by suicide, which is depicted as the transformative trauma of Bond's on-screen life. From this moment, Lynd's fate is sealed, but her death will become Bond's tragedy.

Quantum of Solace (Forster 2008) is a surprising exception to many franchise rules, and yet is a film rife with trauma – not only Bond's but also that of his companion, Camille Montes (played by Olga Kurylenko), and the people of Bolivia who are subjected to the environmental terrorism of Dominic Greene and his associates. Incidentally, the hoarding of water could also be seen as a reference to Vesper Lynd, whose memory lies hidden in Bond's heart, destabilizing him like it destabilizes the world around him in Bolivia. Montes is a unique 'Bond girl', in that her individual quest to avenge the death of her family intersects with and significantly influences Bond's own pursuit, without specifically relying on him. In this sense, her narrative privilege and potential for empathy are nearly equal to that of Bond himself. Indeed, Bond apologizes to Montes for compromising her first opportunity to kill General Luiz Medrano and he prepares her for the physiological responses she might experience when she tries again.

Both Bond and Montes face their final showdown in the Perla de las Dunas, an empty hotel that Nick Jones describes as a space that Bond and Montes both 'invest with meaning and value by imbuing it with their psychological trauma that they have then overcome' (2015: 87). Bond finds Montes curled up on the floor of a burning hotel room. She has succeeded in killing the man responsible for the rape of her mother and the murder of her family, but the cumulative trauma has rendered her unable to escape the room. Bond crouches with Montes, cradling her, and we see her reduced to the child that has carried such an emotional burden for so long. Bond may have grievously injured Greene, but his real triumph comes in liberating himself and Montes from the hotel by blowing out the side of the building.

In the end, though, Bond is unable to liberate himself. When Montes asks, 'Do you think you'll be able to sleep now?' Bond replies incongruously, 'I don't think the dead care about vengeance.' His conversation is not with Montes, but with himself, as he struggles to reclaim his masculine rationality. Montes recognizes that Bond has not – and perhaps cannot – reach the level of healing that she has. 'I wish I could set you free', she tells him before leaving him, 'but your prison is in there.' Camille Montes remains a unique woman in Bond's world, both because she walks away, clearly understanding that she is incapable of healing him, and because her character rejects all normative conventions for her role and finds at least the hope of healing from her trauma. However, the movie only shows her walking away from Bond, without any indication that she may be moving towards a future where her trauma is resolved. Her absence drives home the depth of Bond's suffering by forcing him to confront it alone. It is interesting to note that the film that showed the most complex depiction of women feeling and responding to trauma is also the film that received the poorest reviews at the time of its release, resulting in a franchise pivot and return to familiar narrative territory in *Skyfall*.

Bond's relationships with women, and their character arcs, return closer to form in the following films. *Skyfall* opens with a chase scene that sees a woman operative (later revealed to be Moneypenny) shoot and allegedly kill Bond. As a result of this, Moneypenny (Naomie Harris) is suspended from field work and assigned as an assistant to Gareth Mallory. When they are reunited at MI6's new headquarters, Moneypenny offers an apology, letting the emotional toll her actions took show on her face. 'It's only four ribs, some of the less vital organs, nothing major', Bond responds, showing that he is not only willing to absorb Moneypenny's bullets, but her emotional burdens, as well. He follows this up with a prophetic observation that field work 'isn't for everyone'. Again, having absorbed her emotional experiences into his own identity and body, Bond's role at the centre of the story is ensured, while 'Moneypenny's origin story is minimized and made instrumental to Bond's narrative of success' (Shaw 2015: 72). Later in the film, she comes to Bond's hotel in Shanghai, explaining that 'My official directive was to help', further emphasizing the extent to which her professional and personal identity has been diminished to a role of caretaker. Although Bond offers a sign of trust by allowing her to shave his face with a straight razor, the act reinforces her new, thoroughly subservient, feminized role (Shaw 2015: 78). Following this interaction, Moneypenny abandons fieldwork, taking up a job behind a desk and in service of men who serve as superior(s). Throughout the rest of the franchise, her narratives revolve around aiding Bond, even to the extent of abandoning a lover to help him negotiate the complexities of SPECTRE. The only indication of an emotional or psychological reality in the character comes in her worrying about or mourning Bond, who has been recentred as the focus of her world.

While in Shanghai, Bond also encounters Séverine (Bérénice Marlohe), a woman who at first appears confident and powerful. Within moments of their meeting, however, Bond exposes her history as a victim of child sex-trafficking

Gender, Trauma and Resilience in Daniel Craig's James Bond   89

and her current inescapable relationship with the villain Silva, reducing Séverine to a trembling, helpless damsel-in-distress (Funnell 2015: 86). Bond is thus able to establish physical and psychological power over Séverine, promising to rescue her from Silva if she will show him to Silva's hideout, and engaging in sex with her in her shower. This scene shows how completely the franchise has doubled down on a narrow depiction of women's trauma since Montes in *Quantum of Solace*. When he comes up behind her in the shower, Bond whispers that he prefers Séverine without her gun, prompting her to respond, 'I feel naked without it.' Séverine is disarmed and vulnerable in this moment, forcing the audience to question if the sexual encounter that happens next is something to which she felt able to give consent. The shower sex scene further recalls Bond's previous shower scene with Vesper Lynd, reframing Séverine as an object on which he can work out his own feelings of loss and betrayal by 'stealing' and 'conquering' his enemy's property. Later, her death at Silva's hands offers Bond the opportunity to murder Silva's henchmen and capture the villain. The scene unfolds like a redemption arc for Bond, who overcomes physical injury and psychological hesitancy to dominate Silva, demonstrating his tenuous shift from embattled sufferer to masculine hero, but the cost of that transformation is Séverine's victimization, dehumanization and death (Funnell 2015: 86).

Skyfall also sees the culmination of Bond's relationship with Dame Judi Dench's M, whose starring turn alongside Bond in this film comes at the cost of her pride, her authority and ultimately, her life (Kunze 2015: 245). The final showdown of the film comes when Bond takes on the emotional trauma and physical threat posed by Silva on himself, removing M to his childhood home and forcing her to rely on him and Skyfall's elderly caretaker Kincade (Albert Finney). At the beginning of this film, M authorized the shot that nearly killed Bond, deeming the risk to his person worth the reward of accomplishing the mission. This is in keeping with her character, who adopts 'a traditionally masculine stoicism' in the face of threats to her person, her position, and her country (Kunze 2015: 242). The Craig films, however, consistently challenge her authority, framing her as both 'Bond girl', bantering with Bond and permitting his reckless behaviour, and as mother, soothing his hurt and providing the strongest relationship Bond has throughout the films (Holliday 2015: 271). When her authority directly harms Bond, he invades her home to berate her, telling her she lost her nerve in authorizing the kill shot. Unable to bear the weight of his own pain, Bond lashes out at M, forcing her to endure personal guilt and shame for a professional mistake.

This comment proves ominous, foreshadowing the loss of M's position, self-confidence and life in rapid succession. While waiting for Silva and his men to storm the lodge, M mutters 'I fucked this up, didn't I?' Hunched over and weak, she is no longer the woman who called Pierce Brosnan's Bond 'a sexist, misogynist dinosaur'. Instead, her age, her isolation and her complicity in the villain's violence render her helpless. She sits behind Bond, who stands facing the coming enemy with a gun resting on his shoulder (Figure 5.2). While this Bond superficially rejects this premise, assuring her 'No. You did your job', his words are not absolution. Instead, they transform M into an object on which Bond can build his confidence back. In Skyfall Manor, M is transformed into a relic, equated in dialogue and visually with the ancient house around her, wearing a shawl and unable to fire a gun. Kincade, the gamekeeper, misunderstanding Bond's introduction, refers to her as 'Emma', exchanging her title for an anonymizing feminine name. By diminishing her agency, Bond also refocuses the story onto himself. As with Lynd, M's death is framed as Bond's trauma which drives his pursuit of SPECTRE into the next film. However, her death also removes a character who has thoroughly compromised Bond's masculine confidence and stoicism by provoking and providing an outlet for his emotions and suffering. In the final scene of *Skyfall*, Bond enters the office of the new M (a man now, played by Ralph Fiennes), where Moneypenny sits docilely behind a desk. The Bond music sounds in the background, showing that any threats to Bond's masculine heroism have been vanquished (Boyce 2015: 283).

The final two films of the franchise introduce Dr Madeleine Swann (played by Léa Seydoux), the daughter of the SPECTRE assassin, Mr White, who swiftly becomes the focus of all of Bond's repressed emotions and lingering trauma.

Figure 5.2 *Skyfall* (Eon Productions et al. 2012).

From the moment she and Bond first meet, Dr Swann offers the chance for escape from Bond's history of traumatic repetition and repression. She invokes memories of Vesper Lynd, appearing as a professional woman, dressed in black, rebuffing Bond's questions with ruthless calm, but also dispels them by appearing for their dinner date on the train in a white dress that highlights both her femininity and her innocence, in stark contrast to the duplicitous Vesper Lynd. As a psychologist and a trauma victim herself, Dr Swann is in a unique position to understand Bond's manifestation of trauma and guide him past his traumatic repetitions to an eventual revelation. In a conversation on the train, Dr Swann interrupts Bond's suave prattle by asking him what would happen if he stopped, forcing him to admit that he doesn't know. She guides him through the uncertainty of this choice by holding his hand as he walks away from the later confrontation on Westminster Bridge and, assumedly, into retirement. Her home later provides Bond a place of refuge where he has his first (and only) chance to explore domestic happiness by cooking breakfast for Mathilde, helping him visualize the possibilities of a world where he did not have to be the heroic masculine ideal.

While both *Spectre* and *No Time To Die* attempt to complicate Madeleine Swann's character by showing her as a resilient victim of trauma, the nature of that trauma and her eventual character arc further emphasize the limits of the women's independent emotional development and potential for healing after trauma. The first indication of the harm Dr Swann has suffered comes in L'Americain, where she references the comfort that she requires over the loss of her 'dead daddy' and unconsciously re-enacting her childhood trauma by miming firing a shot at Bond to keep him from following her to bed. In this scene, she is intoxicated and pouting like an overtired child in need of Bond's protection. This image is further reinforced once Bond discovers the secret room in the hotel, where Dr Swann cries while examining the baby pictures her father posted on the room's walls (Figure 5.3).

No Time To Die further delves into the realities of her trauma, showing how a young Madeleine was responsible for caring for a drunken, apparently uncaring mother. Incidentally, Dr Swann is never seen to tell Bond anything about her mother, showing that women who don't live up to gendered expectations disappear, no matter who is telling the story. While her father is away, Lyutsifer Safin invades her home and murders Swann's mother before a young Madeleine shoots him repeatedly. Safin does not die, however, and saves Swann when she falls through the ice attempting to escape him, reinforcing her alignment to the

Figure 5.3 *Spectre* (Eon Productions et al. 2016).

men in her life: her father, Safin, and now Bond. The film generously refocuses from Bond to Dr Swann for this scene, validating her trauma in a unique and important way. However, it also insistent that, in the end, the 'cure' for all of Dr Swann's suffering is to become a mother herself and preserve Bond's memory for their child. She assumes the feminine role of caretaker, which Bond wished to do, but was denied. In her motherhood, gendered order is restored to the world of the films.

'Sounds like you lost another one!': The limits of resilience

There are three noteworthy moments when Bond is shown weeping: at the deaths of Lynd, M and before his own death when speaking with Dr Swann from Safin's secret island. These relationships, which challenge Bond's ability to vanquish enemies and complete his missions, represent the trauma which this Bond can neither resolve nor repress. For this Bond, physical trauma is bound up with masculinity, and thus something that can be negotiated. However, Bond's grief requires him to perform a gendered, feminine form of emotional introspection that cannot stand within the framework of the films.

Throughout Craig's time as James Bond, the role of mourning and grieving has always been taken up by women. Lynd is, unbeknownst to Bond, mourning the loss of her lover; Dr Swann mourns both her father and her lost time with Bond; M, we learn in *Skyfall*, has lost a husband, and is also grieving her loss of identity and career. Grief is also one of the most personal and self-defining of emotions, forcing a recognition of the emotions and desire that make us vulnerable. By embracing his grief, his inability to touch his love or their daughter again, Bond gives in to the introspection that has been threatening to undo his manly resolve for five films. His death, on one hand, represents an escape from the traumatic repression and repetition that has ensnared him since the death of Vesper Lynd, and thus the obliteration of his previous identity. On the other, it represents Bond's willing objectification, accepting a passive position to provide agency and a future to Dr Swann and Mathilde. He chooses his emotions over the orders given to him by M, a kind of feminine betrayal in the world of the franchise. By assuming the position of a traumatized and grieving woman, within the logic of the films, Bond's death was a tragic but necessary eventuality.

Bond's ending transferred the role of grief to the audience, forcing them to feel how loss renders us vulnerable. That this death came during the Covid-19 pandemic, when societies around the world were being asked to repress their reactions over the loss of millions of individuals, this loss became even more significant and profound. By invoking these feelings and provoking so much discussion about Bond's psychological evolution over the years, Craig's Bond accomplished something remarkable. The films guided a historically immature character toward maturity and emphasized that emotions could be a source of strength and heroism, rather than just a weakness to be overcome. They also justified Bond's presence in a post-Cold War world by prompting discourse about heroism, sacrifice and the tolls that these both take on a person forced to enact them. However, in these successes, the films also shone a light on the utter lack of emotional complexity among women in the franchise, and highlighted that audiences were ambivalent about them when they did appear. Ultimately, though the Craig quintet advanced discourse regarding men's trauma and emotions, they did very little to shift the subjectivity of trauma narratives to women, holding the suffering man in the frame at all costs.

References

Amacker, A. K. and D. A. Moore (2011), '"The Bitch Is Dead": Anti-Feminist Rhetoric in *Casino Royale*', in R. G. Weiner, L. B. Whitfield, and J. Becker (eds), *James Bond in World and Popular Culture: The Films Are Not Enough*, 144–55, Newcastle upon Tyne: Cambridge Scholars Publishers.

Bold, C. (2009), '"Under the Very Skirts of Britannia": Re-Reading Women in the James Bond Novels', in C. Lindner (ed.), *The James Bond Phenomenon: A Critical Reader*, 2nd edn, 205–19, Manchester: Manchester University Press.

Bourke, J. (1999), *An Intimate History of Killing: Face-to-Face Killing in Twentieth Century Warfare*, London: Granta Press.

Boyce, M. (2015), 'Property of a Lady: (S)Mothering Judi Dench's M', in L. Funnell (ed.), *For His Eyes Only: The Women of James Bond*, 274–83, New York: Columbia University Press.

Brody, R. (2021), 'Review: "No Time to Die" Leaves Daniel Craig's James Bond Legacy Unfulfilled', 12 October. Available online: https://www.newyorker.com/culture/the-front-row/review-no-time-to-die-leaves-daniel-craigs-james-bond-legacy-unfulfilled.

Brown, A. D. et al. (2010), 'Trauma Centrality and PTSD in Veterans Returning from Iraq and Afghanistan', *Journal of Traumatic Stress* 23 (4): 496–9.

Chamorro-Premuzic, T. and D. Lusk (2017), 'The Dark Side of Resilience', 16 August. Available online: https://hbr.org/2017/08/the-dark-side-of-resilience.

Cotter, P. (2021), 'Daniel Craig Is Responsible for *Casino Royale*'s Most Emotional Scene', 13 September. Available online: https://screenrant.com/being-james-bond-daniel-craig-casino-royale-most-emotional-scene/.

Cox, K. (2014), 'Becoming James Bond: Daniel Craig, Rebirth, and Refashioning Masculinity in *Casino Royale* (2006)', *Journal of Gender Studies* 23 (2): 184–96.

Cunningham, D. A. and R. Gabri (2009), '"Any Thug Can Kill": ReWriting the Masculine Bond', in C. Lindner (ed.), *Revisioning 007: James Bond and Casino Royale*, 81–98, New York: Columbia University Press.

Daub, A. and C. Kronengold (2015), *The James Bond Songs: Pop Anthems of Late Capitalism*, Oxford: Oxford University Press.

Dodds, K. (2012), 'Shaking and Stirring James Bond: Age, Gender, and Resilience in *Skyfall*', *Journal of Popular Film and Television* 42 (3): 116–30.

Ebert, R. (2008), 'A Q only in Quantum', *Roger Ebert*, 1 November. Available online: https://www.rogerebert.com/reviews/quantum-of-solace-2008.

Funnell, L. (2011), 'Negotiating Shifts in Feminism: The "Bad" Girls of James Bond', in Melanie Waters (ed.), *Women on Screen: Feminism and Femininity in Visual Culture*, London: Palgrave Macmillan.

Funnell, L. (2015), 'Objects of White Male Desire: (D)evolving Representations of Asian Women in Bond Films', in Lisa Funnell (ed.), *For His Eyes Only: The Women of James Bond*, 79–90, New York: Wallflower Press.

Funnell, L. (2018), 'Reworking the Bond Girl Concept in the Craig Era Films', *Journal of Popular Film and Television* 20 (46): 11–21.

Gleiberman, O. and P. Debruge (2021), 'Critics Debate: Is *No Time to Die* a Triumph or a Letdown? And Where Does the James Bond Series Go from Here?', *Variety*, 9 October. Available online: https://variety.com/2021/film/opinion/no-time-to-die-critics-dialogue-james-bond-daniel-craig-1235084265/.

Holliday, C. (2015), 'Mothering the Bond-M Relation in *Skyfall* and the Bond Girl Intervention', in Lisa Funnell (ed.), *For His Eyes Only: The Women of James Bond*, 265–73, New York: Wallflower Press.

Holliday, C. (2018), 'London, the Post-7/7 Bond Films, and Mourning Work', *Journal of Popular Film and Television*, 46 (1): 56–63.

Jones, N. (2015), *Hollywood Action Films and Spatial Theory*, New York: Taylor & Francis.

Kunze, P. C. (2015), 'From Masculine Mastermind to Maternal Martyr: Judi Dench's M, *Skyfall*, and the Patriarchal Logic of James Bond Films', in Lisa Funnell (ed.), *For His Eyes Only: The Women of James Bond*, 237–45, New York: Wallflower Press.

Murray, J. (2017), 'Containing the Spectre of the Past: The Evolution of the James Bond Franchise during the Daniel Craig Era', *Visual Culture in Britain*, 18 (2): 247–73.

Palmer, B. (2020), 'Things I Learnt Rereading My GCSE Essay on Sexism in James Bond', *The Mary Sue*, 14 March. Available online: https://www.bustle.com/entertainment/can-james-bond-ever-be-feminist-lessons-from-my-gcse-essay-on-the-subject-22615436.

Petch, T. (2015), '10 Reasons Why James Bond Suffers from Post-Traumatic Stress Disorder', 3 December. Available online: https://www.tompetch.com/blog/10-reasons-why-james-bond-suffers-from-post-traumatic-stress-dis (accessed 4 October 2021).

Scott, A. O. (2008), '007 is Back, and He's Brooding', *New York Times*, 13 November.

Shaw, K. (2015), 'The Politics of Representation: Disciplining and Domesticating Miss Moneypenny in *Skyfall*', in Lisa Funnell (ed.), *For His Eyes Only: The Women of James Bond*, 70–8, New York: Wallflower Press.

Shields, D. M. (2016), 'Military Masculinity, Movies, and the *DSM*: Narratives of Institutionally (En)Gendered Trauma', *Psychology of Men & Masculinities* 17 (1): 64–73. Available online: http://dx.doi.org/10.1037/a0039218.

Showalter, E. (1985), *The Female Malady: Women, Madness and English Culture, 1830–1980*, London: Virago.

Swatman, R. (2015), 'Latest Bond Adventure Spectre Sets Record for Largest Filmstunt Explosion Ever—Watch Incredible Clip', *Guinness World Records*. Available online: https://www.guinnessworldrecords.com/news/2015/11/daniel-craig-accepts-certificate-for-largest-film-stunt-explosion-in-latest-bond-405307.

Tremonte, C. M. and L. Racioppi (2009), 'Body Politics and *Casino Royale*: Gender and (Inter)national Security', in C. Lindner (ed.), *The James Bond Phenomenon: A Critical Reader*, 2nd edn, 184–204, Manchester: Manchester University Press.

Vejvoda, J. (2012), '007 Responds to IGN Readers', *IGN*, 12 May. Available online: https://www.ign.com/articles/2008/09/22/007-responds-to-ign-readers.

Waling, A. (2019), 'Problematizing "Toxic" and "Healthy" Masculinity for Addressing Gender Inequalities', *Australian Feminist Studies* 34 (101): 362–75.

Part Two

Disembodiment

6

For Your Servers Only

Surveillance and Infonationalism in Craig-era Bond

Kathryn Hendrickson and John Brick

The mimetic qualities of fictional narrative – that is, the elements drawn from reality that shape the dimensions of a fictional world – do more than populate a story with fictional characters, devices and situations: they also imbue the story with a distinct perspective of the world. Fiction encodes information about the world that subsumes audiences into an interpretive framework that extends beyond the boundaries of the story itself. As J. Furman Daniel and Paul Musgrave put it, popular narratives 'affect how people interact with the real world through pathways similar to memory and knowledge derived from textbooks or data analyses' (2017: 506). Simply put, fiction offers a lens through which to interpret the world: the stories we build, hear and share filter forward, informing our perspectives and beliefs.

Popular fiction often supplements this interpretive power with *repetition*: reiterated formulae that build patterns of expectations between readers and writers, which also reveal and shape cultural patterns of expectations (Cawelti 1976). The strength of these patterns can hardly be underestimated; in their study of popular culture's impact on common impressions of international relationships, Daniel and Musgrave found that '[m]ovies, television shows, and novels … may be at least as influential — or, under some conditions, even more influential — in shaping people's worldview as more "respectable" sources' (2017: 503). For some audiences, popular media constitutes the dominant (or only) medium through which they encounter or develop ideas about particular concepts or relationships, according those media outsize influence in establishing how they understand those concepts.

Serial franchises like James Bond transmute real-world tensions, anxieties, policies and threats into exciting (and lucrative) entertainment by compressing complex geopolitical issues – foreign relations, the role of the state in a global community, the obligations and limits of national security – into an approachable narrative framework. Spy fiction in particular blossomed in popularity after the Second World War and into the 1960s, 'when popular anxieties were growing over the credibility of government processes' (Seed 2003: 115) and the narrative formula allowed books and films to serve as sites for a concerned audience to explore their worries. Ian Fleming's perennially popular spy burst onto the scene in 1953 with *Casino Royale*; that initial success rapidly expanded into multiple novels, short stories and the ongoing blockbuster film series featuring, as of 2022, no fewer than six different leading men. Early Bond media saw the spy embodying 'the imaginary power that England might once again be placed at the center of world affairs during a period when its world power status was visibly and rapidly declining' (Bennett and Woollacott 1987: 82). James Chapman, a popular culture historian, saw the Bond novels as representing 'a nationalist fantasy, in which Britain's decline as a world power did not really take place' (1999: 38). In his analysis of the evolution of Bond as a cinematic figure, historian Jeremy Black similarly identifies Bond as 'a figure designed to resist the threat to empire' (2001: 4). As the Cold War drew to a close and political fears shifted in response to world events, so too did the foes and threats matched against Bond.

In the first decades of the twenty-first century, the controversially-cast Daniel Craig plays a 007 who must cope with a changing world of increasingly powerful technology, shadowy cyberterrorist threats and shifting global tensions. Craig's first turn as James Bond in the 2006 adaptation of Fleming's *Casino Royale* (Campbell) deliberately rebooted the character, who returned in *Quantum of Solace* (Forster 2008), *Skyfall* (Mendes 2012), *Spectre* (Mendes 2015) and *No Time To Die* (Fukunaga 2021). The first four films enjoyed various measures of critical and commercial success, offering a self-contained story arc from Bond's licensing as a 00 agent in *Casino Royale* through his decision to turn his back on MI6 and walk away with Dr Madeleine Swann in *Spectre*. Despite Craig's growing antipathy toward the role, his return for a surprising fifth instalment presented an opportunity for a second coda. Faced with the challenge of returning Bond, at least temporarily, to MI6, *No Time To Die* invoked the shadow of Vesper Lynd to break Bond's tether to a secretly pregnant Swann and a family life after espionage – and gave the Craig films one final opportunity to repeat their

Surveillance and Infonationalism   101

mimetic formulae to shape audiences' perceptions of real-world events, tensions and threats in a milieu Christopher Holliday describes as 'hing[ing] upon terrorist domination, homeland security, surveillance, and nanotechnology as increasingly threatening' (2018: 61–2).

New Bond, new threats

Bond media have always incorporated real-world analogues into their narratives, but during Craig's tenure as Bond a different sort of anxiety, unique in the franchise's history, may be seen to emerge as a preeminent concern: the mass harvesting of raw data on a staggering scale. While the golden age of espionage pitted nation against nation through the bodies of their agents, present tensions over the ambiguous threat of data-harvesting, its attendant surveillance apparatuses and their implications for national security lend new dimensions to the Craig films, which gradually but inexorably adopt the view that data and its means of collection must be brought under the jurisdiction of the state, and all efforts – legal or extra-legal – to harness them are matters of security and patriotic duty. All five of the Craig films present a world in which the mass-collection of data is inescapable, and rather than any glimpse of a possible alternative, they can only imagine a world in which data and its collection apparatus must be gained, fought for and defended exclusively by the state. Bond's foes, no matter their colourful background or the scale of their motivations, all reside within networks of information that amplify their reach, transforming them from individual criminals into global threats to be conquered, not just by the embodiment of state control but by the incarnation of the state's own data-collection power. Furthermore, villains are no longer to be neutralized; their data collection and capabilities are to be subsumed into the apparatus of the state, and the networked nature of their threat justifies the exercise of licensed state violence in the pursuit of producing and maintaining mechanisms of information collection and control. Making a privileged resource into a central plot point is, of course, a trope of the Bond franchise's mimetic narrative, but data and the apparatus of its harvest constitutes a sufficiently unique type of resource so as to distinguish it from previous iterations like nuclear arms, oil or dwindling natural resources. In their promotion of what we are describing as an *infonationalist* perspective, the Craig films normalize and indeed valorize unlimited state control of data and surveillance as both necessary and patriotic, thereby reiterating the franchise's traditional hierarchies of closed, nationalist and anti-globalist security.

Infonationalism, as we apply it to the Craig films, draws from the concept of techno-nationalism, a term introduced in 1987 by Robert Reich to describe the broad scope of intersections between technology and the self-perpetuating, self-preserving interests of the nation-state (1987: 63–9). Creso Sá, Andrew Kretz and Kristjan Sigurdson identify the primary drives of techno-nationalism as originating within the complex socio-political identity of the state, and employ the term to designate the 'strategies and policy orientations that favor the nation and its innovative capabilities and technological autonomy' as well as a state's 'actions that seek to enhance the innovative capabilities and competitiveness of national industries within globally integrated networks'. In contrast to a techno-globalist orientation, which regards technology as an ideally neutral platform upon which to strengthen international cooperation, trade and cross-cultural exchange, a techno-nationalist position favours 'policies that limit both technological dependence on foreign countries and international knowledge spillovers from domestic research … to ensure national competitiveness within international markets' (Sá et al. 2013: 446). Infonationalism, by extension, operates on a similar logic, seeking to advance strategy and policy orientations designed to ensure state primacy in the harvesting, preservation and use of data and the apparatuses of its collection. At the broadest possible level, all espionage fiction deals with 'information', but it is specifically the unprecedented scale of *data*: the breadth and depth of its collection, and the precision and ubiquity of the tools that harvest it, that compel the consideration of infonationalism as a distinct phenomenon. Furthermore, where techno-nationalism uses 'technology' as a broadly construed abstract category which serves as a nonspecific and self-justifying rationale for nationalist control (Adria 2011: 45), infonationalism uses data to achieve a similar rhetorical goal. Where a specific computer chip or software system, a proprietary algorithm or the engineering specs for a hydroelectric dam or cruise missile might be the focal objects of techno-nationalist policy, invocation of 'technology' as a rhetorical abstract – something, for example, like 'we can't let China outpace us in the technology sector' – serves a political and ideological function. Analogously, infonationalism uses the abstract figure of data harvested on a grand scale to achieve similar political and ideological goals: goals which the mimetic narrative of the Craig films have been uniquely positioned to advance.

Casino Royale debuted in 2006 to a world still grappling with the 9/11 attacks and the subsequent proliferation of domestic and international mass surveillance. The Patriot Act, signed into law in 2001, helped centralize the authority to order surveillance within the executive branch while diminishing norms of oversight from both domestic and foreign courts. The Stellar Wind programme, under which American telecommunications, internet activity and financial records could be data-mined without a warrant was exposed in the *New York Times* in 2004, while *Casino Royale* was in active development. In 2006, two short years before *Quantum of Solace*, WikiLeaks began its regular publication of sensitive and top-secret documents, some of which directly or indirectly substantiated reports of extensive government surveillance circulating in the press that year. In 2013, just after *Skyfall* and two years prior to *Spectre*, National Security Agency whistle-blower Edward Snowden's sensational disclosure of the PRISM programme, which described mass surveillance of internet giants like Microsoft, Yahoo!, Google, Facebook, YouTube, AOL and Apple, permanently altered public perception of mass government surveillance. Between *Spectre* (2015) and *No Time To Die* (2021), public concerns over data-harvesting had grown into the corporate sector, as the 2018 Cambridge Analytica data scandal pitched concerns over data collection and use into the sphere of domestic politics. It can hardly be surprising, then, that during Craig's tenure Bond's villains are increasingly meshed in data, wielding the ability to point and click their way to the destabilization of companies, governments and nations.

The films' dramatization of the anxieties of surveillance and data become increasingly concentrated as the narrative arc winds toward its endpoint for Craig's Bond – and, in doing so, school audiences in the infonationalist imperative: as a matter of national security, authority over data and its collection must reside with no other entity but the state. As intelligence scholars McCrisken and Moran convincingly argue, 'Bond and intelligence should be thought of as co-constitutive; the series shapes representations and perceptions of intelligence, but it also performs a productive role, influencing the behaviours of intelligence agencies themselves' (2018: 817). Bond reaches outside the boundaries of the text and affects both the field of espionage itself and how the public understands and views that field, serving as an ongoing propaganda machine simultaneously glamorizing and justifying the work of the spy. Similarly, the Craig films' response to the rise of infonationalism shapes public perception of the threats posed by data and mass surveillance and serves the infonationalist project of governing attitudes about appropriate, secure control of data and the tools of its harvest.

Information and the spy: *Casino Royale* and *Quantum of Solace*

Bond media has traditionally fictionalized techno-nationalist concerns, deftly replacing real-world anxieties with more palatable fictional ones. Both the 1958 Fleming novel and the 1962 adaptation of *Dr. No* (Young) engages with the fear of Russian space superiority, but rather than subverting the polished magnesium-alloy hull of *Sputnik-1*, James Bond derails a radio-jamming attack against launches at Cape Canaveral. Bond deals with the 1973 energy crisis in *The Man With the Golden Gun* (Hamilton) not by patiently queueing to gas up his Aston Martin DB5, but by preserving the balance of global security and the world's energy economy by assassinating a rogue actor and blowing up his solar power plant. The 2006 remake of *Casino Royale*, however, resituates the franchise, removing the emphasis on Cold War geopolitics and technology and placing it instead on what Tobias Hochscherf describes as 'a new world order of asymmetric threats' (2013: 299), an order inextricably meshed in large-scale data-gathering. Within this new, opaque order, information – more so than money or natural resources – must be protected and breaches of secrecy punished because of its increased and increasing use as leverage: not only in the service of nations but also of corporations and individuals, and against terrorist and other anti-state organizations. Film scholar Seung-hoon Jeong argues that *Casino Royale* 'highlights the linked issues of global security and economy' as 'the black market of terrorism is no longer detached from the official financial sector prospering through dynamic globalization' (2020: 212). This black market, as Jeong rightly points out, requires the traditional financial assets, but also relies on strict regulation of information, blurring the familiar lines between financial currency and the currency of information.

Casino Royale signals its paradigmatic shift by emphasizing the primacy of surveillance and secrecy in its opening. Before assassinating Dryden, Bond chides the Prague section chief: 'M doesn't really mind you earning a little money on the side, Dryden. She'd just prefer if it wasn't selling secrets.' Despite the laconic humour, the line sets the tone for the renewed franchise, making it clear that information is a more valuable currency than money. The film's emphasis on cameras, CCTV images and database information centralizes secrecy and the collection of information as both a unifying theme and the narrative impetus for Bond. Bond's parkour pursuit of Mollaka into the Madagascar embassy earns Bond a scolding from M, which, as with Bond's reprimand to Dryden, is couched in terms of the value of information: Bond's actions have put MI6 in the media spotlight and therefore under public scrutiny, and Bond has failed to apprehend the *correct* criminals, as defined by the data gathered and analysed by MI6. *Casino Royale* does not grapple with mass data harvests and ubiquitous surveillance apparatuses in the way that later films do, but in its attitudes toward the prime value of surveillance and information, it nevertheless positions the series to engage with the growing anxieties over data.

Indeed, even Le Chiffre, the treasurer for powerful criminal organizations and played to a turn with Mads Mikkelsen's restrained menace, acknowledges the primacy of information, gloating over a captured Bond that '[e]ven after I killed you and your little girlfriend, your people would still welcome me with open arms because they need what I have'. Le Chiffre is ultimately proved correct, though not in the manner he expects: before shooting Le Chiffre in the head, Mr White echoes Bond's words to Dryden: 'Money isn't as valuable to our organization as knowing who to trust.' Lynd's death proceeds from the blackmail that compels her to exchange a lesser currency – the poker winnings – for the life of her lover. Information, correctly spent, can purchase redemption; human life may serve as a third form of currency, but not the most valuable one.

Quantum of Solace reiterates the supremacy of information, raising the stakes by increasing the scale of the data and its importance to the film's contending entities. Lisa Funnell and Klaus Dodds highlight the film's 'theme of resource security' (2017: 146) taking place within 'a complicated and shifting web of geopolitical relations in which allies like the United States and Britain compete against one another for energy security' (154). The glib revelation that the precious resource under the Bolivian desert is not oil but water elides the fact that both the United States and Britain are primarily interested in securing the trove of geological data related to Quantum's intended land purchase. Before MI6 or the CIA learn that Greene's organization is damming Bolivia's water supply to leverage their monopoly for political power – that is, for most of *Quantum's* run time – both agencies show themselves willing to legitimize violent revolution on the strength of singularly important data. Though the information that drives much of the action in *Quantum of Solace* does not quite reach the scale that mass-harvested surveillance data does its centrality to the plot and its increased scale accord it more concrete features than Le Chiffre's or Mr White's abstracted invocations of information in *Casino Royale*.

The rhetorical dimension of infonationalism, however, asserts itself more prominently here, quietly manoeuvring the state into the position of the

106   *Resisting James Bond: Power and Privilege in the Daniel Craig Era*

sole legitimate authority over data. The antagonistic entity in *Quantum* is not a single nation but a multinational corporation; Britain, while under no immediate national security threat, endorses Bond's continuing investigations. While the film assigns a weak moral relativism to the pursuit of conventional resources – giving the Foreign Secretary the job of explaining to M, 'If we refused to do business with villains, we'd have almost no one to trade with. The world's running out of oil, M ... Right or wrong doesn't come into it' – *Quantum of Solace* puts its stamp of moral approval on extreme measures in pursuit of information. After Bond's passport and credit cards are revoked by MI6 following the death of a Special Branch agent during Bond's infiltration of the Quantum conference in Austria, Bond violently escapes MI6 custody, flees the country, makes decisions that lead to the deaths of retired French agent René Mathis and British agent Fields, and launches an attack on the meeting between Greene and the power-hungry General Medrano in the Atacama Desert. Bond's retroactive justification by MI6 (on a timeline the film leaves deliberately vague), a device repeated in the later films, once again dramatizes for audiences the central infonationalist tenet that national control of data is paramount. As Hochscherf points out, 'At times, the only difference between Bond and members of Quantum is the respective justification for their actions' (2013: 307) – and as *Quantum* vividly demonstrates, in the Craig films, the acquisition of data can justify anything.

Information is the agent (*Skyfall* and *Spectre*)

The next two Craig films steadily escalate the scale and significance of data, amplifying their reiterations of the state as the sole correct authority for control of its gathering, storage and analysis. Large-scale data finally makes its full debut in *Skyfall*, with the theft of a sensitive hard drive containing the identities of MI6 agents as the opening act for a remote bombing of MI6 headquarters, a high-tech jailbreak and an attack on a government hearing. This was all masterminded by the cyberterrorist Raoul Silva and facilitated by his extensive capabilities to extract, analyse and leverage data. Indeed, Silva's first confrontation with Bond not only serves as a demonstration of his data-given power but as an expository lecture on the value of information and the danger of it falling into the wrong hands (Figure 6.1). After taunting Bond with the actual scores from his recent MI6 evaluations, Silva, framed against a blinking array of monitors and server

Figure 6.1 *Skyfall* (Eon Productions et al. 2012).

banks, describes the impending obsolescence of the secret agent in the face of ubiquitous surveillance and data-harvesting on a massive scale:

> Chasing spies. So old fashioned. Your knees must be killing you. England. Hah. The Empire. MI6. Hah. You're living in a ruin as well … If you wanted, you could pick your own secret missions, as I do … Destabilize a multinational by manipulating stocks. Bip, easy. Interrupt transmissions from a spy satellite over Kabul. Pop, done. Mmm, rig an election in Uganda, all to the highest bidder … Just point and click.

This confrontation scene is perhaps the most effective encapsulation of infonationalism in film, simultaneously elevating data as the resource most worthy of acquisition and defence while threatening viewers with a terrifying example of precocity should a non-state actor gain a measure of control.

What is perhaps *Skyfall*'s most overt articulation of an infonationalist position occurs during the Parliament inquiry, which grills M to justify the existence of MI6 against the accusation that its agents 'still live in a golden age of espionage where human intelligence is the only resource available'. M's response – 'Can you see a face, a uniform, a flag? No! Our world is not more transparent now; it's more opaque. It's in the shadows' – confirms the shift in paradigm from conventional espionage to recherché territory of data that Silva inhabits. James Smith accurately views *Skyfall* as the franchise's first real grappling with the role of the agent in the digital intelligence age, in which constant, secret surveillance, enabled by technology to extract data of unprecedented breadth and depth, is the norm. '[T]he surface-level politics', Smith argues, 'mask the deeper ideological work of the film, which attempts a highly conservative mythologizing of the contemporary secret state and its growing reach in the world' (2016: 147). Put another way, *Skyfall* reassures its audiences that the empire is alive and well, expanding for the common good into the territories of surveillance and data, dramatizing the crucial infonationalist dictum that the state is the supreme curator of information, its collection and its analysis – and, by extension, that its human agents are heroic and deserving of all trust. Bond – or whatever real-world person or persons correspond to his mimetic-narrative function – will always be watching over us.

Of the five Craig films, *Spectre* deals most directly with surveillance and mass harvesting of data. Crucially, while it dramatizes the notion of surveillance and data as a threat, *Spectre* deliberately avoids locating the true root of that threat in surveillance or data itself as existential dangers. The film's Nine Eyes intelligence-sharing alliance (an almost absurdly light fictionalization of the real-world Five Eyes alliance of the US, UK, Canada, Australia and New Zealand), a global network of continual surveillance, data-gathering and behavioural analysis, appears as a remarkably neutral device; the grave danger lies not in the raw capability for universal surveillance or mass data but merely (!) in those capabilities falling into the wrong hands (Figure 6.2). The core infonationalist tenet is very nearly spelled out explicitly here: state control good, non-state control – dramatized in the form of the titular SPECTRE – very bad indeed.

Like any good spy movie, however, *Spectre* offers a twist, serving up a dramatic interpretation of the possibility of undemocratic malfeasance *within* the nation-state, a narrative setup which serves to reinforce the film's core infonationalist attitude. The film feints toward an internal threat with the introduction of Max

Figure 6.2 *Spectre* (Eon Productions et al. 2016).

Denbigh, Director-General of the Joint Security Service, a walking incarnation of the Parliamentary inquiry in *Skyfall*. Denbigh, however, is permitted just enough screen time to voice his clearly insidious support for Britain's participation in the Nine Eyes programme before revealing him as a pawn of Franz Oberhauser, later unveiled as Bond arch-nemesis Ernst Stavro Blofeld. Denbigh's role as the figuration of non-virtuous state control over data is thus carefully quarantined, relegated to the lesser of two threats, and his continual coding as an outsider – from his calculating eagerness against M's composure, to Bond's obvious contempt for him, to his status as secondary villain to Blofeld – neuters Denbigh's weight as a true threat originating from within the state. Simply put, Denbigh is allowed to be the exception that reinforces the infonationalist rule: the rare anomaly within the state's administrative apparatus upon which Bond, M, Q and MI6 can enact the function of the righteous state – and simultaneously reinforce that righteousness as a justification for infonationalist supremacy. In this way, the infonationalist state is presented as always right, for any instances in which it is *not* right may be ascribed to bad actors who do not represent the 'true' state. Indeed, Denbigh's ultimate fate reinforces the notion that the state is fully capable of overcoming any internal wrongdoing: simply put, the state will always have the power to effectively police itself, without the oversight or even knowledge of its citizens. Bond himself operates as both the avatar of the righteous state and its self-policing capability: the agent who, within the new paradigm of a data-driven world, can occasionally overstep his nominally legal bounds (as in the unauthorized Mexico City mission that opens the film and the trip to Rome in defiance of M's orders), but who, unlike Silva, always returns to shore up the bulwarks of the state.

'Information is all, is it not?'

As an unexpected second coda to the Craig films, *No Time To Die* carries the infonationalist logic of the previous films to its natural conclusions. Despite Denbigh's death and the scuttling of Blofeld's designs for Nine Eyes in *Spectre*, *No Time To Die* opens with a Britain still intently invested in a massive project of both national and global surveillance. Heracles, a new British bioweapon developed by Valdo Obruchev under the oversight of Mallory himself, relies for its functionality explicitly on a programme of mass harvesting, storage and analysis of genetic information, requiring access to vast banks of genetic data in order to customize its lethality to specific targets. For the second time in as many films, Mallory's dabbling in mass surveillance grows beyond his control, losing both the weapon and its essential data first to SPECTRE and subsequently to the terrorist Lyutsifer Safin. Heracles' efficacy in translating data into killing power is vividly demonstrated in the first act of the film when Obruchev, revealed as a double agent of Safin, quickly re-programs the weapon's gene-targeting nanobots, frustrating the incarcerated Blofeld's plot to kill Bond and instead gruesomely assassinating the gathered heads of SPECTRE. *No Time To Die* renders data a literal threat, but, tellingly, the film can only interpret that threat through an expressly infonationalist lens (Figure 6.3).

Even when amplified to the degree that it threatens the entire population of the world, the Heracles bioweapon, along with the databanks and surveillance apparatuses that furnish its lethality, are only ever construed as elements to be controlled and leveraged. *No Time To Die* – indeed, all the Craig films – cannot begin to conceive of something like disarmament, eradication or deletion. Having taken his revenge on Blofeld for the murder of his family, Safin proceeds seamlessly (if rather inscrutably) to employ Heracles in a programme of global genocide. While their intentions for Heracles differ – Safin seeks vengeance, and Mallory, vaguely, 'answers to the interests of [his] country' – their goals are never the neutralization of Heracles but only its recovery and the resumption of control. The film's positioning of Safin as a mirror of Bond – and, by extension, MI6 and Britain – exposes the underlying relativism of infonationalist control, in which morality is determined by perspective, not by ends. Safin himself draws attention to this symmetry, remarking: 'James Bond. History of violence. License to kill. Vendetta with Ernst Blofeld. In love with Madeleine Swann. I could be

Figure 6.3 *No Time To Die* (Eon Productions et al. 2021).

Surveillance and Infonationalism

111

speaking to my own reflection.' Armed with the bioweapon and the data to use it, Safin represents a genuine threat to Britain's infonationalist security, and his status as villain is continually framed in terms of his threat to the state – even as it is dramatized on the personal level by his relationship with Bond and the threat to Swann and Mathilde.

No Time To Die's unprecedented choice to kill off Bond ratifies the film's infonationalist inability to consider anything other than total control. The data-reliant nature of Heracles implies a different scope of control than a nuclear missile or an orbital weapons platform; the genetic data that ensures Heracles' efficacy is implied by the film to be essentially universal in scale. Heracles subsumes every individual twice: first on the level of information, and again on the level of biology. Heracles' nanobots, once released, become a permanent part of every person they touch. Prior to the Craig era, the reliably techno-nationalist Bond films drew a notional line between individuals actively participating in technology – its development, construction, maintenance, security and political dimensions – and those who did not actively participate. The former group, quite reasonably, could be pulled into the sphere of international espionage, whereas those who did not actively participate – the de facto 'civilians' – were far more likely to stay safely on the sidelines. Heracles, however, dramatizes one of the fundamental differences between infonationalism and techno-nationalism: the wholesale blurring of any distinction between participants and nonparticipants. A techno-nationalist view still acknowledges a need for agents, state actors endowed with special powers, but under a system of ubiquitous surveillance and mass-harvested data, *everyone* is a participant in infonationalism. There are no non-combatants; the sphere of international espionage now encompasses everyone. In this grim system, each person, not just special agents, is responsible for maintaining the state's grip on the system – and anyone is expendable in service of that cardinal principle. The death of both Bond and Felix Leiter may be understood as the grand finale of the Cold War-era agent and the inauguration of a new era marked by the primacy of data. Bond's powers as a special agent are wholly inadequate against the scope and complexity of a data-driven bioweapon; he is powerless to repair or eliminate the dangers it poses to the world. Mallory deflects Bond's criticism for his development of Heracles by saying, 'If you have nothing left to give, you are irrelevant. You've done your bit and we thank you for your service, again.' Bond's final sacrifice is relevant in that it preserves rather than destabilizes the new infonationalist order. Mallory's programme of mass surveillance initiates the causal chain that results in Madeline and Mathilde's endangerment by a literally toxic Bond, who is ultimately stripped of his superspy capabilities and reduced to the only real agency anyone has under infonationalism: the capacity for self-sacrifice.

Bond's choice to sacrifice himself is never presented as a cold, calculated stratagem; the film wreathes it in warm emotional tones and weights it with familial profundity. It is hardly an accident that both the Heracles bioweapon and the conclusion of *No Time To Die* both rely on genetics. The story told by Madeline Swann to young Mathilde is a matter of family, not geopolitical intrigue. This, simply put, serves the film's didactic function, making palatable the logic of infonationalism as simply the way the world works, and (re) framing individual sacrifices in the service of the infonational state as good and righteous. The primacy of data under infonationalism dovetails neatly with this basically neoliberal view of social responsibility wherein the locus of responsibility resides almost exclusively within the individual, construing blame for the overreaches and missteps of the state as a failure of its citizens to make the necessary sacrifices. Bond, of course, does make the appropriate sacrifice, and his death at the conclusion of *No Time To Die* supports the same core messaging as the previous four films, dramatizing the ideals of right action under infonationalism. In this light, despite its ostensibly heroic circumstances, Bond's exit is also wholly logical: his survival would threaten Britain's infonationalist order, while his death enshrines the primacy of data and the incorporation of everyone into the responsibility for maintaining state hegemony over data and surveillance. Thus, in the instant of his atomization by his own country's missiles, Bond renders infonationalism an incontestable assumption: simultaneously an inevitable force of nature and a perpetually precarious arms race that requires eternal vigilance, the responsibility for its maintenance not concentrated in licensed agents, but rather spread out across an entire population who can be exploited and sacrificed to maintain the state's preeminent hold on the means, product and use of mass-harvested data.

Conclusion

In his 1984 *Delightful Murder: A Social History of the Crime Story*, Ernest Mandel observes that 'In real life, political intrigue and espionage can be woven together so intricately as to obscure or completely eliminate the boundary between "legitimate" politics and criminal activity' (62). Such a weave is hardly new to Bond or indeed many popular franchises; however, few update the formula against a background of infonationalism with the clarity – or regularity – of the Craig films. Taken as a whole, the five instalments school audiences in the proper orientation toward the regime of data-extraction that infiltrates virtually all aspects toward modern life. Even Bond himself, the dynamic hero in whom is balanced the licence to kill and who is continually traumatized, worn down and broken, struts his hour upon the screen governed by nothing so much as the growing importance of data. The metonymic relationship in the Craig films between Bond and his nation situates Bond's physical body as the canvas upon which data – and instruction in the appropriate infonationalist perception of data – is played out. The Craig era ends with Bond's physical body replaced by a story; *No Time To Die*'s final sequence sees Swann telling Mathilde about her father: 'His name was Bond. James Bond.' Narrativized within his own fictional world, Bond survives, fittingly, as data: continually useful, in death as in life, to the needs of the infonationalist state.

From the assassination of Dryden in *Casino Royale* through Lynd's betrayal, the death of M at the hands of the cyberterrorist Silva, to his final decisions in *No Time To Die*, Bond's choices, his triumphs and his tragedies are all framed against the cryptic currents of surveillance and data on an increasingly massive scale. As James Smith puts it, 'The expanding reach of the secret state now poses one of the greatest political and privacy debates facing the present time, with advocates insisting that such powers are necessary in order to engage with the asymmetrical terrorist threats and online battlefields of the twenty-first century, while critics argue that it offers a dangerous and undemocratic reconfiguring of the state's powers' (2016: 146), but the dizzying geopolitical complexities of the present world are rendered small and personal by their translation to film: for Bond, and also for his audience. At the end of Craig's tenure as James Bond, the spy dies a hero's death, awash in personal sacrifice and nobility. This, in the end, is the final necessary lesson of infonationalism, and indeed of all flavours of nationalism, a lesson first drafted in *Casino Royale*: the currency of human life is precious indeed, but not as precious as information.

References

Adria, M. L. (2011), *Technology and Nationalism*, Montreal: McGill-Queen's University Press.

Bennett, T. and J. Woollacott (1987), *Bond and Beyond: The Political Career of a Popular Hero*, London: Macmillan International Higher Education.

Black, J. (2001), *The Politics of James Bond: From Fleming's Novels to the Big Screen*, Westport, CT: Praeger.

Calhoun, D. (2015), "Daniel Craig Interview: 'My Advice to the Next James Bond? Don't Be Shit!', *Time Out*, 7 October. Available online: https://www.timeout.com/film/daniel-craig-interview-my-advice-to-the-next-james-bond-dont-be-shit.

Cawelti, J. G. (1976), *Adventure, Mystery, and Romance: Formula Stories as Art and Popular Culture*, Chicago, IL: University of Chicago Press.

Chapman, J. (1999), *Licence to Thrill: A Cultural History of the James Bond Films*, London and New York: I.B. Tauris.

Daniel, J. F. and P. Musgrave (2017), 'Synthetic Experiences: How Popular Culture Matters for Images of International Relations', *International Studies Quarterly* 61 (3): 503–16.

Funnell, L. and K. Dodds (2017), *Geographies, Genders and Geopolitics of James Bond*, London: Palgrave Macmillan.

Hochscherf, T. (2013), 'Bond for the Age of Global Crises: 007 in the Daniel Craig Era', *Journal of British Cinema and Television* 10 (2): 298–320.

Holliday, C. (2018), 'London, the Post-7/7 Bond Films, and Mourning Work', *The Journal of Popular Film and Television* 46 (1): 56–63.

Jeong, S. H. (2020), 'Global Agency between Bond and Bourne: Skyfall and James Bond in Comparison to the Jason Bourne Film Series', in J. Verheul (ed.), *The Cultural Life of James Bond*, 207–25, Amsterdam: Amsterdam University Press.

Mandel, E. (1984), *Delightful Murder: A Social History of the Crime Story*, Minneapolis: University of Minnesota Press.

McCrisken, T. and C. Moran (2018), 'James Bond, Ian Fleming and Intelligence: Breaking Down the Boundary between the 'Real' and the 'Imagined'', *Intelligence and National Security* 33 (6): 804–21.

Reich, R. (1987), 'The Rise of Techno-Nationalism', *The Atlantic Monthly* 259 (5): 63–9.

Sá, C. et al. (2013), 'Techno-Nationalism and the Construction of University Technology Transfer', *Minerva* 51 (4): 443–64.

Seed, D. (2003), 'Spy Fiction', in Martin Priestman (ed.), *The Cambridge Companion to Crime Fiction*, 115–34, Cambridge: Cambridge University Press.

Smith, J. (2016), '"How Safe Do You Feel?": James Bond, Skyfall, and the Politics of the Secret Agent in an Age of Ubiquitous Threat', *College Literature* 43 (1): 145–72.

7

Spectres of Capitalism

Globalization in the Craig-era Bond Films

Milo Sweedler

The James Bond films of the Daniel Craig era provide a fascinating snapshot of capitalism in the twenty-first century. Featuring villains involved in such quintessentially neoliberal endeavours as high-stakes gambling with leveraged capital as in *Casino Royale* (Campbell 2006) and the privatization and commodification of a hitherto public natural resource notable in *Quantum of Solace* (Forster 2008), the movies situate us in a globalized world where high finance and the phenomenon that political economist David Harvey calls 'accumulation by dispossession' have become dominant modes of capitalist accumulation (2005a: 137–82). When we learn, in *Spectre* (Mendes 2015), that these villains ran subsidiaries of the movie's eponymous crime syndicate, the image of a vast megacorporation bent on world domination begins to emerge. Emblematized in the film by an octopus spreading its tentacles, SPECTRE is a brilliant caricature of the multinational conglomerate in the era of unbridled capitalism. When a villain channelling the energy of the alt-right eradicates this organization in the last Craig-era film, *No Time To Die* (Fukunaga 2021), the movie evokes ongoing battles between factions of the twenty-first-century right. However, although the crypto-fascist triumphs over his capitalist rival in *No Time To Die*, nearly every salient aspect of SPECTRE leads us to anticipate the syndicate's revival in a future Bond film.

This chapter examines how the Craig-era Bond movies reflect the vicissitudes of contemporary capitalism, showing how the five films synthesize and fictionalize macroeconomic and socio-political developments in the early twenty-first century. Analysing the films in chronological order, it shows how the movies give audio-visual narrative form to the global financial crisis of the late 2000s, to international class struggles in the developing world, to the emergence of the 'new right', and to the spectre of capitalism haunting the world.

High finance and bad bets: *Casino Royale* as allegory

Martin Campbell's 2006 adaptation of *Casino Royale* follows fairly closely to the general plotline of Ian Fleming's 1953 novel of the same title. This proximity of the film to its source material makes the narrative differences between the two works all the more noteworthy. Whereas some of the changes that the screenwriters effected to the storyline serve the function of enlivening the material for the audio-visual medium of film or of adding layers of complexity to Fleming's straightforward plot, others update the material for a twenty-first-century audience. The latter are particularly instructive.

The most obvious revision of this sort is the elimination of the novel's Cold War-era references to communism and the Soviet Union. Let us take the example of Le Chiffre, *Casino Royale*'s villain. In both the book and the movie, he is an underground paymaster who finds himself in a precarious position due to a bad investment he makes with funds entrusted to him by a powerful organization. In both works, he then attempts to recuperate his losses at the card table. However, in the novel, the organization whose funds he mishandles is 'the communist-controlled trade union in the heavy transport industries of Alsace' (8), whereas the film's Le Chiffre (Mads Mikkelsen) loses money entrusted to him by the Lord's Resistance Army (LRA) of central Africa. Moreover, in the original story, the organization for which Le Chiffre works is SMERSH, a Soviet counter-intelligence agency that appears in many Bond novels. Correspondingly, Fleming's Le Chiffre is 'in nearly all respects an admirable agent of the U.S.S.R.' (8–9). The operation that the head of S (the anti-Soviet branch of MI6, absent in the film) proposes to M is therefore to degrade this 'powerful Soviet agent' and to bankrupt 'his communist trade union' by defeating him at the tables (12). The film likewise narrates MI6's assault on Le Chiffre's finances at the casino, but it shows little regard for the effect that this operation might have on the African freedom fighters (although it does dutifully present them as bad guys who get their comeuppance), while the organization behind Le Chiffre, and therefore the movie's ultimate enemy, remains unspecified. It is only in *Spectre*, released nine years later, that this anonymous organization gets a name.

However, the film's 'de-communization' of its source material is nothing new. Although, as Lisa Funnell and Klaus Dodds observe, more than half of the Bond films feature Soviet or Russian characters and locations while still others include references to them (2017: 77), many films in the franchise, even those from the Cold War era, substitute SPECTRE for SMERSH as MI6's arch-enemy. The overt threat that Soviet espionage poses in the Bond novels is overshadowed in the films by an international crime ring that often pits the superpowers of the USA and the USSR against one another but has no particular political affiliation. What makes Campbell's *Casino Royale* symptomatic of its historical moment is therefore less the de-emphasizing of Russian influence per se than it is the particular phenomenon that comes to replace it.

By a nearly 180-degree shift, the film substitutes Soviet-era tropes of cloaks and daggers with the language of the market. When Steven Obanno (Isaach De Bankolé), the LRA leader, asks Le Chiffre whether he believes in God, for instance, the latter responds that he believes in 'a reasonable rate of return'. Obanno, unphased by the paymaster's irreligion, informs his de facto money manager that he wants 'no risk in the portfolio'. We soon learn that Le Chiffre has no intention of placing a low-risk bet with Obanno's money. Upon receiving the funds from the freedom fighter, he immediately places a phone call to his stockbroker (a non-existent character in the novel), instructing him to 'short another million shares of Skyfleet stock'. When the broker tells his client that he is 'betting against the market', informing him that 'no one expects this stock to go anywhere but up', Le Chiffre orders the financier to place the bet, nonetheless. Some forty minutes later in the film, after Bond foils Le Chiffre's plot to downgrade the Skyfleet stock, Le Chiffre's broker informs his client that 'the put's expired', using unadulterated market jargon to explain to the investor that he has lost his high-stakes bet.

This introduction of the language of stock portfolios, share prices, rates of return, short bets and put options, none of which appears in the novel, is symptomatic of a macroeconomic shift that took place between the novel's publication in 1953 and the film's release in 2006. Not only has capitalism supplanted communism in nearly every country formerly in the Soviet sphere of influence, but the form of capitalism that has come to prevail in the age of globalization is finance. Whereas industrial capitalism (entailing the manufacture of consumer goods) predominated in free-market economies during the thirty-year period that began around 1945, since the late 1970s, finance capitalism (based on speculative investments in stocks and bonds) has increasingly become the global economy's driving force. This rise of finance capital has had two major socio-economic effects. On the one hand, it has exacerbated wealth inequality; on the other, it has produced a high degree of volatility in the market. *Quantum of Solace*, the second of the Craig-era Bond films, thematizes the first of these two trends. *Casino Royale* allegorizes the second.

It is worth taking a moment at this point to historicize the Bond franchise reboot in 2006. While *Casino Royale* was in production, new-fangled financial instruments called collateralized debt obligations had increasingly become 'the beating heart of Wall Street' (Lewis 2010: 123). When, in 2008, these arcane financial instruments became worthless, it turned out that the Wall Street banks that had been peddling them to unsuspecting investors as though they were virtually risk-free were holding enough of these toxic securities to sink every one of them. Leveraged at ratios as high as thirty to one (meaning that they had invested up to thirty times the companies' net worth), every major investment bank on Wall Street would have collapsed if the US Treasury had not bailed them out with 700 billion tax dollars. Some Wall Street investment firms, such as Goldman Sachs, which had the good fortune of having its former CEO at the helm of the US Treasury at the time, came out of the 2008 debacle virtually unscathed. This particular firm, about which I have more to say below, received 100 cents on the dollar for its 'troubled assets'. Other firms, such as Bear Stearns, which JPMorgan Chase engulfed at two dollars per share (later upgraded to ten dollars), and Lehman Brothers, which declared bankruptcy in September 2008, did not survive the crash.

In this context, Le Chiffre's plight allegorizes before the fact the fate of a firm like Lehman Brothers. It harks back to the 2001 demise of Enron, an energy corporation that, on the eve of its dissolution, was invested almost entirely in financials and barely at all in energy production, but the full force of the movie's allegorical thrust is revealed only in retrospect, when the world's population came to appreciate the extent of the rot at the core of the global financial system in 2008. Le Chiffre's attempt to short the Skyfleet stock, made with funds leveraged from an unsuspecting investor, takes on its full significance in the context of the event that Michael Lewis, author of the definitive account of the 2008 financial meltdown, famously called 'the Big Short' in his 2010 book of that title. Le Chiffre is the Bond franchise's Lehman Brothers. He ends the film with debts he cannot repay and suffers the same consequence as the embattled firm: he is put to an unceremonious death by his peers.

Meanwhile, Vesper Lynd (Eva Green), *Casino Royale*'s Bond girl, who in the novel is the personal assistant to the head of MI6's anti-Soviet S branch, becomes a representative of the UK Treasury in the film. In view of the interpretation sketched above, it may come as no surprise that this character turns out to be a traitor who, however reluctantly, steals the money Bond won at great pains (literally) from Le Chiffre at the tables of Casino Royale and gives it to the unnamed mega-organization behind the scenes. Playing a role not entirely unlike the one enacted in real life a few years later by Henry Paulson, the US Treasury Secretary who bailed out the Wall Street banks with taxpayers' money when it turned out that the banks had misplaced their bets, Lynd, admittedly under duress, compensates this anonymous organization's losses with money confiscated from Bond. The latter, for his part, in this Bond film where 007 unquestionably loses in the end, plays the part of the hapless taxpayer left holding the bag.

I do not mean to suggest that the scriptwriters foresaw the demise of a venerable institution like Lehman Brothers, the fourth largest investment bank in the United States, which had been in operation since 1850. What they do, rather, is put their collective finger on the pulse of macroeconomic developments of the 2000s and integrate them into their screenplay. Faced with updating Fleming's story for the new millennium, the screenwriters grasp the socio-economic zeitgeist and decide to slot finance capitalism in the position previously occupied by international communism as the principal threat facing the free world.

That *Casino Royale* is an allegorical tale is already apparent in Fleming's novel. Indeed, notwithstanding the repeated assertions that Le Chiffre is a communist, it reads very much like an allegory of capitalism in which high-stakes betting at the casino transcodes gambling on the stock market. Joyce Goggin and René Glas make this argument in a fascinating chapter on casino capitalism included in Christoph Lindner's edited volume, *Revisioning 007: James Bond and 'Casino Royale'*. Reminding us that Fleming's narrator draws implicit parallels between the casino and the stock market on two separate occasions, Goggin and Glas argue that 'Fleming was keenly aware of the rapid erosion of the nineteenth-century distinction between speculation and gambling, market and casino, that was occurring as he wrote' (2009: 71). In their view, the salient political-economic shift evident in Campbell's adaptation, a shift which the authors locate in the change from Fleming's baccarat game to the movie's poker match, is essentially a matter of scale. In sum, as Goggin and Glas demonstrate, the resemblance between gambling on stock prices and betting on cards is at the core of Fleming's *Casino Royale*. The film, in turn, sheds the novel's outdated references to communism to reveal the capitalist allegory at its core.

Accumulation by dispossession: Neoliberalism in *Quantum of Solace*

Whereas *Casino Royale* obliquely allegorizes contemporary finance, *Quantum of Solace* (Forster 2008) directly thematizes global neoliberalism. More than other films in the Bond franchise, *Quantum* is openly anti-capitalist. This political orientation is evident in the movie's use of its two primary settings, Haiti and Bolivia, where the majority of the narrative takes place. These two countries provide much more than a picturesque backdrop for the film action. Haiti for its rich history of anti-colonialist struggle and Bolivia for its heroic stance against capitalist exploitation at the turn of the twenty-first century both emblematize international class conflict. This section examines how *Quantum* mobilizes pivotal moments in these two countries' histories to issue a damning indictment of capitalist globalization.

Continuing the narrative thread begun in *Casino*, Bond arrives in Port-au-Prince, Haiti's capital city, on the trail of a certain Mr Slate when a stack of tagged bills, marked by MI6 to track Le Chiffre's money-laundering operation, is deposited into Slate's account. MI6 conducts a quick online inquiry that shows Slate staying at the Hôtel Dessalines in Port-au-Prince, where it dispatches 007. The film signals the agent's arrival at his destination with a Bond's-eye-view shot of the entrance to the Hôtel Dessalines that clearly displays the hotel sign above the open archway (Figure 7.1). This fixed shot of the hotel entryway lasts a full second. In a film characterized by dynamic handheld camerawork and fast-paced editing, this second-long static shot stands out. It is as though the filmmaker wanted to make sure that we caught the name of the hotel. It refers to Jean-Jacques Dessalines, the fiercest leader of the Haitian Revolution of 1791–1804, who became the first ruler of the newly independent nation in 1804 and oversaw the permanent abolition of slavery in the country. A controversial military and political leader who went to extreme lengths to guarantee the freedom of former slaves, Dessalines is anything but a neutral figure.

Although *Quantum* does not dwell on Haiti's early history, allowing instead the signifier 'Dessalines' to vaguely conjure it, the film does provide a nice

Figure 7.1 *Quantum of Solace* (Eon Productions et al. 2008).

synopsis of the country's more recent history. This synopsis, issued from the mouth of Dominic Greene (Mathieu Amalric), *Quantum*'s villain, provides a poignant anti-climax to the national history inaugurated by Dessalines. Strolling along the docks of Port-au-Prince with General Medrano (Joaquín Cosio), a deposed Bolivian dictator whose business Greene is soliciting, Greene uses the pair's current location to illustrate the type of service his organization can offer: 'Look at what we did to this country. The Haitians elect a priest who decides to raise the minimum wage from thirty-eight cents to a dollar a day. It's not a lot, but it's enough to upset the corporations who were here making T-shirts and running shoes, so they called us, and we facilitated a change.' The unnamed priest Greene mentions here can only be Jean-Bertrand Aristide, a liberation theologian thrice elected president of Haiti, who commanded enthusiastic support from the people but antagonized powerful elites both inside the country and abroad. As Peter Hallward shows in his authoritative account of recent political history in Haiti, Aristide's attempts to improve Haitians' living conditions at the expense of the multinational corporations that were paying starvation wages did little to endear him to his detractors (2007: 131–40 and *passim*). When right-wing paramilitaries overthrew him in 2004, the deposed president claimed that the CIA orchestrated the coup. Greene, for his part, gives the credit to his own organization. A conversation between this odious Bond villain and CIA section chief Gregg Beam (David Harbour) in a private jet en route from Haiti to Austria allows us to imagine that both men may be right.

The reason Greene boasts about his syndicate's power as a behind-the-scenes kingmaker is because he wants to convince Medrano to strike a quid-pro-quo deal with him. What Greene proposes is to put the general in power in Bolivia in exchange for drilling rights to a large tract of barren land. For much of the film, we are led to believe that the resource Greene plans to extract is oil. It is only when Bond and Camille Montes (Olga Kurylenko), *Quantum's* unconventional Bond girl, discover that Greene's company has been secretly damming Bolivia's water supply in view of creating a monopoly that we begin to understand the rapacious CEO's scheme. This substitution of water for oil in the film narrative is highly topical. Long considered a public resource to which populations were entitled by right, in recent years fresh water has become a commodity like any other.

A prime example of the logic of neoliberalism, a doctrine whose 'primary aim', David Harvey writes in *A Brief History of Neoliberalism*, 'has been to open up new fields for capital accumulation in domains hitherto regarded as off-limits to the calculus of profitability' (2005a: 160), the commodification of water represents one in a long list of recent privatizations of hitherto public goods and services. As Susan Buck-Morss observes, 'nothing – not schools, not prisons, not human genes, not wild plants, not the national army, not foreign governments – nothing is exempt from this process of privatization' (2013: 72). *Quantum* offers a fictional account of how such a process unfolds by showing how a multinational corporation ironically called Greene Planet appropriates a country's most vital natural resource.

Harvey names this type of process 'accumulation by dispossession'. Rather than building or inventing something new, this modality of capitalist accumulation looks to create wealth by gaining possession of existing resources or services and selling them for a profit. Such processes have been part of capitalism's historical geography since its origins, but 'in our times', Harvey writes, 'the techniques for enriching the ruling classes and diminishing the standard of living' for everyone else through processes of accumulation by dispossession 'have proliferated and multiplied' (2010: 309).

Accumulation by dispossession takes diverse forms. Of particular interest here are the 'colonial, neo-colonial, and imperial processes of appropriation of assets (including natural resources)' from developing countries (Harvey 2005b: 145). One country where such techniques took a particularly acute form is Bolivia, the very nation whose water supply Greene strives to control in the film. Dubbed 'la guerra del agua' (the water war) by local activists, the confrontation between Bechtel, a US-based multinational that had purchased Bolivian water rights in 1999, and citizens who could not afford Bechtel's sharply elevated water prices erupted into violence in April 2000 when Bolivian armed forces

Globalization in the Craig-era Bond Films 123

opened fire on protestors. Fortunately, in 2005, three years before the release of *Quantum*, the Bolivian government terminated its contract with Bechtel, and concessions for the supply of water returned to municipal governments (Anandakugan 2020).

The film portrays Bond as an anti-capitalist crusader fighting against a corporation like Bechtel. I do not mean to suggest that the movie depicts Bond as a man of the people, who leads or participates in a grassroots struggle. On the contrary, the shots of locals discussing the water shortage intercut with images of Bond and Montes strolling past the distressed Bolivians without stopping to mention that they just discovered the location of the sequestered water, create the impression of a hero decidedly aloof from the people whose well-being he nonetheless safeguards by his actions. Bond's role in the film is to combat directly the forces of private capital, not to involve himself in the immediacy of the embattled Bolivians' situation.

In a sense, this narrative line is nothing new. Many Bond films depict the hero foiling a villain's attempt to corner the gold market, control the heroin trade, dominate online news and information with 'fake news' websites, monopolize oil pipeline routes or execute some other nefarious money-making scheme. However, rather than inventing a get-rich conspiracy or obliquely referencing a real-world development, the *Quantum* scriptwriters take an example directly from history. The Bolivian water war is not merely a cultural reference point but the film's actual referent. Instead of drawing the spectator into Bond's world, the movie inserts him into ours. This direct engagement with historical events and the film's decidedly resolute stance on them make *Quantum* one of the great anti-capitalist propaganda films of the early twenty-first century. More clearly than *Casino* or any other Bond film, *Quantum* enables the viewer to perceive the machinations of global capital and to take a position relative to them.

The spectre haunting the world: *Skyfall* and *Spectre*

Following the far-reaching critiques of capitalism presented in the first two films of the Bond franchise reboot, *Skyfall* (Mendes 2012) represents something of a retreat. A much more politically conservative film than its predecessors, *Skyfall*'s principal themes are cyberterrorism and threats to England's homeland security. The prominent British flag waving in the wind on a Whitehall rooftop behind 007 at the end of the film, after he has defeated Raoul Silva (Javier Bardem), the movie's sexually ambiguous punk hacktivist villain, is emblematic of the film's overall political perspective.

That said, the premise behind Fredric Jameson's brilliant treatise on the 1970s conspiracy thriller applies here: 'If everything means something else, then so does technology' (11). Exploring what he calls the 'laterality' of levels, in which social, political, economic and technological motifs reflect and refract one another, Jameson shows how a dozen popular movies from the 1970s audio-visually encode global capital in ways not immediately apparent in their manifest narrative content. In this vein, I would propose that the shot of Bond sitting handcuffed in the cavernous main hall of Silva's lair, surrounded by six-foot towers of wires that snake their way around the room and a half-dozen illuminated computer screens, connotes the processes of capital accumulation as much as it does computer hacking or cyberterrorism (Figure 7.2)]. At this point in the film, we do not yet know of Silva's plans. The shot provides our first glimpse not only into the villain's lair but of the villain himself as he exits an elevator at the far end of the room and slowly approaches his captive. It is only later, as the plot develops, that we learn of Silva's personal vendetta against M (Judi Dench) and his elaborate plan to exact revenge. Appearing in a Bond film released shortly after *Quantum* and *Casino* and a few short years before personal online data overtook oil as the world's most precious commodity, this shot of a makeshift computer lab in the villain's den leads us to wonder whether Silva is an evil media tycoon mining people's data for profit.

Skyfall self-consciously comments in its own way on the 'laterality of levels' later in the computer lab scene when Silva, trying to entice Bond to join him,

Figure 7.2 *Skyfall* (Eon Productions et al. 2012).

Globalization in the Craig-era Bond Films   125

enumerates a few activities Bond could pursue if he joined Silva's ranks. Walking over to a computer, he touches the screen and says: 'Destabilize a multinational by manipulating stocks? Easy!' Proceeding to another computer, he continues: 'Interrupt transmissions from a spy satellite over Kabul? Done! Rig an election in Uganda? All to the highest bidder.' The film draws a narrative equivalence here between multinational capitalism and international politics, which are equally vulnerable to remote manipulation by computer. However, the multinational corporation plays a dual role in this overview of Silva's operation. On the one hand, it provides an example of the type of institution Silva can undermine with a keystroke. Yet, on the other hand, this mini-exposé reveals that Silva's operation is also an institution of this sort. Like Scaramanga (Christopher Lee) in *The Man With the Golden Gun* (Hamilton 1974), Silva puts his services up for sale to the highest bidder. In sum, a for-profit hacking service, Silva's operation is situated at the intersection of the narrative 'levels' of capitalism and high tech.

The overlapping of corporate capitalism and surveillance technology, suggested in passing in *Skyfall*, becomes a bona fide theme in *Spectre* (Mendes 2015). The film presents this theme in a subplot pitting the new M (Ralph Fiennes), director of the 00 programme, against C (Andrew Scott), the head of the new Joint Intelligence Service. Much of the film presents this rivalry as a clash between the traditional M, who still believes in the importance of having human beings in the field, and the up-and-coming C, a thirty-something whiz kid who argues that drones and computers have made the 00 programme obsolete. Presented in this way, the clash recalls a similar opposition set up between Bond and Q (Ben Wishaw), the MI6 quartermaster and in-house computer geek, in *Skyfall*, but the confrontation between M and C goes far beyond the generational divide implicit in the Q-007 exchange in *Skyfall*. Evoking perennial debates over the advantages and disadvantages of human resources versus technological resources, the dispute between M and C also involves the funding of international espionage services. Providing a direct rebuttal to the neoliberal mantra that privatization is always good, the funding source for C's privately backed security programme proves to be none other than SPECTRE. When it turns out that C is, himself, a SPECTRE agent, his pro-capitalist arguments about the superiority of computer power over human labour power and the merits of privately financed public services retroactively implode.

The revelation that C is a SPECTRE agent forms part of the film's larger revelation that this criminal organization is a boundless entity with a seemingly limitless reach. A cartel reunion in Rome that looks simultaneously like a corporate board meeting, an assembly of mob bosses and an occult ritual enumerates several sectors in which the organization is invested. They include pharmaceuticals, human trafficking and prostitution as well as global surveillance. Later, when Q discovers that Le Chiffre, Greene and Silva, along with a handful of lesser villains from the Craig-era films, all ran branches of SPECTRE, the image of a vast commercial enterprise working across countless sectors emerges. Run by Ernst Blofeld (Christoph Waltz), 007's arch-enemy from the early Bond films, this international crime syndicate bent on world domination brilliantly caricatures the multinational conglomerate in the age of globalization.

The film uses a modified version of the SPECTRE insignia first seen in the Cold War-era *From Russia With Love* (Young 1963) to represent this sprawling crime syndicate, but this iconic image of a ghost that resembles an octopus takes on new connotations in the 2015 film (Figure 7.3). For one thing, it comes across like a visualization of the biting turn of phrase that *Rolling Stone* contributor Matt Taibbi famously used in 2010 to describe Goldman Sachs. Appalled both by the firm's role in the financial meltdown of 2008 and by the way it profited afterwards from the crisis, Taibbi dubbed Goldman the 'great vampire squid wrapped around the face of humanity'. Combining a different incarnation of the living dead with a different type of eight-limbed mollusc, the SPECTRE insignia similarly represents a predatory institution with global reach as a ghoulish life form spreading its tentacles. Moreover, appearing in a Craig-era Bond film released shortly after the debacle of 2008, when capitalism as we knew it teetered on the verge of collapse, the SPECTRE emblem also connotes an economic system that refuses to die. As Chris Harman shows in *Zombie Capitalism*, this

Figure 7.3 *Spectre* (Eon Productions et al. 2016).

'undead' system emerged from its mortal crisis in 2008 stronger and meaner than before. 'The dead are alive', an intertitle asserts at the beginning of *Spectre*. The statement applies aptly not only to SPECTRE and Blofeld, who died in two previous Bond films before being resurrected in 2015, but also to the economic system they represent. The phantom haunting the world in *Spectre* is capitalism.

The rise of the extreme right: *No Time To Die*

No Time To Die (Fukunaga 2021), which brings the narrative arc begun in *Casino Royale* to its conclusion, recounts the liquidation of SPECTRE not by Bond, but by Lyutsifer Safin (Rami Malek), the film's principal villain. In contrast to Blofeld and his acolytes, this villain appears to be motivated more by an obscure genocidal desire than by monetary gain. The mass murder that the criminal envisions is difficult to discern. One of the rare clues we are given appears in a few short sentences Safin says to Bond: 'We both eradicate people to make the world a better place. I just want to be a little tidier.' According to Q, this cryptic Bond villain could potentially wipe out 'whole ethnicities' from the face of the earth. The film refrains from naming the groups targeted for extermination, with one exception. When Valdo Obruchev (David Dencik), the European scientist who develops Safin's lethal bioweapon and praises his master's 'vision', informs 00 agent Nomi (Lashana Lynch), who is Black, that he could 'exterminate [her] entire race', the film's white supremacist subtext rises momentarily to the surface.

Like a dog-whistle term suddenly made audible to everyone, Obruchev's ugly remark to Nomi feels like a throwback to another era, when people felt more comfortable expressing racist views in public. Or, rather, it would feel like a throwback to a less enlightened era if so many societies in Europe and the Americas had not made such great strides backwards in the past few years. From Scandinavia to the Mediterranean and from the Atlantic coast to Russia, nearly every European country currently has either a right-wing populist government in power or a significant extreme-right opposition. The electoral victories of Donald Trump in the United States and of Jair Bolsonaro in Brazil provide proof positive that this surge of right-wing populism is not a uniquely European phenomenon. One common element that unites these diverse movements, beyond their authoritarian leadership and their nationalism, is their overt racism. Whereas, until very recently, right-wing politicians in Western democracies tended to use innocuous sounding dog-whistle terms like 'cutting

128 *Resisting James Bond: Power and Privilege in the Daniel Craig Era*

taxes' to promote racist agendas, their contemporary counterparts use racist language to pass legislation benefitting the wealthy. Donald Trump, for example, who made his foray into politics by promulgating the racist 'birther' conspiracy theory that Barack Obama was not a US citizen, who speaks disparagingly about people of colour on a regular basis, who campaigned on the promise of building a wall along the US's southern border and who openly promotes (even if he does not directly condone) white supremacist groups, passed only one major piece of legislation while in office: a massive tax cut for the rich.

In this context, Obruchev's vile comment to Nomi, together with Safin's obscure remarks about tidying up the world, come across like dog-whistle phrases in reverse. Although the film does not clarify the specifics of Safin's financial situation any more than it does his worldview, it does portray him as a capitalist of sorts. It does this in several ways. On the one hand, the villain's operation is run like a factory where a small army of workers in hazmat suits cultivate his garden of poison plants and convert them into nanobots. In addition, an overhead shot of Safin's island compound reveals what look to be container ships – as good a symbol of multinational capitalism as one could hope for – docked at port. Finally, the island's location in a no-man's-land situated between Japan and Russia evokes the unregulated, unmonitored and untaxed export processing zones that have multiplied around the world since the 1980s. On the other hand, what we do know of Safin's finances is that he inherited his apparently vast wealth from his father. This, too, is emblematic of capital in the twenty-first century. As French economist Thomas Piketty shows, one of the salient features of the neoliberal revolution that began in the 1980s has been the increasing importance of inherited wealth relative to money earned from income (2014: 238–42). Granted, Piketty's thesis rests on the idea that inheritance babies increase their wealth through investments – the money multiplying itself inexorably on the stock market without the owners having to do a day's work – and we do not know whether Safin has any of his money invested, but the single piece of information we are given about the origin of Safin's wealth conjures a central component of Piketty's theory of social inequality in the twenty-first century.

In sum, the film presents Safin, a super-rich one-percenter who inherited his tremendous wealth as well as his poison garden and presumably his crypto-fascist worldview from his father, as a capitalist racist bent on destroying his capitalist rivals and making the world great again by eliminating certain groups of people. Regarding the character in this light (and bracketing his physical appearance and mannerisms as well as some of the finer details of his backstory), Safin comes across as a caricature of a man like former President Trump. The film thereby nicely concludes the series of films that began in 2006 with *Casino Royale*. Moving from the 'casino capitalism' and the neocolonialism of the 2000s through the unbridled expansion of the multinational conglomerate and the interpenetration of private capital and surveillance technology in the 2010s to the rise of the alt-right *c.* 2015, the Craig-era Bond films offer a fine cognitive map of global capitalism in the twenty-first century. Viewed chronologically and placed in their historical contexts, they bring into relief the vicissitudes of multinational capitalism in the new millennium, synthesizing macroeconomic and socio-political developments in the real world and transposing them into sounds and moving images. The criminals that 007 faces in *Casino Royale*, *Quantum of Solace*, *Skyfall*, *Spectre* and *No Time To Die* are spectres of twenty-first-century capitalism.

References

Anandakugan, N. (2020), 'Hopes for a Rainy Day: A History of Bolivia's Water Crisis', *Harvard International Review*, 2 July. Available online: https://hir.harvard.edu/hopes-for-a-rainy-day-a-history-of/.

Buck-Morss, S. (2013), 'A Commonist Ethics', in S. Žižek (ed.), *The Idea of Communism*, 2nd edn, 57–75, London: Verso.

Fleming, I. (2012), *Casino Royale*, Las Vegas, CA: Thomas & Mercer.

Funnell, L. and K. Dodds (2017), *Geographies, Genders and Geopolitics of James Bond*, London: Palgrave Macmillan.

Goggin, J. (2020), '*Skyfall* and Global Casino Culture', in J. Verheul (ed.), *The Cultural Life of James Bond: Specters of 007*, 289–307, Amsterdam: Amsterdam University Press.

Goggin, J. and R. Glas (2009), 'It just Keeps Getting Bigger: James Bond and the Political Economy of Huge', in C. Lindner (ed.), *Revisioning 007: James Bond and Casino Royale*, 67–78, New York: Wallflower.

Hallward, P. (2007), *Damming the Flood: Haiti and the Politics of Containment*, London: Verso.

Harman, C. (2010), *Zombie Capitalism: Global Crisis and the Relevance of Marx*, Chicago, IL: Haymarket.

Harvey, D. (2005a), *A Brief History of Neoliberalism*, Oxford: Oxford University Press.

Harvey, D. (2005b), *The New Imperialism*, Oxford: Oxford University Press.

Harvey, D. (2010), *Companion to Marx's 'Capital'*, London: Verso.

Jameson, F. (1992), *The Geopolitical Aesthetic: Cinema and Space in the World System*, Bloomington: Indiana University Press.

Lewis, M. (2010), *The Big Short: Inside the Doomsday Machine*, New York: Norton.

Piketty, T. (2014), *Capital in the Twenty-First Century*, Arthur Goldhammer (trans.), Cambridge, MA: Harvard University Press.

Taibbi, M. (2010), 'The Great American Bubble Machine', *Rolling Stone*, 5 April. Available online: https://www.rollingstone.com/politics/politics-news/the-great-american-bubble-machine-195229/.

8

Bond, Race and Coloniality

No Time to Die(versify) …

Harshad Keval

My personal, creative and cultural relationship to the 'James Bond phenomena' is one filled with uncomfortable and problematic ambiguities, themselves sourced within my multiple cultural, class and racialized identities. As a British Asian, cis-gendered male living in the UK, with origins and belongings spanning Africa, India, UK and Europe, as well as multiple class locations, James Bond has been a stable, problematic and ambiguous feature of my consumer imagination and experience. These ambiguities are productive in *problematizing* what could be seen as a 'treacherous bind' of uncomfortable consumption. It is inside the racialized, gendered, classed and dis/ableist colonial imaginaries that James Bond is situated. Modern social complexities allow the fluid unfurling of identities in response to the winds of any geopolitical moment, bringing forth negotiations of personal, global and local socialities. Given the UK's long and winding relationship with its racialized migrant and non-migrant 'Others' (Fryer 1984; Hirsch 2018), the consumption of cinematic heroes and models is even more significant as moral, ethical and escapist signposts.

Into this complex milieu, Connery's legendary delivery of the Bond formula on screen in *Dr. No* (Young 1962) started a representational fantasy demarcating exclusionary boundaries beyond class, extending global, racial and colonial frames. Thus, heroes are born and emblazoned onto psychic consuming lives as they generate and write the conditions of what is possible for someone to be, aspire to and live through, however peripherally or superficially. However, these possibilities were only ever conditional. It is precisely these conditions of limited representational capacity that connect with a wider racializing complexity that this chapter aims to unpack.

132   *Resisting James Bond: Power and Privilege in the Daniel Craig Era*

This chapter speaks to the many ways in which the idea and practice of 'race', race-thinking and historiographies of race constitute colonial and imperial pasts and presents. Firstly, I provide a socio-structural, historical and political context to the imperial, colonial race-making circuitry of representations, followed by some specific, selective issues that can help us to identify examples of how racial thinking is made and unmade as the Daniel Craig Reboot (DCR) negotiates this arena. Who actually portrays Bond is situated as an existential, commodified racial system and perpetuates powerful myths around black and people of colour in film and TV. In unravelling these issues, I discuss specific characters, such as Felix Leiter, as well as the symbolic representations of Englishness, and racial purity. The five films that make up the DCR to varying extents represent this ambivalent *un-racing and re-racing*. Since, as Pitcher notes, 'race is produced and reproduced in spaces and places that are sometimes dismissed as trivial, insignificant' (Pitcher 2014: 29), 'race-ing' Bond emerges important at this time.

Consuming 'true' heroes ...

The paradoxical consumption *of* the racially 'pure', 'true-blood' hero (Baron 2009: 154), *by* categorically *impure*, dark 'Others' presents a particular problem. The modern associations between nation, state and race (Goldberg 2002) are also underwritten by a historical process of establishing European purity through divine and scientific reasoning. In the context of the colonial/modern world system, what Anibal Quijano (2000) termed the 'colonial matrix of power' and what Mignolo (2007) calls 'Global designs', established since the fifteenth and sixteenth centuries, the idea of nature and 'natural' are constructed for the purposes of oppressing bodies through political and social systems. Racialized distinctions and the subsequent configurations of inequality in humanity were used to categorize Spanish Indian and African bodies in the New World. Blood, as one of the original markers of racial difference and racism, was 'transferred to skin' whilst theology was displaced by secular philosophy and sciences (Mignolo 2007: 8–9). The idea of 'purity of blood' – *limpieza de sangre* – from the mid-fifteenth century onwards institutionalized the prevention of anyone of non-Christian faith from public and religious office, and from positions of authority in the university and army (Gerber 1992, cited in Boatcă 2016: 87). This religion-based oppression was an integral component of the processes of 1492 (notorious in many countries, celebrated in others), with the last Muslim state in Western Europe being conquered by the Spanish Catholic religious and military power. I raise this point to articulate the deeply embedded notions of 'purity' that circulate discourses of representation in Westernized cinema, and the Bond phenomenon is a particularly rich site for this.

There is a need to explore and unpack these troubling negotiations at the borders and boundaries of *difference making*. Although the representational 'leaps' performed in 'post-race' representations in Bond (e.g. Moneypenny, Felix Leiter, Nomi as Agent 007) appear to be nudging the franchise into a new era of equality, diversity and inclusion, this slow, angst-filled move proves that resistance is plentiful. The reasons for the opposition are never too distant from older, essentialist forms of racial purity and its ties with nation-state belonging in imperial and colonial mythologies. By 'post-race' (Lentin 2014, 2021) I refer to the discursive, theoretical and material processes that give the impression of moving beyond the realities of race and racism. There has been and still is a social and cultural pressure to stop talking, writing and activating resistance to different types of racism, pointing at people of colour in positions of power and influence (e.g. Barack Obama, Jay-Z, Beyoncé, etc.). Such refutations of racialized realities usually come from progressive, liberal perspectives and multicultural 'tolerance' models, rather than outright anti-racist perspectives, and can be comfortable models of thinking and practice in media representation, education, work and employment. The implication is that as long as we dismiss 'race' as a concept, and embrace liberal progressive, multicultural perspectives, racisms will eventually disappear. These 'moves' (Tuck and Yang 2012) are seen in cinematic representations, and here in Bond in multiple forms.

Licence to 'race'

Since Umberto Eco's classic text, 'The Narrative Structure in Ian Fleming' in 1965, the 'phenomena' of James Bond has cyclically given rise to academic and popular discourse and discussion. There was always a complex interplay of gendered, raced, classed, imperial and colonial intersections woven into the books and films (Baron 2009; Everett 2020) with a complicated relationship to social and political landscapes in each era. There is a rich literature of analysis of the Bond phenomena regarding race and/or gender and the imperiality of the undertaking (e.g. Baron 2009; Funnell and Dodds 2017). Ann Everett (2020) dives deep in the murky, often grey socio-political structures that facilitate so much

134   *Resisting James Bond: Power and Privilege in the Daniel Craig Era*

of how Bond is mis/understood, consumed and celebrated through persistent re-representations of raced bodies in the Bond films. The analytical themes have focused on representations of gender and sex (e.g. Bennett and Woollacott 2009; Bold 2009; Miller 2009; Funnell 2015), race, colonial and postcolonial themes (e.g. Baron 2009; Eco 2009; Gehlawat 2009), and commodification, international security and intersectionality (e.g. Chapman 2000; Lindner 2009; Funnell and Dodds 2017).

Bond films are a consistently un-raced problematic, a structure that has thrived on how whiteness legacies are colonial traces (Wolfe 2016) of ideologies of inferiority. Such legacies in the US for example, with its particular history of brutalities of plantation slavery, leave powerful traces of race and racialization that connect with multiple forms of oppression in the UK and other global sites of racial production (Boatcă 2016). While these histories and particularities are different, they converge in racialized, gendered and classed projections of imagery on screen, in print and media-consuming consciousness (Stam and Spence 1983). The Bond films, including the DCR, show us in many ways how race is absent and omnipresent, through troubled 'negotiations' with intersectional boundaries. Race is nowhere, while *race-making* is everywhere.

The power of visual imagery and narrative constructions of the 'Other' are crucial in the Bond films when set against the historical, colonial and anthropological backdrop of inscribing otherness on the black body (Young 1996), in what Lola Young called 'the right to look' (1996: 48). For example, a staple Bond experience is the obligatory 'tour' of exotic lands, with exotic peoples, as Bond negotiates his missions. There are echoes here of Michael Dennings' essay (2009: 64) unpacking the narrative of 'tourism' in Fleming's writing. The relative silencing and disappearance of the *peopled* realities of locations, and the indigenous populations therein, is a result of the cinematic frame demanding what Edward Said (1978) called 'orientalist' gazes. This way of looking, constructing and representing 'sees' the foreign land without the troublesome irrelevance of either the people, history, culture, language or the impact of Bond's 'work' on them. This very process *is* 'race' doing its work, so to speak, by reducing, essentializing and stripping away the complexity of 'Other' cultures.

In the commodification and politics of representation, we find some insights into the need for commercial media capitalism to consistently reduce 'Otherness' to only its most easily digestible ingredients. Certainly, in the representation of South Asian contexts (e.g. *Octopussy* [Glen 1983]), as Saha (2013: 819) shows, '... the "beauty" of South Asia is reduced to repetitive images of colourful saris, spicy curries, Hindu sages, exotic weddings and Bollywood dance routines'. We see these stereotype-facilitating mechanics at work busy throughout the entire genre (e.g. the complex, colonial and racialized history of Haiti and Harlem reduced to simplistic rendering of 'voodoo' in *Live and Let Die* [Hamilton 1973]). Similarly, throughout the Craig-era films, including the latest, *No Time To Die* (*NTTD*) (Fukunaga 2021), we witness literally the marketplace *of* 'locals' without any substantive reference or access *to* the very people who constitute that location ('foreign market places' appear frequently, e.g. *Quantum of Solace*, *Skyfall* (Figure 8.1), *NTTD*). This is in direct contrast for example to M's lament to protect 'this', his reference to Western, liberal, democratic society, in conversation with Bond about his questionable security decisions resulting in the potential threat to humanity (*NTTD*). As Mallory speaks, his head and body gesture that 'this', the society in need of defending (London) is a fully fleshed out, civic richness that must be defended.

As other writers have already established, the Bond character exists in a specific, time-space and political frame that mobilizes 'England' and 'Britain's' positioning as a colonial empire and imperial power. Certainly, the colonial gaze was ever present in the Fleming novels and has been a constant feature – in different ways – in all the Bond films since 1962. As Bennett and Woollacott argue, Bond's timely emergence as a 'political hero for the middle classes' (2009: 16) was part of a complex cultural and ideologically mediated zeitgeist, characterized by post-war anxieties, Cold War political developments and a shifting moral landscape of cultural mores. The character and genre's fixation on solving the problems of international villainy and terror are focused

Figure 8.1 *Skyfall* (Eon Productions et al. 2012).

on nationhood, colonial and imperial prowess, and fundamentally a white, hegemonic structure of racism (Hasian 2014).

The Anglo-American desire to consume and engage in historiographies of espionage, adventure and spy-craft are fundamentally defined by the imperial and colonial powers that still enact postcolonial nostalgia, in the US, UK and Europe (Shilliam 2018). These boys-own-fuelled fantasies are of course indulgencies without consequences to the lives and histories of intersectional 'Others'. Again, racialized and culturalized versions of legitimate citizenship are drawn on time and again (Shilliam 2018) as masculine, racial purity offers fantasy corrections to the 'problem' of change and diversity. Bond became an institutionalized ritual, to be viewed and consumed along with the annual Christmas dinner for British fans. This integration into the routinized rituals of everyday 'normal British folk' is deceptive in the underlying power it carries. The realities of empire and the migrants it produced are erased from the viewing of James Bond, in effect turning the consumption of the filmic imagery into a fetishized vacuum, paradoxically still relaying symbolic, constructionist and ideological power in the representations of foreign 'Others'.

The DCR is *still* negotiating troubled narrative boundaries with the 'Other', in a world where global geopolitical fractures have left much of the conviviality of lived multiculturalism (Gilroy 2005) at risk of being reduced and fractured. We witness the changes through the introduction of Jeffrey Wright as Felix Leiter in *Casino Royale* (Campbell 2006), Naomi Harris as Eve Moneypenny in *Skyfall* (Mendes 2012) and of course the now much-contested Lashana Lynch introduced in *No Time to Die* (Fukunaga 2021) as '007'. Within these changes and outside them, there are multiple issues and problems with the representational complexities across race and gender.

In a global context the contemporary period and its antecedents has demanded race, racism and racist structures are placed firmly back on many agendas. Certainly, the recent resurgence in public interest in anti-racism and race politics through global Black Lives Matter movements, Palestinian Solidarity and other groups has placed 'race' back into collective public spheres. The re-emergence of race in a 'post-race' era (Lentin 2014) is carried in large part by the electoral patterns of recent years (Mondon and Winter 2020). These tectonic shifts also produce collective solidarities filling public spaces with race as a key component of intersectional resistances. Here the modern legacies of colonial oppression, genocide, slavery and imperial power located in statues of key figures at the heart of these histories was publicly expressed, with statues falling around the world (Bhambra et al. 2018). The racialized context of 'hostile environment' policies to migrants facilitated by the Conservative government in 2010 (Goodfellow 2020) requires a longer memory than postcolonial amnesia allows, as the British government has a long history of encouraging racial and racist politics to flow outward and through communities (Gentleman 2019). These sociological contexts have always been a living backdrop against which the relief of Bond emerges and moves across our screens, raising questions about the symbolic and concrete impact of the entity's continued existence.

Impossible missions: Being a 'raced' Bond

The highly anticipated DCR was prefaced by a debate not only concerning who would play the character after Pierce Brosnan's last outing in *Die Another Day* (Tamahori 2002), but interestingly, and not for the first time, what 'colour' they would be. In the DCR and the build-up to it, race, racial difference and race-thinking are nowhere to be seen (or read), and yet race is being discursively maintained throughout. Enter Idris Elba, the highly celebrated British actor, touted as the potential takeover from Craig, and we witness widespread panic. The media signposts familiar anxiety and violence at the thought of Bond's 'replacement' with ... an 'Other'. I use the word 'replacement' with deliberate intention, since it evokes many of the populist, right wing, white nationalist and white supremacy texts and related movements over the last three decades, resulting in mass, racialized terror. Specifically, texts such as *The Great Replacement* (2012) by Renaud Camus and its English translation *You Will Not Replace Us!* (2018), and a more libertarian and widely popularized version of 'white genocide' conspiracy theories, *White Shift* (Kaufmann 2018), speak to the panic in the hearts and actions of groups categorized as apparently 'indigenous white', juxtaposed to 'migrants', and racial others taking 'up space' that is widely recognized as reserved. That such vehement expressions of 'purity' are grounded in multiple racisms is often overlooked.

When we hear the question 'Who will *be* Bond?', the subtext is 'Who can *never be* Bond?'. Here is the heart of unspoken agendas, wishes and fears. The imperial, British, heteronormative, cis-gendered, elite-class, assigned-male-at-birth Bond is consumed and legitimated as much as the action, glamour and product placement. What is being rendered time and again are the unspoken boundaries of racialized existence. The signs, signifiers and symbolic representations on screen spell out in no uncertain terms what *is possible, for whom*, and the raced, gendered and patriarchal hierarchies therein.

The nature of whiteness on- and off-screen (Dyer 1997) is that whiteness is never just a person, but a symbolic collection of unquestioned presences and often silent power that make and remake what is possible, what is right and what is normal. The 'Idris Elba' issue is not without precedent (Fetters 2015). Colin Salmon, a highly esteemed British actor, having played Charles Robinson, the Deputy Chief of Staff at MI6 in three Bond films alongside Pierce Brosnan, was widely celebrated as having the screen presence, skill and physicality to play Bond next. The social media discussion (e.g. '#ElbaAsBond') had been developing for a decade, amid multiple culturally 'sensitive' explanations and justifications for his rejection, such as his 'streetness' (as phrased by the author Anthony Horowitz), his lack of 'English-Englishness' (as identified by Roger Moore) and of course, his (lack of) whiteness (succinctly racialized by the hard-right US conservative commentator Rush Limbaugh) (Romana 2018). The question 'Who will be the next James Bond?' is actually asking 'Who can, legitimately, without uncertainty, and without causing psycho-social and cultural turbulence, be allowed to represent the colonial and imperial fantasies of James Bond?' The Bond series is replete with normative white supremacy, and this is not limited to race or gender. The coding of human legitimacy runs throughout the franchise, across bodies and through geopolitical realms. We may not always *see it*, but race and race-making often reveal themselves *relationally* – that is, through the interplay across other intersectional dimensions of identity, such as gender.

The introduction of Lashana Lynch's character Nomi as '007' in *No Time to Die* presents a striking, cinematic first, and one which many would argue is a bold and brave attempt at replacing tired and tested white, male, uber masculine tropes with a new world of strong, relevant, female central black characters. But this isn't the only instance of a black actor being 'allowed' to break the white casting of Bond films. Felix Leiter, the CIA operative who is key to many of the plot lines, appears in many Bond films as traditionally a white man but in the 2006 *Casino Royale* reboot with Daniel Craig as Bond, Leiter was played by the actor Jeffery Wright. This is not the first time Leiter is played by a black actor. In the 1983 non-Eon produced film, *Never Say Never Again* (Kershner 1983), Bernie Casey, a former professional football player and athlete played the character. Interestingly, throughout the period of US film and TV when it was finally possible to see black actors on screen, it was often only through their already existing sports profile and public persona that they were given access to acting as a career (e.g. Jim Brown, O.J. Simpson, Woody Strode). These inclusions of black actors to play traditionally white characters spell the beginning of *a* transition but is a complex and unstable negotiation easily corrupted. Leiter here is a signifier for the audience that in racial terms, all is well since the character occupies multiple positions for the audience to read the 'post-race-ness' of this moment. As a black African American CIA agent standing on a secret service global platform akin to Bond, Leiter can be hailed as a truly progressive, liberal step in representation, since his self-identification as a 'brother from Langley' (*Casino Royale* 2006) re-codes any previously held notions of racial identity as both equal to Bond in professional stature and indicates a camaraderie and loyalty as friend and ally. Thus, Felix Leiter in this new era dismisses charges of older racializing exclusions, showing audiences what a brave new 'de-racialized' and post-race world might look like. We may also invoke Denning's analysis here on the 'anxiety of the tourist' (2009: 68) articulated by the 1962 Felix Leiter (played by Jack Lord) in *Dr. No*: 'Harlem doesn't like being stared at anymore.' The Leiter of the Craig-era films is in many ways resisting and refracting the colonial, racializing gaze by the fact of his difference – he *is* a person of colour, racialized – but through his *non-difference* he is American, secret service and on the 'same-side'. Binary explanations can sometimes oversimplify racialized representations, which are fluid and dynamic but also show us how both positions are held simultaneously within these depictions (Figure 8.2).

Figure 8.2 *Casino Royale* (Eon Productions et al. 2006).

Race rituals

'Race-rituals' are deeply embedded psycho-social and culturally performed processes, which are consistently repeated, and act as foundational inscription practices. Although the franchise changed quantifiably into something visibly representing global multi-ethnic worlds, where people and communities of colour could appear in the narrative arc, the rituals that characterize Bond still require a formulation of the old before giving to way new methods of existing. We see this for example in *Casino Royale*'s depiction of Isaach De Bankolé as Steven Obanno, and Sebastien Foucan as Mollaka – both playing very minor villain roles, two of the very few black actors in the film. Ideologies of race identity are infused with the ongoing purity of Bond, as an Anglo-American, Western model of heteronormative superiority. From *Skyfall* (2012) onwards, we begin to see something akin to what people working in organizations might witness in equality, diversity and inclusion policies and initiatives. The repetition of narrative structure constitutes a form of empire-memorial ritual, with an important function – they help control 'risky encounters' because 'Boundaries, whether physical or social are places of danger. Strangers are to be feared. Fear is coped with by ritual' (Hume 1986: 72).

Fundamental to the Bond franchise are collective, societal fears and anxieties reflected back through the Bond celluloid. However, as the DCR series was borne into a highly terror-risk conscious and securitized global moment, the rituals of doing battle with foreign enemies were played out closer and closer to home. The rituals re-emphasized the engagement with security measures, but when symbolized through a colonially connected, imperially dominant, white heterosexual hypermasculine figure it is a powerfully commodified and fetishized model of being. The genre *performs the work at the borders* of nation-state, civic socialities and plays with these grey areas, performing useful identity transgressions to demonstrate that fear of strangers can be mitigated, that boundaries can be interacted with and yet it actually reinforces the boundary. Narrative attempts in *Skyfall*, such as showing Moneypenny taking sexual control of her boss or Bond's semi-homo-erotic moment with Javier Bardem's camp, 'foreign' and traumatized villain Raoul Silva, complete with requisite 'villain-esque' physical markers, are revealed as a pseudo boundary transgression moments. This moment reeks of the 'foreign-terrorist amongst us' trope, so wilfully constructed and politically mobilized by successive governments of two decades, clearly demonstrated in government PREVENT strategies,

Expendables

The re-codification of black and other minority actors in this way demonstrates the tensions and tussles going on here: there is presence, and yet there is redundancy. *No Time to Die* bids farewell to Felix Leiter, making his role fatally more redundant than his 'failure' to play poker as well as Bond in *Casino Royale*. We could argue there is a significance to his death that demonstrates what can be called the 'One-in-One-out' syndrome – where black presence in film, TV, comedy, stage or in fact any representation can only be countenanced as one-off gestures. We can see this with for example the UK comedy scene, where two black artists are very unlikely to be booked consecutively (Ling 2020), or major acting roles in TV or film consisting of one or two black or minoritized actors. The Leiter death suggests that given the screen time afforded to Lashana Lynch's character Nomi, the race-representation equation demanded balancing. These social and cultural 'equations' can also be witnessed across the multiple global politics of equality, diversity and inclusion policies and practices (Ahmed 2017) and is therefore not limited to just film and TV. Rather it shows us the widespread limitations of racial thinking in representation, where 'presence' is still limited to tokenism.

As a technology of power (Lentin 2020) race is everywhere and nowhere, with the ability to fuse onto 'culture' as a disguise. Bond's complex placement within national heritage, nostalgia (Hasian 2014), and the throes of post-imperial angst reveals a hegemonic, white, representational fixity. The (un)raced possibilities of being Bond signifies a particular symbolic belonging. Bond is fundamentally *un-raced*, in a cloak of whiteness, surrounded by raced 'Others'. In the commercial fantasy of global capitalist film consumption, the dark and 'dangerous brown' men (Bhattacharyya 2009) that occupy the 'shadows' spoken of by Judi Dench's 'M' in *Skyfall* are not only 'in the shadows' where the new global terror threat emerges. It is precisely *with* these shadows that the empire will do battle. Intersectionally constructed bodies are caught in a representational trap – as villains (disfigured, disabled, pathologized, 'unstable', 'foreign') or as

142   *Resisting James Bond: Power and Privilege in the Daniel Craig Era*

supporting figures, existing as mere 'help' to Bond's dominant hero (e.g. Vijay Amritraj in *Octopussy* [Glen 1983]). The commercial enterprise represents the hetero-racial-normative archetype of what bell hooks called 'imperialist white-supremacist capitalist patriarchy' (2006: 60). The dark, dangerous and comic representations of disposable 'Others' in the Bond franchise serves to remind us of the impossibility of *being* for profound raciological reasons and is predicated on what James Trafford calls the human 'waste matter' of colonial and imperial power (2020).

The 'Other' is fixed in a position of alterity within the filmic representations, as a *race ritual*. Countless dark-body counts can be established from *Dr. No* through to *NTTD*, beginning with the representation and death of 'innocent native' Quarrel (played by John Kitzmiller) in *Dr. No*, a character so deeply imbued with the deepest racialized stereotypes that when viewed now, are barely believable. The absurdly demeaning depiction of the 'island native' Quarrel resonates with how poorly black actors were treated on stage, screen and real life, and renders Kitzmiller's long and rich acting history in European and America cinema (Fikes 2014) (making forty films) totally invisible. That he died three years after the release of *Dr. No* is a detail mostly forgotten. These 'waste matter' mechanics run through the films, even in the Craig era, with peripheralization and disposal of people of colour across gender and ethnicity. This pattern although seemingly interrupted in the Craig era with new presences from hitherto ignored diversities, also struggles to break free from these 'race-rituals'. From *Casino Royale*'s depiction of Congolese military assassins, through to the minor on-screen moment of the late Paul Battarcharjee we witness peripheralization. Battarcharjee was a celebrated actor of stage and screen but in the opening film of this 'new' era, pigeon-holed into the 'Asian Doctor' category, a stereotypical fixation in the US and UK (Ahmed 2017) representational arenas. It seems rather striking that in this multicultural, diverse era of Bond films, so few people of colour – including British Asian actors have thus far been on screen. While *Skyfall*'s introduction to Naomi Harris changes patterns somewhat, as I discuss later, this also represents a troubling negotiation, reinforcing Bond as the white, masculine symbol of professional competency and vitality, against which others continue to fall short – a '*race ritual*' first seen in *Dr. No*.

These negotiations are signs of struggle for a literary and movie franchise seemingly infinite in its ability to periodically dominate global box office. Such variability can be seen in how gendered representations punctuate *Spectre* (Mendes 2015), with established veteran actors such as Monica Bellucci limited

Bond, Race and Coloniality: No Time to Die(versify)

to playing the 'wife' of a villain, and existing only to satisfy Bond's need to re-affirm his sexual vitality. However, *Spectre* in many ways is also an explicit refusal of the 'new' politics of diversity in representation, given the paucity of roles given to any actors of colour, regardless of gender. For example, the Congolese actor Marc Zinga playing 'Moreau', or the established Algerian actor Miloud Mourad Benamara playing 'street sweeper'. You cannot be the hero, if the very object of the empire's gaze and target sites are you, your belonging, histories, people and culture. If, as Frantz Fanon wrote, 'Europe is literally the creation of the Third world' (2004: 102) then that world is always positioned as inferior but essential to imperial gazes.

Boundaries: Made and unmade

The early Bond films narrate post-war, Cold War and commonwealth migration anxieties into the scripture of Bond's cinematic journey (Everett 2020). The DCR appears to somewhat fragment and destabilize this process, in effect reaffirming the boundaries already configured by introducing *flex* in race and gender. As Kristen Shaw (2015) indicates the repositioning of a 'new' Moneypenny is ambivalent since she simply performs the same function as the Felix Leiter character (played by Jeffrey Wright). The only two black actors have peripheral 'helper' roles, never appearing on screen together or in the same film until *NTTD*, and are effectively seen as less talented, able and competent than Bond, and in Moneypenny's case even demoted from fieldwork to desk duty in *Skyfall*. Leiter bids farewell to the franchise in *NTTD*, almost as if without Bond, there can be no Leiter. This killing off is significant in its differential impact. Although Bond too is killed in the final scenes of *NTTD*, the symbolic power relations involved mean that Bond's death is simply a narrative detail filled with his own reproduction and continuity. Leiter's death, and perhaps Moneypenny's demotion, re-inscribe intersectional limitations and boundaries to show that *this* Felix Leiter's life exists only in relation to an un-raced Bond. Bond's narrative needs for emotional redemption as 'brother' far outweigh the continuation of Leiter's narrative arc, producing Leiter as *raciologically* tied to Bond's existence.

We can see echoes of this 'needful' and necessary expendability in many other forms of cinematic representations of limited 'black moments', so much so that the early-in-the-film black death has been satirized by writers and creatives such as Keegan-Michael Key and Jordan Peele (2012) with filmic references in works such as *Get Out* (Peele 2016). Although the 'black-person-dies-first' trope (TV Tropes n.d.) has been a consistent feature of films and TV for many decades, it is the 1968 George A. Romero zombie classic *Night of the Living Dead* that stimulates our life-death narrative here. As a film where the only black character manages to survive a never-ending apocalypse of zombie attacks, it is in the final moments that the lead character played by Duane Jones ('Ben') is shot by a white police officer that the film is a full revelational statement of the US's relationship with racial terror. Here then the black actor is the last to die, and yet forms the foundation for the always limited presence of black people and people of colour in so much of representational history. Leiter's death could be seen as a timely reminder of normative ideals still so prevalent in black presences in film.

National Bonds

This troubled negotiation with race-thinking in the UK is exemplified in 2012, the year of London hosting the Olympics, and the release of *Skyfall*. Danny Boyle's direction of the Olympic Games opening was a celebration of lived multicultural (Parekh 2000) reality and rather cleverly situated the UK's state-funded National Health Service as central to this. The emphasis on Britain's long and deep relationship with its 'dark visitors' – or what M might call 'shadows' was key to this. Since its inception in 1948, the National Health Service's delivery of health care to the nation has been fundamentally underpinned by the work, skills, labour and expertise of a huge and diverse range of multicultural, multi-ethnic and global people, despite a persistent, powerful and damaging pattern of racism in the NHS, and public attitudes towards Black and Asian workers of colour (Joliff 2020; Kapadia et al. 2022).

As part of the introduction to the Olympic Games, in a six-minute-fifteen-second sequence filmed specifically for the 2012 London Olympics ceremony (Olympics 2012), Queen Elizabeth II accompanies Bond onto a waiting helicopter which then flies over London, as the camera gaze takes in (for our consumption) major historical (tourist) sites, including statues and celebrated figures, such as Winston Churchill. As the helicopter arrives at the Olympic stadium, Bond opens the helicopter door, allowing the 'Queen' to jump out, followed closely by Bond. As their parachutes open into Union Jacks (a nod to *The Spy Who Loved Me* [Gilbert 1977]), the Bond theme tune by Monty Norman plays us into the beginning of the games. Although interesting and entertaining, no doubt because of Craig's skill in self-parody and a demonstrable comedy talent, the entire sequence of film and music fell short of its intended aims, seen in the lack of enthusiasm and disinterest in the audience. The anxieties at play here were exemplified by the Conservative MP, Aidan Burley, who tweeted 'Thank God the athletes have arrived! Now we can move on from leftie multicultural crap. Bring back red arrows, Shakespeare, and the Stones … !' (Watt 2012).

The emblematic presence of Union Jacks to signify British Island unity and sovereignty, as well as enduring imperial and colonial reminders of global superiority – albeit historical, also deeply signify many centuries of racial reclassifying of black people as subhuman (Olusoga 2016). Britain's long relationship with slavery and human trafficking through the much-celebrated Royal African Company, and its nostalgic, postcolonial amnesia or 'postcolonial melancholia' (Gilroy 2005) in the twentieth century results in intimate connections between Bond, the royal monarchic system of governance and the Union Jack (Figure 8.3).

Although writers focusing on British spy fiction and empire (e.g. Goodman 2015) allude to notions of grief and loss experienced by 'the British' throughout a period of decolonization, there is little engagement with the brutality of what the empire came to mean for its dispossessed, impoverished and decimated darker subjects (Gopal 2019). The very notion of a *vanishing empire* (Goodman 2015) can reproduce the very nostalgia it purports to identify. In other words, if empire is vanishing, then what is left in the resulting space? This is interesting because

Figure 8.3 2012 Summer Olympics Opening Ceremony (BBC 2012).

if the Craig-era Bond is repositioning itself relationally – that is, in relation to a range of diverse peoples, cultures and possibilities – then in the context of a vanishing empire, what happens to those who previously *were* its subjects? If we take empire to be associated with 'civilizational' modern achievements but also bound up with deadly, colonial and imperial extractive processes then what of empire's counter-objects if the former is vanishing? 'Post-racial' perspectives might argue that nothing is left to discuss, since the problem of race and racism vanished with the empire. But the contemporary landscapes of racialized lives and racial thinking in so many aspects of society, such as education, employment, media and incarceration (Hirsch 2018) tells a different story.

This is what the Bond franchise appears to be negotiating, and resultantly produces a re-inscription of parallel, representational colonialities through race and class. The space that is left can *potentially* be re-defined by new, radical progressive, multicultural, ethnic, gendered and classed lives that break away from *essentializing categories*, as exemplified by the mass protests all over the globe. The late Stuart Hall, writer, theorist and intellectual, argued consistently for an honest engagement in the complexity of the politics of identities and representation, here quoting the writer and director Hanif Kureishi (1985) on this subject:

> If there is to be a serious attempt to understand Britain today, with its mix of races and colours, its hysteria and despair, then, writing about it has to be complex. It can't apologise or idealise. It can't sentimentalise and it can't represent only one group as having a monopoly on virtue.
>
> (Kureishi qtd. in Hall 2021: 255)

It is this new-ness and complexity that may ultimately force Bond, 007 and the franchise to accept that the franchise must be unravelled totally to embrace the realities of racial, classed and gendered difference, rather than just the fantasy of tokenistic inclusion.

Performative rituals: Playing in the shadows

The DCR emerges and responds at a time when anxieties over nation and identity are reaching fever pitch. Reflections of this are seen in *Skyfall* in the figure of Bond sprinting through traffic to M's rescue, as she, while being questioned on infringements to civil liberties, surveillance and security governance, recites Tennyson. The scene in question concerns the accountability of M's secret service operations, and the way in which they undermine the fabric of British civil life and democracy itself. The defence which M mobilizes is to quote from the poem *Ulysses* (1842 [1991]), as scenes outside the room begin to unfold with the villain Raoul making his way to assassinate M. The crux of this narrative segment is that Bond, in all his anti-political correctness, serves as the ultimate defender of all that is required in the name of civilized British progress. M states:

> I am frightened because our enemies are no longer known to us […] they do not exist on a map […] they are not nations they are individuals […] look around you, who do you fear? […] it's in the shadows, and that's where we must do battle.

The melancholy regarding loss of nation, imperial and colonial power, and the requisite and resulting sense of (in)security, is palpable in the celluloid and the visual fabric of two sections of the film in particular. M quotes Tennyson:

> Though much is taken, much abides; and though / We are not now that strength which in old days / Moved earth and heaven; that which we are, we are / One equal temper of heroic hearts / Made weak by time and fate, but strong in will / To strive, to seek, to find, and not to yield.

A range of fears and fantasies can be projected onto the figure of Bond, whose 'exceptional services are still required in a world where people, ideas and terror can travel everywhere' (Dodds 2003: 149) and overlaid with the hyper-vigilance, anxiety and violence meted out against *any* form of stranger as emerging with contemporary political scenes. The emergent risks of terror are weighed against the risks of 'xeno-racism' (Fekete 2001) as an acceptable price to pay.

Deep belonging

The palpable unease that is present when the issue of 'an-*Other*' Bond is raised signposts the reimagining of belongings. Hence 'an-*Other*' Bond would be to reimagine the postcolonial, and to enter into a phase of social, cultural and political expression in the arts which might mobilize a reflective, truthful, backward glance at histories. However, Lashana Lynch's 007 introduction is not entirely constitutive of progressive liberal forward motion. These (racialized) bodies out of place and space, what Nirmal Puwar called 'space invaders' (2004), represents a retro-injection of liminality. If we view heritage and nationalist/imperial belonging and identity as forming a series of mirrors which surround

148   *Resisting James Bond: Power and Privilege in the Daniel Craig Era*

the memory, always reflecting back the essentialized and idealized structures of power, then the introduction of *an(Other)* Bond into this imaginary would involve a shattering of those long enduring reflective images. It *could* serve to fracture the imagery of white British colonial power and supremacy. As Hall (1999) argues, the British sense of heritage is 'keeping what already exists – as opposed to the production and circulation of new work in different media ...' (1999: 3). Mallory, played by Ralph Fiennes, ominously foretells, 'They're going back in time. Somewhere we will have the advantage.' The *advantage here* is not only the connection to soil, and the psychic-architecture that is occupied in the mindscape, but in the comfort of a distant place, space and time which cannot be owned or connected to by anyone other than a 'true' imperial representative.

Being able to rely on 'personal and public memory [...] increasingly hung on a conception of "National Heritage"' (MacPhee 2011: 142), however mythical or imagined it might be, is an advantage 'the enemy' cannot have, since they cannot occupy these racial-psycho-social landscapes. We can ask who is *allowed* to belong and be a part of all that is symbolized by the Bond genre? As Wright explains,

> To be a subject of Deep England ... is above all to have been there ... one must have had the essential experience ... one must have grown up in the midst of ancestral continuities and have experienced that kindling of consciousness which the national landscape and cultural tradition prepare for the dawning national spirit.

> (2009: 81)

The celluloid stitching together of a postcolonial tearing performs a 'post-race', post-imperial adventure, seeking to make sense of globalized world anxieties, by re-massaging, re-narrating and relying on the invisible ways in which the 'abyss' (Wright 2009) of the future can be made more bearable. The Bond books and films were, are, a filmic stitching together of that which has been politically, culturally constructed as torn and broken in the postcolonial demise of mythical imperial superiority.

Universal export?

It is not only the Bond genre that would need a systematic rethinking, but Britishness and Englishness itself, to work out ways of re-presenting the full reality and changing dynamics of human social life. The opportunity to reimagine Bond

Bond, Race and Coloniality: No Time to Die(versify)

as re-presenter of diverse inclusivity was always mired in doubled consciousness, and in many ways echoes current societal undulations in the *decolonizing* (Keval 2019) arena. Universal Exports, the fictional cover company employing Bond beginning in the inaugural *Dr. No*, was always suffering from a crisis of the meaning of 'universal' (Everett 2020), and what exactly was being exported. The 'Other' appears in the narrative neither fully formed nor ephemeral, but only as part-life. Lashana Lynch as 007 provides an example of the (im)possibilities of being a dominant other, since regardless of how physically and intellectually skilled she may be, her function is to be ultimately subordinate to Bond, regardless of his demise. In one of the final scenes of the film, the preparation for the final encounter that could contestably be a denouement, Nomi requests Bond's 007 licence to be reinstated, as a parting gesture of respect. We can read this in multiple ways, for example a show of authority by the new 'agent on the block', because after all, it requires a commanding position to be able to return someone else to a position they previously held. However, reading this against the backdrop of racializating signifiers, it can also be interpreted as the normalized micro-oppressions experienced through gender power relations in the workplace. Ultimately, Nomi has to acquiesce to Bond's history and the legacies that it carries, symbolically demonstrating the power of whiteness structures to accomplish positions of power and superiority, despite the presence of 'Others'.

In Bond we can identify both the apparent 'safety' and solidity of race as it appears ascribed to black and brown bodies but also simultaneously read the precarity and instability of race through the constant attempt to redraw and re-fashion the racial order. That these tropes and codifications somewhat dissolve in the later films is only a dissolution masked in multiple racial assemblages sensitive to a new, 'woke' film industry. The re-coding of race and colonial power simply shifts its axes and performs what Stuart Hall in 1996 identified as the floating signification of race. That race is *still* written onto the bodies of Felix Leiter, Moneypenny and Lashana Lynch, but never onto M, Bond or Q is a mesmerizing racial trick that only modern/colonial media power structures can pull off.

In the final moments of *NTTD*, the title an ironic nod to Bond's last filmic breath, Bond is infected with a virus that will prevent the very intimacy that his life has been without, and which in this film was thought to be a real possibility. Such normal life possibilities such as a partner and family for the world's greatest secret agent of course were always going to be thwarted in one way or another.

It is here in a final act of bravery and self-sacrifice that Bond accepts his own death, while serving his country – indeed, protecting the entire world. Though death is inevitable, even in his moment of finality there is a declaration in the title of the film that human mortality cannot outweigh the systemic power structures that drive the imperial, colonial, extractionist and heteronormative surveillance capitalist system that generated the entity of Bond. On the one hand, it is an intimate, sombre and melancholic moment for the character who has throughout the Craig-era films been yearning for something beyond the death and destruction meted out by his sworn duties, something Daniel Craig performs skilfully. Wearing battle weariness, wounds and a child's teddy bear as a visual link to a life that could have been lived but never was, correcting the missile door malfunction, he is left standing, accepting of his fate. On the other hand, we are also left with the reality of what Bond represents: a systemic, historical force, borne of racial, imperial practices, which although mobilizes individuals to carry out missions, cannot be reducible to those individual acts. As such, Bond's death is merely a statistic, worthy of a toast back at headquarters by M, after which the show must go on. It is this 'show', the continuing global, military, extractionist project that produces racial and social injustices that I refer to as having *No Time To Die*, a reference to continuity and system endurance.

As George Yancy writes, there is an urgency to racial justice that has never been satisfied, reckoned with or paid-in full (2018: 269). In other words, whether it stems from the early beginnings of resistance to the racial terror of transatlantic and plantation slavery or global civil rights actions of the twentieth and twenty-first century, representation, like racial justice, must be waited for. With *NTTD*, we witness a potential moment that transcends the colonial renditions of racial bodies and minds, an instant potential representative reparation. The possibilities are presented as real, and *now*, and in the full splendour of a black, female 007, the waiting *could* finally be over. The incessant clamour for certain types of fictitious certainties, long held in race-thinking, will need to cope in a world where people will no longer tolerate the unquestioned celebration of monuments and historical figures central to genocide, murder and systemic brutality (Keval 2020). In this world Lashana Lynch can confidently, without hesitation tell Mr Bond to 'stay in your lane'. Here is where the duplicity and insidious nature of empire reminds us that coloniality and imperial violence take place as much internally as they do elsewhere (Nandi 1983). For 007, business will be as usual, as systemic and structural violence gets exported, universally.

Conclusion

The Bond franchise has always been about the spatial and temporal fields of infinite colonial whiteness. Such structures necessarily operate on a zero-sum game of existential being: some people can never *be* Bond, it is an impossibility rooted in what Maldonado-Torres calls the 'coloniality of being' (2007). This requires a rethinking of modernity to be reframed not as a purely civilizational, natural European superiority, but as a racial enlightenment (Eze 1997) fuelled, colonial modernity (Mignolo 2007). The cinematic Bond is a psycho-social container for national, cultural and sociological tensions which weave their way through different nation contexts but are always calibrated against a baseline of racial, gendered and classed embodiments.

In order to break such a cycle of representation and narrative, a fundamental dismantling of what can *legitimately be* is required. To show a range of diverse, fully fleshed out characters that do not exist primarily as supporting actors for the main characters who are white, is to also legitimate deeper existential realities. When we consume imagery on screens, we see not just reflections of a societal context but also the production and constitution of that society. This means that where there are racial hierarchies involved in actor presence, depth of character, length of appearance, nature of engagement and richness of the story lines they are a part of, then a fundamental racialized social action is being asserted. The Bond franchise is an ongoing troubled negotiation in the Craig era, where hierarchies are being disrupted and reasserted. To see, hear and viscerally engage with deep representation on screen that reflects the richness of real lives is reflective of lived realities, but also functions to re-establish what a complex, global, multi-ethnic, gendered and classed world looks like. This is what I refer to as the legitimations of *being* – representations matter because they reflect and reproduce what and who is allowed to exist in certain ways.

In a world so deeply troubled by the ongoing effects and legacies of imperial and colonial expansions, consumer and media capitalism, and social media consciousness is implicated in the celebration and condemnation of violence that appear distant and disconnected from real lives. The titular declaration of Daniel Craig's last outing suggests and reinforces the infinite power of racialized systems beyond the control of individuals. In such a world the continuation of 007's licence to kill should rightly be fully questioned, discussed and unpacked to understand and re-narrate positive change. Whatever direction and form the franchise takes, the presence of intersectionally diverse actors and characters reflecting different realities of this world will ensure it will not be a settled, straightforward negotiation, but one whose struggle has many parallels in real lives.

References

Ahmed, R. (2017), 'Airports and Auditions', in N. Shukla (ed.), *The Good Immigrant: 21 Writers Reflect on Race in Contemporary Britain*, 159–62, London: Penguin.

Baron, C. (2009), 'Dr. No: Bonding Britishness to Racial Sovereignty', in C. Lindner (ed.), *The James Bond Phenomenon: A Critical Reader*, 153–68, Manchester: Manchester University Press.

Bennett, T. and J. Woollacott (2009), 'The Moments of Bond', in C. Lindner (ed.), *The James Bond Phenomenon: A Critical Reader*, 13–33, Manchester: Manchester University Press.

Bhabha, H. K. (1983), 'The Other Question …', *Screen* 24(6): 18–36.

Bhambra, G. K. et al. (2018), *Decolonising the University*, London: Pluto Press.

Bhattacharyya, G. (2009), *Dangerous Brown Men: Exploiting Sex, Violence and Feminism in the 'War on Terror'*, London: Bloomsbury Publishing.

Boatcă, M. (2016), *Global Inequalities beyond Occidentalism*, London and New York: Routledge.

Bold, C. (2009), '"Under the Very Skirts of Britannia": Re-reading Women in the James Bond Novels', in C. Lindner (ed.), *The James Bond Phenomenon: A Critical Reader*, 205–19, Manchester: Manchester University Press.

Camus, R. (2018), *You Will Not Replace Us!*, Chez L'auteur.

Chapman, J. (2000), *Licence to Thrill: A Cultural History of the James Bond Films*, New York: Columbia University Press.

Denning, M. (2009), 'License to Look: James Bond and the Heroism of Consumption', in C. Lindner (ed.), *The James Bond Phenomenon: A Critical Reader*, 56–75, Manchester: Manchester University Press.

Dodds, K. (2003), 'Licensed to Stereotype: Geopolitics, James Bond and the Spectre of Balkanism', *Geopolitics* 8(2): 125–56.

Dyer, R. (1997), *White: Essays on Race and Culture*, London and New York: Routledge.

Eco, U. (2009), 'Narrative Structures in Fleming', in C. Lindner (ed.), *The James Bond Phenomenon: A Critical Reader*, 34–55, Manchester: Manchester University Press.

Everett, A. (2020), 'Shaken, Not Stirred Britishness: James Bond, Race, and the Transnational Imaginary', in J. Verheul (ed.), *The Cultural Life of James Bond: Specters of 007*, 187–206, Amsterdam: Amsterdam University Press.

Eze, E. C. (1997), *Race and the Enlightenment: A Reader*, New Jersey: Blackwell.

Fanon, F. (2004), *The Wretched of the Earth*, Richard Philcox (trans.), New York: Grove Press.

Fekete, L. (2001), 'The Emergence of Xeno-Racism', *Race & Class* 43 (2): 23–40.

Fetters, A. (2015), 'A Brief, Depressing History of the Quest for a Black James Bond', *GQ Magazine*. Available online: https://www.gq.com/story/brief-history-black-james-bond.

Fikes, R. (2014), 'John Kitzmiller (1913–1965)', *Blackpast*. Available online: https://www.blackpast.org/global-african-history/kitzmiller-john-1913-1965/.

Fryer, P. (1984), *Staying Power: The History of Black People in Britain*, Edmonton: University of Alberta.

Funnell, L., ed. (2015), *For His Eyes Only: The Women of James Bond*, New York: Columbia University Press.

Funnell, L. and K. Dodds (2017), *Geographies, Genders and Geopolitics of James Bond*, London: Palgrave Macmillan.

Gehlawat, A. (2009), 'Kamasutra Bond-ing', in C. Lindner (ed.), *The James Bond Phenomenon: A Critical Reader*, 268–84, Manchester: Manchester University Press.

Gentleman, A. (2019), *The Windrush Betrayal: Exposing the Hostile Environment*, London: Faber & Faber.

Gilroy, P. (2005), *Postcolonial Melancholia*, New York: Columbia University Press.

Goldberg, D. T., ed. (2002), *The Racial State*, Malden, MA: Blackwell Publishing.

Goodfellow, M. (2020), *Hostile Environment: How Immigrants Became Scapegoats*, London: Verso Books.

Goodman, S. (2015), *British Spy Fiction and the End of Empire*, New York and London: Routledge.

Gopal, P. (2019), *Insurgent Empire: Anticolonial Resistance and British Dissent*, London: Verso Books.

Hall, S. (1999), 'Un-settling "the Heritage", Re-Imagining the Post-Nation: Whose Heritage?', *Third Text* 13(49): 3–13.

Hall, S. (2021), 'New Ethnicities', in P. Gilroy and R. W. Gilmore (eds), *Selected Writings on Race and Difference*, 246–56, Durham, NC: Duke University Press.

Hasian, Jr., M. (2014), 'Skyfall, James Bond's Resurrection, and 21st-Century Anglo-American Imperial Nostalgia', *Communication Quarterly* 62 (5): 569–88.

Hirsch, A. (2018), *Brit(ish): On Race, Identity and Belonging*, London: Jonathan Cape.

hooks, b. (2006), 'Understanding Patriarchy'. Available online: https://imaginenoborders.org/zines/.

Hulme, P. (1986), *Colonial Encounters: Europe and the Native Caribbean, 1492–1797*, London: Methuen.

Joliff, T. (2020), *Time to Speak Up: Some Necessary Words about Racism*, Kings Fund. Available online: https://www.kingsfund.org.uk/blog/2020/07/necessary-words-racism.

Kapadia, D. et al. (2022), *Ethnic Inequalities in Healthcare: A Rapid Evidence Review*, London: NHS Race and Health Observatory.

Kaufmann, E. (2018), *Whiteshift: Populism, Immigration and the Future of White Majorities*, London: Penguin.

Keval, H. (2019), 'Navigating the "Decolonising" Process: Avoiding Pitfalls and Some Do's and Don't's', *Discover Society*, 65. Available online: https://archive.discoversociety.org/2019/02/06/navigating-the-decolonising-process-avoiding-pitfalls-and-some-dos-and-donts/.

Keval, H. (2020), *Black Lives Matter, Toppling Statues and Anti Racism: Joining the Dots*, Canterbury Christ Church University Expert Comment. Available online: https://blogs.canterbury.ac.uk/expertcomment/black-lives-matter-toppling-statues-and-anti-racism-joining-the-dots/.

Key, K. M. and J. Peele (2012), *Key & Peele* [TV Comedy Series]. Cindylou, Monkeypaw, productions, Comedy Partners, Martel & Roberts Productions, Principato-Young Entertainment.

Lentin, A. (2014), 'Post-Race, Post Politics: The Paradoxical Rise of Culture after Multiculturalism', *Ethnic and Racial Studies* 37(8): 1268–85.

Lentin, A. (2020), *Why Race Still Matters*, Medford, MA: Polity Press.

Lindner, C., ed. (2009), *The James Bond Phenomenon: A Critical Reader*, Manchester: Manchester University Press.

Ling, T. (2020), '"Sorry, We've Already Got a Black Act": The Insidious Racism of UK Comedy', *Vice*. Available online: https://www.vice.com/en/article/5dze7b/racism-uk-comedy-scene.

MacPhee, G. (2011), *Postwar British Literature and Postcolonial Studies*, Edinburgh: Edinburgh University Press.

Maldonado-Torres, N. (2007), 'On the Coloniality of Being: Contributions to the Development of a Concept', *Cultural Studies* 21(2–3): 240–70.

Mignolo, W. D. (2007), 'Introduction: Coloniality of Power and De-Colonial Thinking', *Cultural Studies* 21(2–3): 155–67.

Miller, T. (2009), 'James Bond's Penis', in C. Lindner (ed.), *The James Bond Phenomenon: A Critical Reader*, 232–47, Manchester: Manchester University Press.

Mondon, A. and A. Winter (2020), *Reactionary Democracy: How Racism and the Populist Far Right Became Mainstream*, London: Verso Books.

Nandi, A. (1983), *The Intimate Enemy: Loss and Recovery of Self under Colonialism*, Oxford: Oxford University Press.

Olusoga, D. (2016), *Black and British: A Forgotten History*, London: Palgrave Macmillan.

Olympics (2012), James Bond and The Queen London 2012 Performance. Available online: https://www.youtube.com/watch?v=1AS-dCdYZbo.

Parekh, B. C. (2000), *The Future of Multi-Ethnic Britain: Report of the Commission on the Future of Multi-Ethnic Britain*, London: Profile Books.

Pitcher, B. (2014), *Consuming Race*, New York and London: Routledge.

Prashad, V. (2013), *The Poorer Nations: A Possible History of the Global South*, London: Verso.

Puwar, N. (2004), *Space Invaders: Race, Gender and Bodies Out of Place*, Oxford: Berg.

Quijano, A. (2000), 'Coloniality of Power and Eurocentrism in Latin America', *International Sociology* 15(2): 215–32.

Romano, A. (2018), 'Celebrating 10 Years of Idris Elba Becoming James Bond Any Second Now', *Vox*. Available online: https://www.vox.com/2018/8/10/17674666/idris-elba-james-bond-casting-history-daniel-craig.

Saha A. (2013), '"Curry Tales": The Production of "Race" and Ethnicity in the Cultural Industries', *Ethnicities* 13(6): 818–37.

Said, E. (1978), *Orientalism*, New York: Pantheon Books.

Shaw, K. (2015), 'The Politics of Representation: Disciplining and Domesticating Miss Moneypenny in *Skyfall*', in L. Funnell (ed.), *For His Eyes Only: The Women of James Bond*, 70–8, New York: Columbia University Press.

Shilliam, R. (2018), *Race and the Undeserving Poor: From Abolition to Brexit*, Newcastle upon Tyne: Agenda Publishing.

Stam, R. and L. Spence (1983), 'Colonialism, Racism and Representation', *Screen* 24(2): 2–20.

Tennyson, A. T. (1991), *Alfred Lord Tennyson: Selected Poems*, ed. A. Day, New York: Penguin Books.

Trafford, J. (2020), *The Empire at Home: Internal Colonies and the End of Britain*, London: Pluto.

Tuck, E. and W. Wang (2012), 'Decolonization is not a Metaphor', *Decolonization: Indigeneity, Education & Society* 1 (1): 1–40.

TV Tropes (n.d.), 'Black Dude Dies First'. Available online: https://tvtropes.org/pmwiki/pmwiki.php/Main/BlackDudeDiesFirst.

Verheul, J., ed. (2020), *The Cultural Life of James Bond: Specters of 007*, Amsterdam: Amsterdam University Press.

Watt, N. (2012), 'Olympics Opening Ceremony was "Multicultural Crap" Tory MP Tweets', *Guardian*, 28 July. Available online: https://www.theguardian.com/politics/2012/jul/28/olympics-opening-ceremony-multicultural-crap-tory-mp.

Wolfe, P. (2016), *Traces of History: Elementary Structures of Race*, London: Verso Books.

Wright, P. (2009), *On Living in an Old Country: The National Past in Contemporary Britain*, Oxford: Oxford University Press.

Yancy, G. (2018), 'Afterword', in A. Johnson et al. (eds), *The Fire Now: Anti-Racist Scholarship in Times of Explicit Racial Violence*, 266–74, London: Zed Books.

Young, L. (1996), *Fear of the Dark: Race, Gender and Sexuality in the Cinema*, New York and London: Routledge.

Younis, T. (2021), 'The Psychologisation of Counter-Extremism: Unpacking PREVENT', *Race & Class* 62(3): 37–60.

9

Licence to Urbicide

Defusing Bond's Acts of Terrorism for a New Era

Fernando Gabriel Pagnoni Berns

It is a simple plan. Using a fake name and identity (Arlington Beech, professional card player), James Bond (Daniel Craig) has to check into Hotel Splendide in Montenegro. After entering the lobby, Bond gives the receptionist his real name, immediately blowing his cover. Vesper Lynd (Eva Green), the film's Bond girl and his partner on the mission, is livid with rage. It is worth noting that Bond is fairly certain that the film's main villain, Le Chiffre (Mads Mikkelsen), would know anyone who was registered for the poker tournament based on how well connected he is. Thus, for Bond, pretending to be someone else is futile and he does not even attempt to hide his presence in Montenegro.

The scene described above is from *Casino Royale* (Campbell 2006). One of the most striking differences regarding the pre-Craig-era Bond franchise is how little concern 007 has now for his status as a spy. There is no subtle infiltration within dangerous organizations, nor fake identities, nor even invisibility. This shift from 'covert spy' who tries to pass unnoticed to assigned-male-at-birth hero action figure operating in the open follows the changes produced through the franchise, especially after the departure of Sean Connery as Bond. After the initial efforts of the first films, the franchise became 'more action-oriented, with the huge set pieces taking over some of the movies' (Budnik 2017: 3). This shift towards spectacle includes high(er) tech gadgets, long and more dynamic action scenes, a greater emphasis on fashion, fast cars and, of course, developments to the character of Bond himself. Bond now is highly visible, leaving behind him a trail not only of broken hearts and corpses but of urban destruction as well.

When Daniel Craig assumed the mantle of Bond, the franchise acquired a grimmer approach in which cities in addition to people now become victims of his British exceptionalism, including the destruction of urban spaces that were, in the pre-Craig era, safeguarded. If one of the most visible marks of international terrorism is the destruction of buildings and entire cities, then James Bond can be considered, in this post-9/11 era, as a terrorist with a 'license to destroy' (Funnell and Dodds 2017: 17). After all, 007 is a cultural artefact that changes according to the different sets of ideological, social, historical and cultural contexts through which his adventures are set. Bond is now directly responsible for widespread destruction taking place in urban areas which puts the lives of innocent bystanders at risk. Yet, this kind of destruction is codified as 'collateral damage' with the concept of 'terrorism' only being invoked when the destruction takes place in USA or UK.

While James Bond has always had a 'licence to destroy', he becomes increasingly destructive across the Craig-era films. For instance, various action sequences take place in construction sites where buildings are being erected and/or renovated (Funnell and Dodds 2017: 165–70). While Monika Gehlawat discusses the 'aesthetics of demolition' in *Casino Royale* (2009: 137), Funnell and Dodds have expanded this analysis to include spaces of construction/destruction in *Quantum of Solace* (Forster 2008) and *Skyfall* (Mendes 2012). However, when this action takes place at home (UK) or in public spaces such as the Underground in London, it reveals how the average British citizen (and colonial subject) is being endangered through the actions taken by the (not-so-secret) spy. Wherever Bond goes during the Craig era, highly visible urban wreckage follows. As M (Judi Dench) mentions, spies working during the Cold War era were able, unlike Bond, to cover up their own disasters, especially when they took place at home.

As noted by Stephen Graham, in the post-Cold War era, cities have become 'lightening conductors' for political violence. Referencing the work of Saskia Sassen, he writes:

> The great geopolitical contests of cultural change, ethnic conflict, and diasporic social mixing; of economic reregulation and liberalization; of militarization, informatization, resource exploitation, and ecological change are, to a growing extent, boiling down to often violent conflicts in the key strategic sites of our age: contemporary cities.
>
> (2004: 4)

Defusing Bond's Acts of Terrorism for a New Era   159

As a result, warfare and international terrorism become highly urbanized acts. These links are reflected across the Craig-era films as the franchise redefines transnational power and how it impacts on national security. This chapter will explore how power is topographically localized in the city across these films, where disinterest for the safety of the common citizen is the mark of the new Bond.

The city and James Bond: Shifts

This chapter does not ignore that war (even the Cold War), terrorism and the Bond franchise have been intimately bound together from the outset of the 007 series. In fact, they played a critical role in shaping the dynamic encounters of Ian Fleming's source novels and short stories (1954–66). Transnational travel and the presence of the British spy exerting his power (and, by extension, that of the British government) in foreign countries delineated the early literary adventures of 007. Still, the transnational mobility of the literary Bond was quite low compared with his filmic counterparts (Nitins 2011: 108). In fact, the use of 'Universal Exports' as an organizational cover for MI6 suggests the necessity of travel for the jet-setting spy and the continuation of British/colonial influence around the world.

The pre-Craig-era films were not indifferent to the connection between violence in foreign cities and Bond's state-sanctioned missions. In *Moonraker* (Lewis Gilbert 1979), Bond (Roger Moore) is involved in a gondola chase in Venice where he is pursued by assassins whose bullets miss him and instead hit the old stone arches above the water. To flee those hunting him, Bond converts his gondola into a hovercraft and starts to drive it through the city. The sequence works as a comic set piece where bystanders stare in disbelief and servers accidentally pour drinks on costumers. Even a dove does a 'double take' at the image of Bond driving his 'gondola' through the streets. Thus, the urban intervention is played for laughs. In *The Living Daylights* (John Glen 1987), more reckless behaviour can be seen in the streets of Gibraltar, where citizens are put in danger by a chase that ends with a Land Rover careening down narrow roads. Yet, it is the villain driving the Land Rover, while Bond fights to stop him. Later in the film, Bond is pursued over the roof of the Musée de la Kasbah and the chase ends with Bond jumping over a courtyard filled with scantily clad women, thus giving viewers another form of 'soft' urban intervention played for amusement. Except for the impact of bullets, the buildings are left largely undamaged.

Chases through streets and well-known buildings, such as museums or historical places, are hallmarks of the cinematic Bond franchise. Yet, two narratives prevail through these famous chases. The first is the security of citizens: they may be pushed aside, frightened or amazed by what they see, but the average person is never depicted as being in serious danger. Second, while cities and individual buildings serve as backdrops for fights and car chases, they are left mostly intact. As Lisa Funnell and Klaus Dodds argue, 'although Bond destroys the buildings erected by the villains, he is careful not to damage cultural artifacts and national monuments' (2017: 167). In countries considered 'neutral' or part of a colonial map – and, as such, imperial/colonial properties – 'Bond moves carefully and even respectfully' (169) through the cities. There are exceptions, as noted by Funnel and Dodds: 'In *GoldenEye*, Bond tries to secure the release of Natalya Simonova by chasing after General Ourumov's car with a tank. He leaves a trail of destruction as he makes his way through the streets of St. Petersburg' (2017: 168). At some point, Bond 'crashes through a monument at the center of town' (168). The trail of destruction, however, takes place in a 'rogue' country and, as such, the scene is coded as 'freedom' rather than 'interventionism'.

This has changed in the Craig-era films, mostly due to three shifts. First, as a consequence of Christopher Nolan's Batman trilogy, a new 'grim and gritty' (Weldon 2016: 235) standard was established for action and adventure films. A similar revisionist approach was taken in the Craig-era films through the depiction of Bond's origin story for attaining his '00' licence to kill. Not only was Craig's Bond colder and more detached, but this new 'grim and gritty' attitude affected how Bond interacts with the urban as well, as the destruction of the city blends together spectacle, the trauma of terrorism and a process of globalization that accentuates the inequalities born from 'colonialism, imperialism, racism, and other human failings' (AlSayyad 2010: xv). In relation to the 'grim and gritty' era, the second shift revolves around ideals of masculinity, where Bond's patriotic manliness is revised in favour of 'physical prowess' (Lewis-Vidler 2020: 33) more attuned with the superhero genre. This new Bond, according to Lewis-Vidler, is 'ruthless' (33) and his stamina and destructive capacity are proof of his 'exceptionalism', the latter making him more like a superhero 'than ever before' (33). The third shift was produced by the terrorist attacks of 9/11 in the US, which influenced popular culture as content creators in Hollywood in particular became more conscious of the portrayal of urban destruction. The significant impact of images of ambulances and police running toward different levels of smoking wreckage became more haunting, leaving audiences uncomfortable with film sequences of city destruction (Quay and Damico 2010: 181). Yet the Craig era presents an ambivalent attitude towards urban destruction through the interlinking of these three shifts. The franchise mostly understands terrorism as an act of destruction taking place in the UK. Ambulances, sirens and the horror of urban destruction seem to be visually emphasized only in British spaces. All the other forms of urban intervention pass without further resolution or punishment in the narratives.

Casino Royale opened in 2006, only five years after the terrorist attack on the World Trade Center. The film opens in black and white, a call back to memories (including the Bond of old, his colourful eccentricities now considered passé) and as a way of introducing a more realistic and grittier version of the character, who brutally kills an enemy in hand-to-hand combat. There are neither one-liners nor silly jokes. This is not the Bond of old.

The film's first chase takes place in Madagascar and works as a blueprint of things to come. While chasing Mollaka (Sebastien Foucan), Bond climbs cranes, bulldozes entire buildings and destroys the embassy. His first act of destruction seems to follow the logic of the traditional Bond, with Bond chasing down a suspect using whatever means necessary (in this case, a bulldozer). Yet, *Casino Royale* offers new levels of destruction. Bond smashes the bulldozer into the base of the building under construction. The chase contains a key scene that exemplifies the exceptionality of the new Bond. Running away, Mollaka jumps through a narrow window in the building. Bond, in turn, prefers to destroy the building's wall using the force of his body to smash through it. At this point in the pursuit, Mollaka has killed many people, but Bond has caused more material and structural damage. In the streets, the suspect gets to his destination: the Nambutu embassy (Nambutu being a fictional country in Africa), where he seeks asylum. Bond raids the place, taking the suspect with him while attacking the people who, rightfully so, try to stop 007's wave of destruction. Trapped by the security guards, Bond kills the suspect and produces an explosion that destroys part of the embassy. The face of the ambassador, amazed at the devastation around him, is very telling. Rather than anger, his face reveals numbness and sadness. This reckless destruction goes hand in hand with Bond's disregard of diplomatic international relations and disrespect for foreign frontiers marking the limits of European power, thus emphasizing the character of 'exceptionalism' outlining the British government. Any extreme measure is feasible as a way of counter-terrorism, where structures of power are equated with Bond's physical power. Bond is a figure of British (and, by extension, imperial) exceptionalism and he does not care about the buildings, their security or their policies.

It must be noted that the scene depicts three problematic aspects. First, Bond is a white man assaulting an embassy in Africa where everyone – from the diplomats to the security guards – are black. The resulting imagery evokes notions/memories of colonialism and imperialism. As noted by Lisa Funnell and Klaus Dodds, the people guarding the embassy are depicted as 'largely ineffectual' (2017: 169). As such, the scene contributes to the legitimation of Europeans razing cities under the rationale of words like 'retaken'. Indeed, Bond has 'retaken' a dangerous element that Nambutu is unable to contain. Second, Bond's gunfire within the building evokes images of terrorism, especially in the scene where he shoots at the ceiling in a room filled with scared, screaming women. It may be argued that audiences know James Bond is the 'hero', but dichotomies such as 'good/evil' or 'villain/hero' are highly subjective rather than fixed. It may be argued that, for some viewers, Bond is a terrorist who is risking innocent lives. Third, this scene raises the question of who will pay for the huge damage done to the embassy? Will it be the UK? That is highly improbable.

Bond's acts of material destruction are no longer part of naive amazement, as in the Roger Moore era. *Casino Royale*'s last scene, where Lynd's betrayal is revealed, depicts Venice as another victim of Bond's exceptionalism. Thugs take Lynd hostage and, later, she locks herself within an elevator while the kidnappers fight Bond. Looking for a way to fight the criminals, Bond produces several explosions, causing the flooded building to start sinking. Soon, the whole structure collapses, dragging Lynd with it.

This scene is significant for several reasons. First, it does not engage the politics of 'indulgent' urban intervention where a camp element softens the terrorist act. The sequence cuts between scenes of action within the building and shots of people eating at the small cafes close to the canals, citizens who watch with panic in their faces when the building collapses. Second, Bond is now directly responsible for all the destruction. His intentions may be good (to save his lover Lynd) but the fact remains that he is destroying a whole building in the centre of the city without much care for the people around it. Third, and lastly, this building is not a common edifice, but part of the cultural heritage of Venice (see Figure 9.1). Like terrorists focusing on symbolic urban cultural heritage as a way to produce 'memoricide' (Abujidi 2014: 21), Bond destroys not only a building, but part of the history of the city. Like human beings, irreplaceable

Figure 9.1 *Casino Royale* (Eon Productions et al. 2006).

architecture becomes collateral damage. For Monika Gehlawat, the scene speaks to Bond's exceptionalism: 'when Bond arrives on the scene, [buildings] rapidly transform and ultimately disintegrate' (2009: 133). Nick Jones adds: 'The tourist view of the city as a sun-drenched romantic idyll is literally knocked off balance as Bond invests the building and his experience of Venice with his own personal demons' (2015: 80). This urbicidal scene unites the three shifts taking place in the Craig era: bigger and grimmer spectacle, the haunting effects of terrorism and a protagonist with a superhuman destructive capacity.

The Venice sequence in *Casino Royale* ends with Bond trying to resuscitate Lynd amidst the wreckage of the building, oblivious to all the destruction around him. The sequence also has a coda with Bond speaking to M in the UK on his mobile phone while resting on a gondola. He is now a tourist enjoying the city but his urban impact arguably endures. Venice is a city overwhelmed by the effects of over tourism. An advertisement from UNESCO declared in 2009 that 'Tourism is yet another issue that can help to send the vulnerable Venice to a watery grave' (Standish 2012: 218). This is what Bond does in a double way: he has literally sent a whole building into a watery grave and, in parallel, he is part of the over tourism slowly eroding the city. In fact, one of the problems facing this particular historical quarter is the dislocation of the local people who used to inhabit it to become a space dominated by tourists who, in turn, elevate the prices of everything, from fruits and vegetables to the housing market. Recent surveys have indicated that 'an average of 82,000 tourists now visit Venice daily, while the resident population has decreased from 175,000 in the 1960s to 53,000 today' (Browning and Zupan 2020: 238). As we see in *Moonraker* (also in *From*

Russia With Love [Terence Young 1963]), Venice serves as an ideal location for the James Bond franchise. Exotic, luxurious, highly aestheticized and with a long history, the city is perfectly suited for global consumption, and its destruction in *Casino Royale* belongs to this extreme phase of its condition as a consumable city.

The pre-credit sequence in the following film, *Quantum of Solace*, features a similar approach and aesthetic. Following a dynamic car chase sequence and the failed interrogation of a suspect, Bond pursues a rogue spy into a building (and possibly a church) with a bell tower under construction. The pair crash through a window and struggle for their guns while hanging from ropes and grappling with scaffolding. While Bond comes out on top after shooting the suspect, the *mise en scène* is particularly noteworthy. It looks like the 'peripherical' urban world is constantly under repair or under construction 'effected by the implied resilience of its inhabitants' (Jordan 2010: 145).

The urban destruction increases in later films, demonstrating that *Casino Royale*, which opens a new era of Bond films, is part of a new politics of urbicide, as analysed below. *Skyfall* (Sam Mendes 2012) opens with a traditional Bondian chase sequence, taking place in Istanbul and featuring the 1,500-year-old mosque Hagia Sophia. The scene could fit easily into any other Bond film from the classic era (1962–2002), except for details that highlight how the city and the new 007 interact. Bond is seen shooting recklessly at a plaza filled with little markets, with people running away from the danger. In one of the most baffling scenes in the extended chase, Bond tries to reach a suspect, who is riding a train. To get to him, 007 uses a digger, hitting one of the carriages with the machine's giant shovel. The carriage is filled with people who could have easily been hurt (see Figure 9.2). After boarding the train, Bond adjusts his expensive Tom Ford

Figure 9.2 *Skyfall* (Eon Productions et al. 2012).

Defusing Bond's Acts of Terrorism for a New Era   165

suit, without worrying about the people around him. As in the scenes analysed in _Casino Royale_, this sequence does not play for laughs. Taken together, the first three Craig-era films feature problematic sequences rife with misogyny (Funnell 2015: 1) and led by a Bond who looks detached from any sense of humanity via 'grim and gritty' narratives.

Urbicide: Shaken, not stirred

Urbicide is defined by Martin Coward as 'the widespread, and yet intentional, destruction of the urban environment' (2004: 157). This is the case with the end of _Spectre_ (Sam Mendes 2015), where London is the specific target of the terrorist organization that gives the film its title. Urban destruction is severe here, with M (Ralph Fiennes), one of the film's heroes, looking stupefied at the urban destruction around him. Yet, the story ends with Blofeld (Christoph Waltz) getting his punishment amidst the ruins of a section of London Bridge. The destruction caused in foreign cities, in turn, is part of a complicated scheme where Bond saves the world and, as such, a necessary part of the exceptionalism framing Britain across the era. It is particularly interesting that the menace of Blofeld (who is the leader of the terrorist organization SPECTRE and the power behind the villains of the previous three films) ends in London, where the destruction is more significant than the structural damage that has been caused in other countries. While urban destruction is punished in London, the structural devastation caused by Bond around the world is treated as mere collateral.

In a later scene in _Skyfall_, Silva (Javier Bardem), the film's main villain, escapes with Bond pursuing him through a London Underground station, running through platforms before leaping onto a speeding tube train as the criminal evades him. When 007 finally catches Silva and holds him at gun point in a service area, the mastermind detonates a hole in the roof which results in a train crashing down. This creates a hole through which Silva can escape and he uses the destruction of the Underground system as a distraction to aid him. Emergency services rushing to a London tube station looking for victims in _Skyfall_ probably had a profound impact on audiences who still remembered the 2001 terrorist attacks of 9/11 in the US or the 7/7 London transport bombings in 2005. Arguably, terrorism has been central to the Bond franchise, but while the pre-Craig films engaged with villains who want to conquer the world, the new films emphasize forms of terrorism and urbicide filtered through an ideological lens of exceptionalism. Ambulances, police and firefighters arriving at a scene of utter destruction highlight how this particular geographic location has become a 'victim' and in need of state intervention. When terror strikes in other countries (many times unleashed or at least aided by Bond), there is a lack of consequence: people may die and buildings can collapse, but viewers are left in the dark about how the city copes with this destruction. Invariably, the films abruptly cut to another scene (often, already in another country), without even a brief glimpse of ambulances coming to the rescue. To keep the 'heroic' narrative going, the Bond franchise needs to defuse any critique of British terrorism. As a consequence, the narrative actively emphasizes the idea of 'collateral damage' or deflects the consequences of urban terrorism into nothingness.

Yet, Coward offers another definition of urbicide which does not make reference to the 'intentional' destruction of the urban environment, but rather describes it as a product of 'necessary' military action (Coward 2009: 19). The term 'collateral damage' came to prominence 'through its use by American commanders during the 1990–91 Gulf War' and refers to incidental casualties and property damage resulting from military action: 'On the whole, collateral damage is viewed as an undesirable, and yet possibly unavoidable, consequence of military action' (19).

If the destruction of the urban fabric cannot be understood as simple collateral damage, it can be interpreted or justified as a military necessity. Yet, this last argument does not hold as all of the buildings should have played some role in the logistics and plans of both Bond and/or the UK secret service. There are instances in which such arguments may be credible, such as the destruction of the hotel in *Quantum of Solace*. The levelling of this particular structure, which was built from profits ascertained from the theft of water from the citizens of Bolivia, is a symbolic act in the final scenes of the film. Yet, it cannot erase the urbicide and collateral damage that takes place earlier in the film. During the second chase scene in Siena, Italy, Bond pursues a suspect on top of the roofs of the old city. Like human victims (of which there are many, as the action occurs amidst a horse race in a crowded plaza), the roofs of antique homes are victimized by shooting and the heavy weight of two men (one of them, Bond) jumping onto delicate, frail-looking roofs. This is different from Bond in previous eras where similar chases, such as in *The Spy Who Loved Me* (Gilbert 1977), do not cause similar levels of damage. Through the fighting in Siena, Bond destroys part of a copula undergoing restoration, another antique building

Defusing Bond's Acts of Terrorism for a New Era 167

suffering the effects of terrorism. Antique urban cultural heritage is relentlessly under assault in the Bond franchise as never before. A close shot of an old, frail woman suffering the destruction, as seen in the chase scene mentioned above, is very telling: real people are suffering the effects of this destruction. Considering the urban destruction as 'collateral damage' in the path to major good is one of the strategies the franchise uses to downplay any trace of 'terrorism' coming from Bond. According to Robin Murray and Joseph Heumann, even if efforts were made to 'green' *Quantum of Solace*, the movie fails in its eco message: the film was shot in six countries and this on-location filming was 'among the most expensive and carbon-intense stages of film production', with huge diesel generators used to power the lighting and heating and with thousands of extras overcrowding and congesting the cities (2014: 185).

Another strategy to diffuse the violence perpetrated by Bond is leaving the narrative inconclusive without Bond or MI6 experiencing any consequences. *Spectre's* opening scene represents a clear case of urbicide. Taking place in Mexico City during the festivities of Dia de los Muertos, the sequence not only depicts urban destruction but, also, the endangerment of many human lives. Both are inextricably linked and yet serve as mere backdrops for British exceptionalism in a post-'war on terror' scenario and Bond's 'super' masculinity. After arriving in Mexico City, Bond carries out his plan of killing a terrorist. Watching him from a safe distance, Bond shoots his target and the surviving terrorists return fire. Shortly afterwards, Bond shoots a briefcase containing a bomb, causing the building to explode. No information is given about the building, its function (i.e. business, housing) or its surviving occupants. As the camera tracks horizontally, it shows the complete destruction of the building with blackened walls and smoke pouring out from the wreckage. There is no indication that innocent people have been hurt or killed but neither have we seen any evidence to the contrary. Weakened by the explosion, the building starts to collapse upon another edifice (with Bond on its roof), dragging it in its fall (see Figure 9.3). Bond is seen dropping comically onto a couch. Yet, the camp aspect is undercut by the next scene, where Bond comes out into the street and finds the city covered in dust and debris. The image evokes the aftermath of 9/11, 7/7 and other attacks as well as the horrors of global terrorism.

This linkage, however, is downplayed as the terrorist act takes place in Mexico and the film does not spare a minute in depicting how the event affects the citizens and impacts their lives, if they survived. Unlike the scenes of terrorism taking place in the UK, there are no images of ambulances or firefighters coming to the

Figure 9.3 *Spectre* (Eon Productions et al. 2016).

rescue of potential victims. Surprisingly, the festivities of the Dia de los Muertos continue, as if Mexican citizens are somehow unaware of the destruction of two large buildings mere metres away. This way, the destruction performed by James Bond in Mexico is brushed away, no importance given. There is no consequence to the wide destruction performed by Bond upon the city.

Citizens only react when Bond, now aboard a helicopter and fighting an enemy, loses control of the aircraft. The helicopter spins erratically above the crowded square as Bond wrestles with the controls and finally pulls the plummeting aircraft out of its dive just feet away from crashing into the people below, and then flies off across Mexico City. For urban geographer David Harvey, the end of the Cold War also signified the end of the city for revolutionary politics and the common citizen. The streets and the cities become each day more a space for capitalist-driven philosophies than a space that the common citizen can occupy and walk. Harvey mentions that this change 'has entailed repeated bouts of urban restructuring through creative destruction. This nearly always has a class dimension, since it is usually the poor, the underprivileged, and those marginalized from political power that suffer first and foremost from this process' (2012: 16). In the Craig era, urban areas are not safe anymore for common citizens, nor will the UK Government take responsibility for the destruction. It is noticeable that the urban destruction performed through the Craig era is enacted on poor areas dominated by old buildings or on historic quarters. When working-class people take to the streets to enjoy a festivity, urbicide is hanging (literally in the scene with the helicopter) over their heads, a reminder that the proletariat can make the cities theirs only sporadically.

The Craig era only understands 'terrorism' in terms of violence performed on the United Kingdom. The destruction produced by Bond in other countries is presented as 'heroism' in uncomplicated ways, and the films understand these cases of urbicide as evidence of British exceptionalism. *Spectre*, the film that ended the whole arc of global terrorism sustained by that organization, ends in London, where – following the films' logic of British exceptionalism – violence upon the city must be avenged. It is a fitting location for bringing terrorism to a halt (until the next film, at least).

Conclusions

No Time To Die (Fukunaga 2021), Craig's last film as Bond, depicts a more nuanced version of 007. Looking for an ending to the story arc of Bond, producers chose to (slightly) shift the narrative. Absent is Bond's cold detachment from humanity (he even smiles), offering a more introspective look at the character. *No Time To Die* depicts Bond as a father figure with a capacity for love and self-sacrifice. This 'softer' version, not coincidentally, comes with only a limited amount of urbicide.

In the pre-credit sequence, Bond visits the grave of Vesper Lynd in Matera, Italy. He is attacked by agents of SPECTRE who rig her stone with explosives, causing minor damage at the cemetery. In the chase scene through the old stone-based streets of the city that follows, Bond engages in combat with limited destruction to the surrounding city. Instead, it is his old Aston Martin DB5 that sustains the most damage as he tries to escape with his pregnant girlfriend, Dr Madeleine Swann. This focus on (pro)creation destabilizes the Craig-era Bond trend towards urbicide. This is most notable in the conclusion where Bond sacrifices his life to save his family (and the world at large) from the biological weapon created by the villain Safin (Rami Malek). While a complete island has been erased from earth at the film's climax, it contained a weapon of mass destruction which was being sold to the highest bidder and the location was isolated from innocent citizens. Furthermore, the missiles destroying the facility are sent on the order of M rather than being a consequence of Bond's actions. It is Bond, an agent of the state, who is destroyed rather than innocent people and their spaces around the world.

Urbicide is defined as the killing of cities. Still, the term means more: it implies 'the hollowing out of urban economies' (Gregory and Graham 2009: 794), like what happens with the 'privatization' of water in *Quantum of Solace*. It also means 'the destruction of memory or the erasure of the physical traces of past communities' (Gregory and Graham 2009: 794), as happens with the complete destruction of the Venetian historical quarter in *Casino Royale*. Lastly, it implies the impossibility of heterogeneity and sense of community as the city is lived basically for some citizens rather than all them. The festivities of the Dia de los Muertos in *Spectre*, abruptly interrupted by urban violence, are a clear example of citizens being pushed away from their holiday.

Although *No Time To Die* was released during the Delta wave of the coronavirus pandemic, it opened exclusively in theatres and became a hit at the box office, reaching over $700 million worldwide. The film encouraged people to step out of their homes and invited them to take to the streets again after a global lockdown that kept citizens around the globe at home. Part of the problems generated by the Covid pandemic was the cancellation (global-wide) of different festivities, occasions where the proletariat (as well as other people) could take to the streets, as Mexicans do in *Spectre*. The reopening of theatres and the success of *No Time To Die*, at least, symbolized a return to 'living' streets and a more active, lived experience of the city.

References

Abujidi, N. (2014), *Urbicide in Palestine: Spaces of Oppression and Resilience*, New York: Routledge.

AlSayyad, N. (2010), 'Foreword', in C. Lindner (ed.), *Globalization, Violence, and the Visual Culture of Cities*, xv–xvi, New York: Routledge.

Browning, E. and M. Zupan (2020), *Microeconomics: Theory and Application*, New York: Wiley.

Budnik, D. (2017), *'80s Action Movies on the Cheap: 284 Low Budget, High Impact Pictures*, Jefferson, NC: McFarland.

Coward, M. (2004), 'Urbicide in Bosnia', in S. Graham (ed.), *Cities, War, and Terrorism: Towards an Urban Geopolitics*, 154–71, Malden, MA: Blackwell.

Coward, M. (2009), *Urbicide: The Politics of Urban Destruction*, New York: Routledge.

Funnell, L. (2015), 'Introduction: The Women of James Bond', in L. Funnel (ed.), *For His Eyes Only: The Women of James Bond*, 1–6, New York: Wallflower Press.

Funnell, L. and K. Dodds (2017), *Geographies, Genders and Geopolitics of James Bond*, New York: Palgrave Macmillan.

Gehlawat, M. (2009), 'Improvisation, Action and Architecture in *Casino Royale*', in C. Lindner (ed.), *Revisioning 007: James Bond and Casino Royale*, 131–43, New York: Wallflower.

Graham, S. (2004), 'Introduction: Cities, Warfare, and States of Emergency', in S. Graham (ed.), *Cities, War, and Terrorism: Towards an Urban Geopolitics*, 1–26, Malden, MA: Blackwell.

Gregory, D. and S. Graham (2009), 'Urbicide', in D. Gregory, R. Johnston, G. Pratt, M. Watts and S. Whatmore (eds), *The Dictionary of Human Geography*, 794, Malden, MA: Wiley.

Harvey, D. (2012), *Rebel Cities: From the Right to the City to the Urban Revolution*, London: Verso.

Jones, N. (2015), *Hollywood Action Films and Spatial Theory*, New York: Routledge.

Jordan, S. (2010), 'The Poetics of Scale in Urban Photography', in C. Lindner (ed.), *Globalization, Violence, and the Visual Culture of Cities*, 137–49, New York: Routledge.

Lewis-Vidler, J. (2020), 'The Patriotic Spy: For Queen, Empire, and Dry Martinis', in S. Gerrard (ed.), *From Blofeld to Moneypenny: Gender in James Bond*, 25–40, Bingley: Emerald.

Murray, M. and J. Heumann (2014), *Film and Everyday Eco-disasters*, Lincoln: University of Nebraska Press.

Nitins, N. (2011), *Selling James Bond: Product Placement in the James Bond Films*, Newcastle upon Tyne: Cambridge Scholars.

Quay, S. and A. Damico (2010), *September 11 in Popular Culture: A Guide*, Santa Barbara, CA: Greenwood.

Standish, D. (2012), *Venice in Environmental Peril? Myth and Reality*, Lanham, MD: University Press of America.

Weldon, G. (2016), *The Caped Crusader: Batman and the Rise of the Nerd Culture*, New York: Simon & Schuster.

Afterword

007 and Ableism

Lisa Funnell

For too long, disability activism has functioned as a separate and distinct movement from other social justice initiatives. The history of the disability rights movement in the United States serves as a good example. The Americans with Disabilities Act (1990) was passed nearly thirty years after the Civil Rights Act (1964). Both policies are designed to protect historically marginalized groups from discrimination; however, people with disabilities along with their allies have had to advocate for equity without the strength, support or momentum of broader social justice networks and civil rights movements (see Bryan 2018; Ostiguy-Finneran and Peters 2018). This separation is also evident in the contemporaneous institutionalization of equity, diversity and inclusion (EDI) initiatives in workplaces as accessibility is (often) addressed separately and by a different department/team, a distinction that further contributes to the separation of ableism from broader intersectional conversations about power, privilege and disadvantage.

Regardless of this institutional positioning, ableism needs to be included in our broader discourse on social (in)justice as well as our critique of popular media and, especially, film. Systems of oppression operate on three levels: individual (via bias and bigotry), institutional (via policies and practices) and social/cultural (via narratives and representation). Culture binds individuals and institutions together and creates justifications for the maintenance of the status quo (see Adams et al. 2018). Historically, ableism has also been created by those with intersectional privilege, especially in the context of blockbuster filmmaking with its large(r) budgets and widespread international reach. While some may argue that popular franchises like James Bond are 'only entertainment' and therefore benign, what this volume has shown is that the messages relayed through such franchises are more influential, pervasive and even insidious on closer examination. It is in this context that I offer this afterword on ableism in James Bond with a particular focus on facial scarring

Afterword

in the Craig-era films, which expands upon the problematic tendency to use of physical disability as a proxy for villainy across the series from Ian Fleming's source novels and their cinematic adaptations to the previous era of Brosnan films, thereby raising questions about creative intent, social relevance and legacies of privilege.

Both content and creative context matter when discussing disability on screen. Stereotypes abound for heroic and villainous figures and while a comprehensive discussion of these tropes is beyond the scope of this reflection, it is important to highlight that these representations are almost entirely created and portrayed by people without disabilities. As noted by Elisa Shaholli, 'the power then sits with the non-disabled creator [and performer] in establishing the role' and while 'disability may be physically present on screen, it is simultaneously erased by being created without disabled people behind or in front of the camera' (2022). As a result, these problematic and dis/embodied depictions of disability tap into and extend a longer tradition of misrepresentation that continues to contribute to the stigmatization of people of disabilities.

Villainous depictions are particularly troublesome as they promote the connection between disability and evil/monstrosity. Paul Longmore argues that 'the depiction of the disabled person as "monster" and the criminal characterization both express to varying degrees the notion that disability involves the loss of an essential part of one's humanity. Depending on the extent of the disability, the individual is perceived as more or less subhuman' (1987: 135). Furthermore, Julie Amthor Croley et al. note that since the silent era villainous figures have been depicted with dermatologic features including 'facial scars, alopecia, deep rhytides, periorbital hyperpigmentation, rhinophyma, verruca vulgaris, extensive tattoos, large facial nevi, poliosis, and albinism or gray-hued complexions' (2017: 559). They argue that 'these visual cues evoke in the audience apprehension or fear of the unfamiliar and provide a perceptible parallel to the villainous character's inward corruption. They can foreshadow the future and can efficiently denote a troubled past in a motion picture limited in character development by production constraints' (559). In spite of backlash from organizations like the National Organization of Albinism and Hypropigmentation (NOAH) and various advocacy groups, facial differences and especially scarification continue to be used in the depiction of cinematic villains (559).

In my own writings on James Bond, I have argued that the heroic identity of the title character is created by his interactions with others and defined at

174 *Afterword*

their expense. While most of my scholarly work has focused on the depiction and treatment of women, I have also explored the haptic geographies of James Bond and the history of Bond's diegetic contrasting with villains. In my book with Klaus Dodds, *Geographies, Genders, and Geopolitics of James Bond*, we note that Bond 'is often contrasted with a villain who has a physical impairment that limits him physically and/or socially (as he is perceived as being "freakish")' (2017: 25). This convention was initially used by Fleming in his source novels (1953–66) and Umberto Eco provides a detailed examination of how each villain is written in such a way as to emphasize their monstrosity and difference from Bond (2003). This problematic practice was carried forward into the film adaptations from *Dr. No* (Young 1962) onwards and has continued into the original screenplays that now define the cinematic world of Bond. In addition, Bond is also challenged by an array of hench people who possess abnormal/inhuman strength and abilities such as Jaws in *The Spy Who Loved Me* (Gilbert 1977) and *Moonraker* (Gilbert 1979) who has metal teeth that can cut through flesh, bone and various hard materials (Eco 2003: 26). Through his defeat of these adversaries, Bond's body is positioned as the ideal of masculinity while the physical differences of his adversaries prove to be their downfall (Eco 2003: 27).

Prior to the 1990s, facial differences were not commonly used in the cinematic world of Bond. In the novels, it was Bond who had a thin vertical scar on his cheek (Eco 2003: 35), a characteristic that was not adapted into the filmic versions. Instead, this convention was applied to Ernst Stavro Blofeld, the head of the villainous organization SPECTRE in *You Only Live Twice* (Gilbert 1967), who is presented with a vertical scar across his right eye that extends from his forehead down to his cheek. While facial differences, from disfigurement to scarring, are highly visible and heavily stigmatized not only in film but society at large, there is limited legal recognition of them in current disability laws worldwide ('Our Mission' 2021). The stereotypical use of facial differences in the vilification of characters is dehumanizing and contributes to the negative sentiments and unequal treatment that is being experienced. In spite of increasing calls to stop this antiquated mode of representation, the Craig-era Bond films have increased rather than decreased their frequency.

Casino Royale (Campbell 2006) is a prequel and effectively reboots the Bond brand by providing the origin story of James Bond. The film is revisionist as it deconstructs the classic formula and reworks the core elements gradually reintroducing them across the first three films (see Funnell 2011). While *Casino Royale* introduces a more Hollywood-styled hard-bodied mode of masculinity for Bond (Funnell 2011), it also relies heavily on facial differences to depict the villain LeChiffre who pales in comparison (literally and figuratively) to Bond. Similar to Blofeld, LeChiffre has a scar above his left eye that extends across his eyelid to just under his eye. While Bond is defined by his muscular body and its ability to endure pain, LeChiffre is known for his malformed tear duct from which he 'cries' blood.

The depiction of trauma, scarring and disfiguration creates a dichotomy in which the body of the hero is valorized while the face of the antagonist is vilified. This extends across the orphan origin trilogy which consists of *Casino Royale*, *Quantum of Solace* (Forster 2008) and *Skyfall* (Mendes 2012). As noted by Klaus Dodds, Bond's body serves as a living archive for the trauma he endures (2013). Since his scars can be hidden beneath the surface (via clothing), they do not limit him in social and professional spaces; instead they are revealed and highlighted in private or vulnerable moments when the hero is alone or in close contact with a person. In a similar way, the trauma of his partner Camille Montes in *Quantum of Solace* is 'inscribed' through the burns on her back. While these can also be hidden by clothing, the character is frequently costumed in shirts/dresses that are cut in such a way that her scars remain noticeable and serve as a visual reminder to viewers of her childhood trauma and the vendetta she plans to carry out.

In comparison, *Skyfall* utilizes facial differences for shock value as the villain Raoul Silva recounts his past as a former 00 agent. Sitting in a glass cage in front of M and Bond, Silva discusses the torture he endured at the hands of his captors and his attempt at killing himself using the cyanide capsule implanted in his back left molar. After Silva describes how the chemical burnt him on the inside (literally, although morally is implied), he removes the palette in his mouth to reveal the damage to his cheekbone and teeth on the left side of his face resulting in a drooping of his lower left eyelid. This digital transformation (via CGI) is paired with music that is tense and foreboding, and the 'horrific' results cause M and Bond to turn away to leave, disturbed by what they have seen. While this moment lasts for only thirty seconds, it taps into the pervasive stereotype of disability as monstrosity and promotes a connection between the facial difference/disfiguration and moral integrity of Silva.

Unlike the orphan origin trilogy which is revisionist, *Spectre* (Mendes 2016) is decidedly reversionist as it returns the franchise to the gender- and geo-politics of the 1960s (see Funnell and Dodds 2017; Funnell 2018). This is notable in the return and depiction of the megalomaniac Blofeld. While the figure is played by different actors and depicted in a variety of ways across the Connery (1962–71), Lazenby (1969) and Moore (1981) eras (see Gerrard 2020), *Spectre* relies on the visual conventions featured in *You Only Live Twice* which centre on facial scarring. In fact, I would argue that *Spectre* provides an origin story for Blofeld's facial scar rather than the character himself as the film ends with the bloody reveal rather than the character's death or escape. While this 'creative' choice can be construed as an homage or reversion to Bond tradition, it is also decidedly ableist and essentializes the figure down to his facial scar.

More importantly, the use of scarring draws into question why disabilities and specifically facial scars have more recently become part of the Bond brand. In her analysis of the first four Craig-era films, Fran Pheasant-Kelly argues that the feminization of villains post-9/11 is projected through facial differences and other physical impediments, and provides a visual contrast with the muscular masculinity of Craig's Bond (see 2021). However, this intersectional reading does not account for the use of facial scars in the Brosnan films leading up the Craig era, including *Goldeneye* (1995) for Alec Trevelyan, *The World Is Not Enough* (1999) for Renard and *Die Another Day* (2002) for Tang Ling Zao. Whether the use of facial differences across the Craig era is simply a continuation of lazy storytelling and insidious tropes, a form of homage/reversionism to Bond tradition or a new way to depict gender- and geo-politics, it remains an antiquated form of representation that has been falling out of step in contemporary culture.

As articulated in the 'I Am Not Your Villain Campaign' led by UK charity Changing Faces, film representation plays a critical role in shaping public perception and contributes to appearance-related discrimination. In 2018, the charity put out a call to the film industry to stop using scars, burns and other facial differences as a shorthand for villainy ('Campaign with Us' n.d.). The same year the British Film Institute (BFI) endorsed the campaign and issued a statement that they will no longer fund films featuring villains with facial scarring/differences (Pulver 2018). While the Craig-era films are considered by some to be more progressive in terms of representation – through the casting of Black actors to play Felix Leiter and Eve Moneypenny, for example – the consideration of ableism and especially the use of facial differences in the franchise is not considered in these evaluations.

The most troublesome film of the Craig era is *No Time To Die* (Fukunaga 2021) given its release after the aforementioned campaigns. While the media surrounding the film's release focused on the casting of a black woman (Lashana Lynch) as 007 (Miller 2020; Daley-Ward 2021; Lewis 2021), less attention was paid to the persistent use of facial scarring for THREE villainous figures in the film: Blofeld, Primo and Safin. On the one hand, Blofeld returns and is connected to Primo (aka Cyclops) through a bionic eye that both characters use to communicate. Much like LeChiffre, Primo has scarring around his eyelid and this provides a visual cue about his secret connection to Blofeld. On the other hand, arch-villain Lyutsifer Safin has widespread facial scarring from a poisoning he survived in his youth. In the pre-credit sequence, Safin wears a traditional, albeit broken, Japanese Noh mask to cover his scars (reminiscent of other villains like the Phantom in *The Phantom of the Opera* [Schumacher 2004] and Dr Isabel Maru in *Wonder Woman* [Jenkins 2017]) but appears unmasked for the rest of the film. In a stereotypical fashion, these scars serve as a constant visual reminder of the trauma he endured which has, according to the film, influenced his villainous actions and intentions.

In spite of broader calls across the US and British film industries, among others, to stop the use of facial differences and other ableist tropes in the depiction of villains, the creators of *No Time To Die* continued to use them in defining the world of Bond and shaping his heroic legacy. Any argument for progressive representation in the film (in terms of gender and race) cannot outweigh the frequency and consistency of depicting villains with facial scarring not only across the era let alone its culmination in *No Time To Die*. Moreover, it draws attention to the implicit/explicit bias of the core creative team operating across the Brosnan and Craig eras including scriptwriters Neal Purvis and Robert Wade (1999–2021), producers Barbara Broccoli (1995–2021) and Michael G. Wilson (1985–2021), and directors like Sam Mendes (2012–16), among others.

This raises the question as to whether ableism is a core/generic element of the Bond brand and other action franchises by extension. When stereotypes associated with facial differences are so easily adopted, they not only interfere with the development of creative stories and the depiction of compelling characters, but they also capitalize (socially and economically) on the stigma experienced by historically marginalized and targeted individuals, worsening their conditions in the process. The frequent use of this regressive and antiquated mode of representation in *No Time To Die* in the wake of campaigns and social (media) discourse calling for an end to these practices is an insult to everyone who has to endure the consequences of such irresponsible creative practices. Moreover, this critique of ableism cannot and should not be overlooked in the prioritization of other seemingly positive representational goals.

178 *Afterword*

As the Bond franchise begins the process of revisioning its brand once again with the casting of a new actor in the lead role in the post-Craig era, it is my hope that this volume will provide readers (and, if we are lucky, Bond creators) with moments of pause and reflection. Blockbuster filmmaking conveys powerful messages about power, privilege and identity, and a series like James Bond brings with it sixty years of representational practices that are often upheld by fans as tradition. Just because time passes, it does not mean that the series has progressed and evolved. Bond and his creators have always been defined by privilege and while the figure might not change (quickly enough), the perspectives, social discourse and critical lenses of viewers have. In order for Bond to remain relevant in the years to come, creators will need to take a closer look at the Craig-era films and consider whether the world they *choose* to (re)envision is appealing or off-putting to filmgoers who are both impacted by and contributing to social justice movements of which disability activism is certainly a part.

The old Bond is dead and does not need to be resuscitated. Let us also put to rest the franchise's regressive representational practices, including facial scarring for villains.

References

Adams, M. et al., eds (2018), *Readings for Diversity and Social Justice*, 4th edn, New York: Routledge.

Bryan, W. V. (2018), 'Struggle for Freedom: Disability Rights Movements', in M. Adams et al. (eds), *Readings for Diversity and Social Justice*, 4th edn, 475–80, New York: Routledge.

'Campaign with Us' (n.d.), *Changing Faces*. Available online: https://www.changingfaces.org.uk/get-involved/campaign-with-us/i-am-not-your-villian/.

Croley, J. A. et al. (2017), 'Dermatologic Features of Classic Movie Villains: The Face of Evil', *JAMA Dermatology* 153 (6): 559–64.

Daley-Ward, Y. (2021), 'Lashana Lynch on Making History as the First Black Female 007', *Harpers Bazaar*, 28 September. Available online: https://www.harpersbazaar.com/uk/culture/culture-news/a34517814/lashana-lynch-black-female-007-interview/.

Dodds, K. (2013), 'Shaking and Stirring James Bond: Age, Gender, and Resilience in *Skyfall* (2012)', *Journal of Popular Film and Television* 14 (3): 116–30.

Eco, U. (2003), 'The Narrative Structure in Fleming', in C. Lindner (ed.), *The James Bond Phenomenon: A Critical Reader*, 34–55, Manchester: Manchester University Press.

Funnell, L. (2011), '"I Know Where You Keep Your Gun": Daniel Craig as the Bond-Bond Girl Hybrid in *Casino Royale*', *Journal of Popular Culture* 44 (3): 455–72.

Funnell, L. (2018), 'Reworking the Bond Girl Concept in the Craig Era', *Journal of Popular Film and Television* 18 (1): 11–21.

Funnell, L. and K. Dodds (2017), *Geographies, Genders, and Geopolitics of James Bond*, London: Palgrave Macmillan.

Gerrard, S. (2020), 'Blofeld', in S. Gerrard (ed.), *From Blofeld to Moneypenny: Gender in James Bond*, 167–83, Bingley: Emerald.

Lewis, T. (2021), 'Lashana Lynch, the First Female 007: "I Never Had a Plan B"', *Guardian*, 12 September. Available online: https://www.theguardian.com/culture/2021/sep/12/lashana-lynch-first-female-007-i-never-had-a-plan-b-no-time-to-die.

Longmore, P. (1987), *Screening Stereotypes: Images of Disabled People in TV and Motion Pictures*, Westport, CT: Praeger.

Miller, M. (2020), 'Lashana Lynch Confirms She is James Bond's New 007, Haters Be Damned', *Esquire*, 5 November. Available online: https://www.esquire.com/entertainment/movies/a34585204/lashana-lynch-new-007-james-bond-no-time-to-die/.

Ostiguy-Finneran, B. and M. L. Peters (2018), 'Ableism: Introduction', in M. Adams et al. (eds), *Readings for Diversity and Social Justice*, 4th edn, 467–74, New York: Routledge.

'Our Mission' (2021), *Face Equity International*. Available online: https://faceequalityinternational.org/our-mission/.

Pheasant-Kelly, F. (2021), 'Facial Disfigurement on Screen: James Bond and the Politics of Portraying the Post-9/11 Terrorist', in C. Klecker and G. M. Grabher (eds), *The Disfigured Face in American Literature, Film, and Television*, 151–72, New York: Routledge.

Pulver, A. (2018), 'BFI to Refuse Funding for Films with Facially-Scarred Villains', *Guardian*, 29 November. Available online: https://www.theguardian.com/film/2018/nov/29/bfi-to-refuse-funding-for-films-with-facially-scarred-villains.

Shaholli, E. (2022), 'Disability in a Galaxy Far, Far Away: A Mythology of Villains, "Obsessive Avengers," and Complex Embodiments in *Star Wars*', *Disability Studies Quarterly* 42 (1).

Contributors

Fernando Gabriel Pagnoni Berns works as Professor at the Universidad de Buenos Aires (UBA) – Facultad de Filosofía y Letras (Argentina). He is director of the research group on horror cinema 'Grite' and has authored a book about Spanish horror TV series *Historias para no Dormir* (2020) and has edited books on Frankenstein bicentennial (2017), on director James Wan (2021), on the Italian *giallo* film (forthcoming) and horror comics (2022). He is currently editing a book on horror director Wes Craven and one on Hammer horror films.

John Brick teaches in the English department at Marquette University in Milwaukee, Wisconsin, USA. His research interests focus primarily on American literary journalism of the mid-twentieth century, and his most recent work is a comprehensive annotated variorum of Hunter S. Thompson's 1971 *Fear and Loathing in Las Vegas*, alongside an examination of Gonzo journalism as an ongoing transhistorical and transnational phenomenon.

Mary M. Burke, Professor of English at the University of Connecticut, publishes widely on Irish and Irish-American culture and identities. Her book, *Race, Politics, and Irish America: A Gothic History*, will be published by Oxford University Press in 2023, as was her cultural history of Irish Travellers, *'Tinkers': Synge and the Cultural History of the Irish Traveller* (2009). Her collaboration with Tramp Press on the Juanita Casey *Horse of Selene* reissue appeared in 2022. Burke's public-facing and creative work has placed with NPR, the *Irish Times*, national broadcaster RTÉ and Faber. She is a former NEH Keough-Naughton Fellow at University of Notre Dame, London. A graduate of Trinity College, Dublin and Queen's University, Belfast, she is a 2022 TCD LRH Visiting Fellow.

Colin Burnett, Associate Professor of Film and Media Studies at Washington University in St. Louis, USA, is the author of *The Invention of Robert Bresson: The Auteur and His Market* (2017). He is currently at work on a second book, entitled *Serial Bonds: The Many Lives of 007* which examines the property's distinct cross-media narrative experience and its creative, legal and production contexts.

Contributors

Lisa Funnell is Associate Dean of Creative Industries at Mohawk College in Canada. She specializes in gender and geopolitics in the James Bond franchise and other actions. She is the author of *Geographies, Genders, and Geopolitics of James Bond* (2017) with Klaus Dodds and editor of *For His Eyes Only: The Women of James Bond* (2015), among other award-winning monographs, anthologies and articles.

Ron E. Hassner is Chancellor's Professor of Political Science, Helen Diller Family Chair in Israel Studies, and faculty director of the Helen Diller Institute for Jewish Law and Israel Studies at the University of California, Berkeley, USA. Ron studies the role of ideas, practices and symbols in international security with particular attention to the relationship between religion and violence. He is the editor of the Cornell University Press book series 'Religion and Conflict'. His latest book, *Anatomy of Torture* (2022) explores the archives of the Spanish Inquisition to uncover evidence about the causes, characteristics and effects of interrogational torture.

Kathryn Hendrickson is an Instructional Consultant with the Foundational Course Initiative at the University of Michigan, USA. She earned her PhD at Marquette University, where her dissertation, *Genre and Loss: The Impossibility of Restoration in 20th Century Detective Fiction*, examined detective fiction, its creation and maintenance as a genre, how it is continually conceptualized and re-formed within popular culture and the ways in which it enables critical engagement with questions of genre and boundaries. Her broader research interests lie in genre studies and twentieth- and twenty-first-century transatlantic fiction, with a focus on mystery, crime and detection.

Harshad Keval is a writer and educator specializing in race critical sociologies, anti-racism and decolonial frameworks. He has written across the intersections of race and education, institutions, mental health, gender, representation, disability and history. He has a particular interest in cross-over creative spaces where connections between theoretical, practical and embodied locations of power can be explored, resisted and re-articulated.

Bridget E. Keown is a Teaching Assistant Professor in the Gender, Sexuality, and Women's Studies at the University of Pittsburgh, USA. She earned her PhD in history at Northeastern University, where her research focused on the experience and treatment of war-related trauma among British and Irish women during the First World War and Irish War of Independence. Her writing on this topic, as well as the representation of trauma across media, has appeared in several journals and edited volumes, as well as the blog *Nursing Clio*.

Tatiana Konrad is a postdoctoral researcher in the Department of English and American Studies, University of Vienna, Austria. She is the author of *Docu-Fictions of War: U.S. Interventionism in Film and Literature* (2019), editor of *Cold War II: Hollywood's Renewed Obsession with Russia* (2020) and *Transportation and the Culture of Climate Change: Accelerating Ride to Global Crisis* (2020), and co-editor of *Cultures of War in Graphic Novels: Violence, Trauma, and Memory* (2018).

Marwan M. Kraidy is Dean and CEO of Northwestern University Qatar, founder of the Institute for Advanced Study in the Global South and Anthony Shadid Chair in Global Media, Politics and Culture at Northwestern, Illinois, USA. Supported by Carnegie, Guggenheim and other fellowships, his books include *Hybridity, or, the Cultural Logic of Globalization* (2005), *Reality Television and Arab Politics* (2010) and *The Naked Blogger of Cairo: Creative Insurgency in the Arab World* (2016). He serves on the Board of Directors of the American Council of Learned Societies and of the Center for Advanced Research in Global Communication.

Christoph Lindner is Professor of Urban Studies and Dean of The Bartlett Faculty of the Built Environment at University College London, where he writes about cities, visual culture and social-spatial inequality. His work on James Bond includes the edited volumes *Revisioning 007: James Bond and Casino Royale* (2009) and *The James Bond Phenomenon: A Critical Reader* (2nd edn, 2009).

Milo Sweedler is a Professor of French, Cultural Analysis and Social Theory at Wilfrid Laurier University, Canada. His primary research area is socio-political film criticism. His recent books include *Rumble and Crash: Crises of Capitalism in Contemporary Film* (2019) and *Allegories of the End of Capitalism: Six Films on the Revolutions of Our Times* (2020).

Index

ableism 172–9
'accumulation by dispossession' 122
Amis, Kingsley 68–9
Anderson, Fiona 68
Aristide, Jean-Bertrand 121

Baron, Cynthia 73
Battarcharjee, Paul 142
Bellucci, Monica 3
Black, Jeremy 100
Bold, Christine 86
boy soldier, Bond as 70–1, 72
Brabazon, Tara 50
Brereton, Pat 25
Brexit 73–4
Brisman, Avi 22
Buck-Morss, Susan 122
Burley, Aidan 145
Butler, Judith 15–16

capitalism 115–30
Career Novel 49–50
Casino Royale (film)
    Bond's trauma 83–4
    capitalism 115, 116–20
    ecocinema 24
    emotional vulnerability and physical
        weariness of Bond 73
    environmental injustice and 'slow
        violence' 11, 14, 16–18, 24
    facial scarring use 174–5
    infonationalism and surveillance
        104–5
    'licence to kill' status 69
    Moneypenny 46, 50
    racial thinking 136, 138, 140
    rebranding the franchise 4, 157
    torture 30, 32, 39–40, 69
    urbicide 161–4
    women's trauma 86
Changing Faces campaign 176

Chapman, James 2, 100
clothing 63, 65, 67–9
colonialism 15, 16, 72–3, 135–6, 162
Connery, Sean, Scottish independence 72
Coward, Martin 165, 166
Croley, Julie Amthor 173
Crosby, Alfred W. 15

Daniel, J. Furman 99
data-harvesting and surveillance 99–114
Dessalines, Jean-Jacques 120
Devine, T. M. 66
Diamonds Are Forever (film) 2, 32, 37
Die Another Day (film)
    facial scarring use 176
    Moneypenny 51
    torture 30, 38–9
disability 172–9
Dodds, Klaus 13, 24, 105, 117, 158, 160,
    162, 174, 175
Dr No (film)
    infonationalism and surveillance 104
    Moneypenny 48–9
    racial thinking 131, 142
    sexual violence 2
    torture 32
Dynamite Entertainment comics 46, 48,
    55–60

Ebert, Robert 83
ecocinema 12, 24–6
ecological imperialism 15
Elba, Idris 137, 138
Elizabeth II, Queen 144
environmental injustice 11–27
Everett, Ann 133

facial scarring 172–9
fashions 63, 65, 67–9
Fleming, Ian, Bond as a dull, uninteresting
    character 69

184   *Index*

For Your Eyes Only (film) 32
For Your Eyes Only (short story) 70
Ford, Tom 63, 67
Forster, Greg 70
From Russia With Love (film) 2, 37
Fukunaga, Cary 4
Funnell, Lisa 13, 24, 72, 105, 117, 158, 160, 162, 174, 175

Gehlawat, Monika 163
gender
    PTSD 80–3
    women's trauma 86–92
Germanà, Monica 68
Gilligan, Sarah 63
Glas, René 119
'Glen Check' 68
Glenurquhart (Glen Urquhart) Estate check 67–8
global responsibility 15–16
Goggin, Joyce 119
Goldeneye (film)
    facial scarring use 176
    Moneypenny 50
    torture 32
    urbicide 160
Goldfinger (film)
    Bond's suit design 68
    sexual violence 2
    torture 31–2
Graham, Stephen 158
grief 92–3

Haggis, Paul 4
Hall, Stuart 146, 148, 149
Hallward, Peter 121
Hanley, Tim 71–2
Harman, Chris 126
Harvey, David 115, 122, 168
Hawkins, Gay 20
Held, Jacob M. 73
'heterosexy' 49–50, 53
Heumann, Joseph 167
Highland Rape, McQueen runway show 66–7
Hochscherf, Tobias 104
Holliday, Christopher 101
Houser, Jody 57–60
Hughes, Helen 25

'I am Not Your Villain' campaign 176
imperialism 15, 22–4, 162
infonationalism 99–114

Jameson, Fredric 124
Jeffery, Keith 70
Jeong, Seung-hoon 104
Jones, Nick 163

Key, Keegan-Michael 143
kilts 65
Kretz, Andrew 102
Kureishi, Hanif 146

Lazenby, George 2–3
LeWars, Marguerite 3
Lewis-Vidler, J. 160
'licence to kill' status 69, 70
Licence to Kill (film) 32, 34
Lindner, Christoph vii, viii, 119
Live and Let Die (film) 32, 135
Living Daylights, The (film) 159–60
London Olympics 2012 opening ceremony 144–5
Longmore, Paul 173

MacDonald, Scott 12
Man With the Golden Gun (film) 104
Mandel, Ernest 112
McCrisken, Trevor 103
McQueen, Alexander 63, 66–7
#MeToo movement 1–2, 5
Millard, André J. 24
Monarch of the Glen, The 66, 74
Moneypenny 45–62
Moneypenny (comic) 57–60
Moneypenny Diaries, The (Weinberg) 45, 47–8
Moonraker (film) 32, 159, 174
Moore, Ellen E. 20–1, 22, 25
Moran, Christopher 103
mourning 92–3
Müller, Timo 22, 24
Murray, Robin 167
Musgrave, Paul 99

neoliberalism 120–3
Never Say Never Again (film) 138
Night of the Living Dead (film) 144

Nixon, Rob 11, 13, 15
No Time To Die (film)
 bleak ending reflecting Brexit 73–4
 Bond's suit design 63, 67
 Bond's trauma 80
 capitalism 115, 127–9
 ecocinema 24, 25
 environmental injustice and 'slow
  violence' 11, 14, 16, 19
 facial scarring use 176–7
 infonationalism and surveillance
  109–12
 Moneypenny 53–5
 racial thinking 135, 136, 138, 141, 143,
  149–50
 torture 29, 30, 36, 41
 urbicide 169, 170
 women's trauma 91–2

Octopussy (film)
 Moneypenny 50
 torture 34, 36
On Her Majesty's Secret Service (film) 37,
 50
orphans/orphanage trafficking 70–1

Peele, Jordan 143
Petch, Tom 79
Pheasant-Kelly, Fran 176
Piketty, Thomas 128
Pitcher, Ben 132
post-colonialism 14–22, 23, 72–3, 100,
 145–6, 148
post-traumatic stress disorder 79, 80–3
Potter, Emily 20
Prince of Wales check 63, 67–8

Quantum of Solace (film)
 Bond's trauma 84
 Camille Montes character 82–3, 87–8
 capitalism 115, 120–3
 ecocinema 24
 emotional vulnerability and physical
  weariness of Bond 73
 environmental injustice and 'slow
  violence' 11, 14, 16, 18, 20–2, 23
 facial scarring use 175
 infonationalism and surveillance
  105–6

torture 37, 38
 urbicide 164, 166–7
 women's trauma 87–8

Race, Kane 20
racial thinking 131–55
Racioppi, Linda 82
Ray, Sarah Jaquette 14
Reich, Robert 102
Rejali, Darius 34
resilience 81–2, 83, 92–3
right-wing populism 127–9

Sá, Creso 102
Salmon, Colin 138
Scotland's traumatic past 63–77
Scottish Independence Referendum 72
selkie 65, 71
sex slavery 4, 71–2
sexual violence 2–5, 32–3, 71
Shaholli, Elisa 173
Shaw, Kristen 143
Shields, Duncan 81
Showalter, Elaine 81
Sigurdson, Kristjan 102
Skyfall (film)
 Bond's trauma 84
 capitalism 123–5
 ecocinema 24
 environmental injustice and 'slow
  violence' 19–20
 facial scarring use 175
 gendering of PTSD 82
 infonationalism and surveillance
  106–8
 Moneypenny 50, 51–3
 racial thinking 136, 140, 146–7
 Scotland's traumatic past 63–77
 Séverine as sex slave 4, 71–2
 sexual violence 4, 71
 torture 32, 36
 urbicide 164–5
 women's trauma 88–90
 word-association exercise 74
'slow violence' 11–27
Smith, James 113
Smith, Sam 73
Snowden, Edward 103
Solstice (comic) 46

186   *Index*

Sontag, Susan 16
Spectre (film)
  Bond's trauma 85
  capitalism 115, 125–7
  ecocinema 24
  environmental injustice and 'slow
    violence' 11, 14, 16, 18
  facial scarring use 175–6
  infonationalism and surveillance 108–9
  Moneypenny 53–5
  PTSD ad 79
  racial thinking 142–3
  Sam Smith's theme song 73
  torture 34–5, 36
  urbicide 165, 167–9
  women's trauma 90–1
Spencer, Stephanie 49
Spy Who Loves Me, The (film) 38, 174
Stuart, Caroline, Countess of Seafield 67
surveillance 99–114

tartan register 67–8
terrorism, urbanized 157–71
Thunderball (film) 2, 32, 34, 36
Tomorrow Never Dies (film) 32, 34, 36
torture 29–43, 69

trauma
  Bond's trauma 80, 83–5
  PTSD 79, 80–3
  Scotland's traumatic past 63–77
  women's trauma 86–92
Tremonte, Colleen M. 82
Trump, Donald 73, 128

urbicide 157–71

Vargr (comic) 56–7
Victoria, Queen 65–6

waterboarding 69
Weinberg, Samantha 45, 47–8, 53
Weinstein, Harvey 2
'Widows of Culloden' 67
Willoquet-Maricondi, Paula 12
Winder, Simon 72
World is Not Enough, The (film) 33, 60,
  176
Wright, Patrick 148

Yancy, George 150
You Only Live Twice (film) 35–6, 174
Young, Terence 3

Printed in the USA
CPSIA information can be obtained
at www.ICGtesting.com
LVHW020441040724
784649LV00003B/33